Warring Personalities

Other Books by Dan White:

Crossing the Gnat Line
Hep Cat
Confluence

Warring Personalities

From Bunker Hill to Appomattox

Dan White

ISBN 978-1-959895-40-4 (paperback)
ISBN 978-1-959895-41-1 (ebook)

Printed in the United States of America

Photo Credits
All photos in this book are owned by the author or are within the public domain, with the exception of the photo of Fess Parker as Davy Crockett obtained under license from Getty Images.

Drawings and Cover Design:
All drawings and cover design by Dan White.

Dedication

For my wife, Susie, who has patiently listened to my endless ramblings about Bunker Hill, Appomattox, and all points in between and has encouraged me to write.

Acknowledgement

Special appreciation goes to:

My brother, Walter, and my sister, Anna, who have always encouraged me on everything.

My friend and editor, Zack Gresham, whose invaluable input is greatly appreciated.

Peter Henderson, my long-time friend, who discussed Mexican history with me at length to steer me straight.

Rob Johnson, my buddy from way back, who helped me with the tone and scope of the Roll Call chapter and The Revolutionary War chapter.

Contents

Acknowledgement vii
Chapter 1: Roll Call 1
Chapter 2: The Revolutionary War: From Boston to Yorktown 4
Chapter 3: Remember the Alamo? 80
Chapter 4: The Civil War 157
Bibliography 265

Chapter 1

Roll Call

I was never much interested in history. In fact, I never had a history course that I liked. Eighth grade history was taught by some football coach because he had to, and all I remember is everyone having to get up one at a time to recite the preamble to the Constitution. That was a show. At the end of each person's recitation, Coach Barnes asked, "Who were the two signers of the Constitution from Georgia?"

"Abraham Baldwin and William Few," they replied. Then they sat down. I still remember every word of the preamble, but that's all.

Tenth grade history came in the form of Gene Blakeford, who was 300 years old and droned on and on about dates and places with no reference to who or why. I cannot recall anything we studied that year—not even the general subject matter, time period, or continent. The only excitement in the class was when Mark Baxter climbed out the window most days to sneak off to the gym to play basketball. Baxter was tall and skinny and he always sat next to the windows, which opened out over the courtyard two stories below.

As soon as Mr. Blakeford finished calling the roll and briefly turned his back to the class, Baxter would stand up and quietly slide one leg out the window. Then he would bend over at a right angle so that his upper body was parallel to the floor before ducking it outside the window, followed by the other leg. The whole class watched in gleeful silence. After that, he squatted on the thin concrete ledge below the window for a few seconds and then somehow maneuvered so that he hung from the ledge by his arms. From there Baxter simply let go, landing on his feet in the courtyard.

A lot of people said that senior history taught by Mr. Nault was fantastic, but difficult. I could not imagine that, so I skipped it. In college, Western Civilization 101 was more of the same old thing, just on a grander scale, with lectures three times per week in an auditorium crammed full of 200 people. Henry Ford's claim that "history is bunk" seemed right on the mark.

I had considered going to Davidson College and took a tour of it in 1973. The campus was quiet and beautiful, with red brick buildings all around. Then they showed me the dorms, even letting me look into a room to get an idea of how things would be. The room that they showed me was a single belonging to some guy who had put his mattress on the floor and built a plywood table over it. The table took up so much of the room that I could barely get around it to the window. On the table he had built a replica of the battle of Gettysburg, complete with plastic trees and horses and soldiers. He had even laid down green felt for the fields. That kid was either a nutcase or a history buff or both. Right then and there I decided that I was not going to Davidson.

Twenty-five years later, when worries about work were keeping me up late at night, I decided to read a book that would help me fall asleep. I needed something good and boring. Naturally, I chose history. So I picked up a three-volume, three-thousand-page narrative of the Civil War by Shelby Foote. After the first 50 pages I was wide awake and fascinated. He delved into the people involved, not just what happened where on a particular date. Soon I was staying up late at night reading history.

Thinking back on it now, when I was a kid I was crazy about Swamp Fox of the Revolutionary War, as well as all things related to World War II. We all ran around in the back yard yelling "Kill, Kill, Kill!" and we dug foxholes using folding shovels from the army surplus store, fighting the Nazis most afternoons. My older sister, Anna, expressed concern about my war obsession to my mom, who said it would not last. Mom was right, I suppose.

I also watched a lot of cartoons on Saturday mornings. In 1963, all three channels ran black-and-white cartoons on Saturday. The oddest one to me was *Fractured Fairy Tales*, which took a traditional fairy tale and twisted it. I knew some of the tales beforehand and was puzzled when everything got scrambled in the cartoon. Currently, I find that the more I read about the personalities and motives of people in history, the more like *Fractured Fairy Tales* the whole story becomes. Knowing about the personalities and their backstories upends and enriches the conventional narrative.

My aim here is to provide insight into the people involved. Who were they and why did they do what they did? Sure, military engagements involve positions, headcounts, flanks, abatis, enfilades, amphibious right-turn maneuvers, and so forth. But who cares about that? Endless military factoids suck the life out of what happened. For example, I see many historical plaques that are basically unintelligible. They say things like, "The Second Division, 23rd Army Corps and part of the 14th Corps moved from the high bluff west of Camp Creek 3/4 mile west to the valley floor and attempted to carry Confederate works west of the stream."

Rarely do I read the introduction to a book, so I have put this background information in this first chapter so that you will see it and know where I am coming from. This book is about people, their vanities and strengths, their weaknesses and humanity. For me, the human element is what breathes life into history. I have done my best here to get all the facts straight. I have done a lot of digging. Hell, I even have citations! And as it turns out, the three-volume treatise that initially piqued my interest in the Civil War is spot-on accurate, but the son of a bitch did not put a single citation in his work.

Chapter 2

The Revolutionary War: From Boston to Yorktown

I always thought that the colonists declared independence, fought the British, spent one cold winter at Valley Forge, and then beat Cornwallis (who surrendered at Yorktown, wherever that was), and the war was over in a snap. The Constitution was then written up, if it had not been already, and Washington became the first president right off of the bat.

In reality, the war lasted nearly eight and a half years, though the actual fighting lasted only six and a half. The remaining two years involved negotiations leading to the Treaty of Paris, which officially ended the war. It then took another six years to create the Constitution and for Washington to become president. And I don't remember any discussion in school about the colonists being at each other's throats during the war over whether to be loyalists faithful to Britain or patriots fighting to break free.

This chapter covers the war from the British occupation of Boston to the surrender of Cornwallis at Yorktown, which turns out to be in Virginia. This is about conscience and arrogance, fear and honor, with references to dates and the number of bullets fired only as needed or when interesting.

A Splendid View of Boston

Henry Knox was a Boston badass. He dragged nearly 60 cannon up Dorchester Heights overlooking Boston Harbor and blasted away at the 140 British ships and 9,000 soldiers down below. With no formal military training, Knox was the owner of a Boston bookstore that specialized in British books, with a large selection on military history and strategy. He had married a year before the war broke out and his wife's father, a loyalist, had arranged for Henry to be offered a commission in the British army. But Knox declined, joining the patriot militia instead. The British went into a panic under his cannon fire, turning their ships around and hightailing it to Nova Scotia. It was March of 1776. Henry Knox stood at six foot three and 250 pounds. He was 25 years old.[1]

England was deeply in debt after spending a fortune kicking the French out of North America during the French and Indian War several years earlier, so it had raised taxes on the American colonies, in essence expecting the colonies to pay for that war. The near collapse of Britain's East India Company had made matters worse, so British Parliament passed the Tea Act, giving it a trading monopoly in the colonies. Before then, most American tea had been brought in by the Dutch. The colonists got angry about the new tax and the trade monopoly, so they boycotted British goods, reducing their imports from Britain by a whopping 97 percent. They did not want "taxation without representation" in Parliament. They also dumped 342 crates of tea into the Boston Harbor. That is when King George III decided that America must be made to obey.[2]

Britain declared Massachusetts to be in a state of rebellion and blocked colonial trade with the British West Indies. Britain also barred colonial ships from the cod fisheries in Newfoundland. The colonists began scrambling for guns in April of 1775, so the British tried to take over the patriot arsenal in Concord. That is when the Massachusetts

---

1 McCullough, pp. 59, 107; Puls, pp. 9, 13, 25–27; Brooks (1900), p. 18; http://www.revolutionarywarjournal.com/henry-knox, accessed July 10, 2021.

2 McCullough, p. 6; Calloway, p. 4; Greene and Pole, pp. 155–156; Paine, Kramnick (ed.), p. 21.

battles of Lexington and Concord broke out. The British troops were chased back into Boston by the patriots, who then put them under siege. Boston was a Peninsula connected to the mainland by a skinny "neck" only half a mile wide; it was easy for the patriots to trap the British. The British were bottled up.[3]

In May of 1775, 4,500 British reinforcements arrived by ship from England, including General William Howe, who had learned during the voyage that war had broken out and that Boston was under siege. A few weeks later, Howe was ordered by his commander to lead 2,200 men in a direct attack uphill against 1,000 patriots at Bunker Hill, on the outskirts of Boston. The patriots had the higher ground, but they had fewer soldiers and were low on ammunition. "Don't fire until you see the whites of their eyes," they were told. They indeed waited until the British were only several dozen yards away before firing their muskets, with devastating results. The British regrouped and charged again, with the same outcome. Henry Knox was directing the patriot artillery fire.[4]

Finally, on the third attempt, the British reached the patriot line, engaging in hand-to-hand combat and forcing a patriot retreat. But 1,000 Brisith were killed or wounded—the highest casualty percentage of any battle in the Revolutionary War. The British won the battle of Bunker Hill, but at a very high price. Patriot casualties were also high, but the patriots had learned that they could combat Britain and its superior military might. Howe's commander asked London for more soldiers. Instead, he got replaced by Howe.[5]

George Washington arrived in Boston in early July of 1775, two weeks after Bunker Hill. He had just been appointed by Congress to serve as commander in chief of the armed forces for the colonies. Washington was supposed to design the overall military strategy of the war in cooperation with Congress. He had previously led Virginia militia

---

3 Fischer, p. 76; Ketchum (2014), pp. 18, 54; McCullough, p. 26; Ferling (*Almost A Miracle*), pp. 62–64.

4 Ketchum (2014), pp. 2–9; Puls, p. 29.

5 Ketchum (*Decisive Day*), pp. 151–183; Brooks (1999), p. 237; https://www.history.com/topics/american-revolution/battle-of-bunker-hill, accessed July 21, 2021; McCullough, p. 8; Higginbotham, pp. 75–77.

regiments under British command during the French and Indian War. George Washington was 43 years old.[6]

By the time Washington arrived in Boston, 14,000 patriot soldiers were fit for active duty. The Brits had only 7,000, but were believed to have 11,000. The patriot soldiers were consuming a bottle of rum per day per man. They were untrained, and many of the officers had no idea what they were supposed to do. What's more, the patriots were not accustomed to having someone tell them what to do, so they came and went as they pleased. But they did work on their defenses, expecting a British attack at any moment. Washington viewed his New England soldiers as "dirty and nasty" and he contemptuously referred to them as "these people." As John Adams saw it, Washington's plantation sense of superiority fueled his disdain.[7]

Henry Knox met Washington for the first time shortly after the commander's arrival. Washington wanted to storm Boston with his troops, but was convinced by others that his untrained continental soldiers simply were not up to the task. So he agreed to continue the siege. It was a standoff, with the British not daring to attack after what had happened to them at Bunker Hill. The two armies studied each other day after day through telescopes. But Howe never attacked Washington and Washington never attacked the city. In fact, Howe showed a lack of self-confidence after Bunker Hill that would plague him throughout the war.[8] So the British controlled the city and the Charleston Peninsula (which included Bunker Hill) to the north, but had not bothered to claim the Dorchester Peninsula, which overlooked Boston Harbor from the south. The skinny neck of Boston was only 120 feet wide at high tide.[9]

---

6 McCullough, p. 59; Bell, pp. 3–4; Billias (1969), p. 48; Chernow (2010), p. 186; Lengel, pp. 365–371; Taylor, pp. 141–142.

7 Ibid., pp. 25–31, 38–41, 57.

8 Ibid., pp. 26–27, 53, Frothingham, pp. 100–101; Trevelyan, p. 338; Fleming, p. 44; Ketchum (*Decisive Day*), p. 213.

9 https://www.en.m.wikipedia.org/wiki/Boston_Neck, accessed September 15, 2021.

In 1776, the skinny neck onto the Boston peninsula was only 120 feet wide at high tide.

In November of 1775, four months after Washington's arrival, Henry Knox suggested that the cannon at Fort Ticonderoga in upstate New York be brought to Boston. Ticonderoga was a British fort that had been captured six months earlier by patriots Benedict Arnold and Ethan Allen. After the fort was captured, Ethan Allen and his Green Mountain Boys drank up all the British liquor there, while Arnold went to the far end of Lake Champlain and captured several British ships. (Some say that the idea of using the captured Ticonderoga cannon at Boston was initially Benedict Arnold's. In fact, Arnold had been the one who suggested that the poorly defended Fort Ticonderoga be captured in the first place.) Anyway, Washington agreed right away and put Henry Knox in charge of the mission, which many thought to be impossible.[10]

---

[10] Brooks (1900), p. 38; Martin (1997), p. 106; http://www.revolutionarywarjournal.com/henry-knox, accessed July 10, 2021; Philbrick (2016), pp. 35–36; McCullough,

Knox left Boston in mid-November of 1775 headed for Fort Ticonderoga. He took his 19-year-old brother, William, with him. On his way to Fort Ticonderoga, Knox met a British officer named John Andre, who had been captured at the fort and was headed south to be exchanged for a patriot officer of equal rank. They spent an evening in conversation. Little did Knox know that he would later see that man again under very different circumstances.[11]

On November 21, the first snow fell in Boston. The British began to run short on supplies due to winter storms on the sea and to colonial privateers who were raiding their ships. In fact, food became so scarce that hungry British soldiers began deserting. Smallpox was also rampant in the town. In late November, the British sent 300 loyalists by boat across the Back Bay to Washington. Though many of them were sick and dying, Washington refused to believe that they had been sent as a form of warfare, but when he received an additional 150 from the British, he concluded otherwise. His own men were cold and hungry and only 2,540 of his soldiers had so far reenlisted for the coming year.[12]

The Boston winter was brutal for the British. As one British admiral noted, ". . . the sentinel on shore is frequently found frozen to death upon his post, though relieved every half hour . . ." To stay warm, they tore down more than a hundred houses, along with barns, wharves, old ships, and even the Old North Church for firewood. There were also 4,000 civilian loyalists under siege in Boston. Though food was scarce and horse meat was in strong demand, the British officers did, however, attend plays and balls. General Howe enjoyed himself that winter hosting elegant dinners. Washington considered him to be "blind" to the true condition of the struggling patriot army.[13]

Meanwhile, Washington stayed in a three-story mansion near Harvard. It overlooked the Charles River and had been abandoned by a loyalist who had fled into Boston. Washington had two cooks, a maid, a steward, a tailor, a washerwoman, and eight servants. Martha Washington

---

pp. 59–60.

[11] McCullough, p. 60.

[12] Ibid., pp. 61–64.

[13] Ibid., pp. 73–79.

arrived on December 10 after a month of travel to get there. Congress authorized Washington to destroy the British army at Boston, even if that meant burning down the town.[14] On January 1, 1776, news arrived that King George III had called the patriots "traitors" in a speech to Parliament. With 3,000 miles of ocean between Britain and the colonies, news took a month or more to travel. The patriots were outraged and drew new resolve from it.[15]

Washington's initial war strategy was two-pronged: (1) attack the British where they were bottled up in Boston, and (2) attack the British by surprise in Quebec. In Boston, he still wanted to conduct an all-out assault. But by this time his men were in tents, they had no firewood, winter was upon them, and his enlistments would soon be expiring. His officers continued to talk him out of it, fortunately, since an attack was exactly what the British were hoping for.[16]

Fort Ticonderoga stood in upstate New York at the southern end of Lake Champlain where it meets Lake George. It was 220 miles from Boston as the crow flies. Arriving there on December 5, 1775, Knox organized a "train" of artillery by gathering 58 artillery pieces weighing 120,000 pounds in all. He loaded them onto boats that rowed 40 miles down Lake George. It took eight days to cover that distance. Then he loaded the artillery onto 42 heavy sleds and dragged them over the land by oxen. Knox had to cross the Hudson River four times, with one sled falling through the ice, leaving a hole 14 feet wide. He somehow retrieved the cannon from the bottom of the river and then headed on.[17]

The snow in the Berkshire Mountains of Massachusetts was thick. To slow the heavy sleds on the downhills, Knox had his men tie ropes to trees to check the speed. After that, to move things along, Knox swapped out the oxen for horses at Springfield for the final 90 miles. Hundreds of men were involved, with a total distance traveled of 300 miles. It took nearly three months to accomplish this feat and when Knox arrived in

---

[14] Ibid., pp. 41–42, 66–67.

[15] Ibid., pp. 7, 67–69.

[16] Ibid., pp. 53–54.

[17] Ibid., pp. 82–84.

Boston in late January of 1776 with the cannon, Washington put him in command of artillery for the entire Continental army.[18]

By now, Boston had been under siege for nine months. The British considered it a disgrace to be cooped up by an "undisciplined rabble." One British soldier likened it to being birds in a cage. The British controlled the sea and what it could bring in the way of supplies and troops. But, with the exception of Bunker Hill, the patriots occupied most of the other hills surrounding Boston and its harbor. The patriots, however, had hardly any artillery and only enough musket gunpowder for nine rounds per man—in fact, they were given spears to use in case of a British attack.[19]

The British knew that Dorchester Heights, which loomed above their ships in the harbor, was critical to their safety and success in Boston. But they continued to do nothing about it. As historian David McCullough characterizes it, "Dorchester Heights remained a kind of high, windblown no-man's land, neither side unmindful of its strategic importance, but neither side daring to seize and fortify it." One British officer, Henry Clinton, urged General Howe to take Dorchester Heights. Howe refused and sent Clinton away to invade the Carolinas.[20]

The British considered scrapping Boston as a poor place to attack and moving to New York instead. But by the time London ordered Howe to do so, winter had set in and it was too late for that. Howe decided to wait until spring to depart, replying to London: "We are not under the least apprehension of an attack on this place by surprise or otherwise."[21]

William Howe was never one to rush into anything. He was 43 years old and took the conventional officer's view that winter was not a season for action. But he did say that he would "sally forth" if Washington tried to take Dorchester Heights. So during the winter of 1775, Howe spent a good deal of his time gambling and hanging out with the wife of a Boston loyalist, seemingly giving no thought to what Washington

---

18 Ware, pp. 19–24; Brooks (1900), p. 38; http://www.revolutionarywarjournal.com/henry-knox, accessed July 10, 2021; McCullough, pp. 84–85.

19 McCullough, pp. 17, 25, 28, 60, 80.

20 Ferling (*The Ascent*), p. 100; McCullough, p. 71.

21 Ibid., pp. 70–71; Billias (1969), p. 47; Gruber, p. 82.

might do. Howe had far more military experience than Washington. He also had a much better trained and supplied army, and a massive navy in the harbor.[22]

While Henry Knox was dragging cannon over the countryside toward Boston, Benedict Arnold was on his way to Quebec with 1,200 patriots. Arnold was capable and decisive. But he lost 500 men along the way to starvation, exposure, or desertion in the icy Maine wilderness. He then unsuccessfully attacked the British at Quebec City on December 31, 1775. During the attack, his left leg was shattered.[23]

Arnold then moved south to Montreal, staying there until large British reinforcements under General John Burgoyne forced his further retreat south in May of 1776. The sheer audacity of Arnold's efforts earned him the nickname "The American Hannibal." His men either worshipped or despised him. With Arnold, there simply was no middle ground. When Arnold retreated from Montreal to Lake Champlain, he made sure that he was the last soldier to step onto the last boat and he did so with dramatic flair. That was after he had insisted that he and his aide shoot their horses before boarding the boat, so as not to leave anything of value behind for the British. As historian Nathaniel Philbrick observes: "it added lustre to the swashbuckling tale of his flight from Canada." But word soon spread that Arnold had used military supplies for his own personal gain during the retreat.[24]

On January 17, 1776, in Boston, Washington learned of Arnold's defeat at Quebec. Fortunately, Henry Knox showed up ten days later with the cannon from Ticonderoga. Washington was still itching to attack Boston. In fact, he wanted to transport troops across the Back Bay for a side attack as soon as the ice froze thick enough. But it never got thick enough. In the meantime, his officers talked him out of an attack for the fourth time.[25]

Boston and its harbor were within cannon range of Dorchester Heights, which stood 112 feet higher than the sea-level town. The

---

22 McCullough, pp. 72, 77, 78, 87; Fischer, p. 72.

23 Philbrick (2016), p. 37.

24 Randall (1990), pp. 131–228; Philbrick (2016), pp. 37-38.

25 McCullough, pp. 81, 86–87.

patriots planned to sneak up there in a single night with their cannon. So for several nights before their mission they fired artillery barrages at Boston from other parts of town as a distraction. They also did so on the night of the mission in order to cover their noise while scaling Dorchester. Wagons, carts, 800 oxen, and 3,000 men were rounded up to ascend Dorchester Heights. Washington also placed 4,000 men and 60 flatboats on the far side of the Charles River to invade Boston from that direction if the British attacked.[26]

March 4, 1776, was the night of the secret ascent. The patriots fired their usual nightly barrages and the British responded, creating one hell of a din. The climb up Dorchester then began and, before dawn, the cannon were in place. They were all aimed at Boston and the British ships in the harbor below. The patriots had also filled barrels with stone and sand in order to roll them downhill at advancing British troops if and when they attacked.[27]

The British were in shock the next morning when they saw the cannon above them. They blasted away at Dorchester Heights for two solid hours, but their cannon could not be raised enough to hit their high target. Washington waited for Howe to sally forth. Howe had in fact decided to do so but, as one who never rushed into anything, he decided to launch the assault at nightfall.

By nightfall, however, a winter storm had hit Boston with snow and sleet. Howe, naturally, postponed. By the following morning, he cancelled the attack altogether and instead issued orders to evacuate Boston. Many of his officers said that the storm had provided him with an easy out. Howe's recent uphill disaster at Bunker Hill likely played a large part in his decision.

With their vulnerability readily apparent, the British troops and Boston loyalists were in a frenzy. Washington refrained from firing while the British frantically loaded boats with supplies and water.[28] Howe soon sent a message to Washington saying that he would burn down Boston

---

26 Ibid., pp. 88–89.

27 http://www.revolutionarywarjournal.com/henry-knox, accessed July 10, 2021; McCullough, pp. 89, 93, 95.

28 McCullough, pp. 94–98.

if the patriots attacked the evacuees during their departure. Meanwhile, in town, all items that would not fit onboard and might be of use to the patriots were destroyed. Barrels of flour, sugar, and salt were dumped into Boston Harbor. Furniture, wheelbarrows, and wagons were smashed. While the escaping loyalists saw themselves as law-abiding subjects, they viewed the patriots as lawless rebels. The Declaration of Independence did not yet exist.[29]

Two weeks later, the British troops boarded their ships at four in the morning. By nine o'clock, 1,100 loyalists and nearly 9,000 soldiers departed on what became known as Evacuation Day. The passengers were not told where they were going, and the ships sat downshore for ten days before hightailing it to Halifax, Nova Scotia. Among the loyalists on the British ships were the parents of Henry Knox's wife. They did not return after the war. She never saw them again.[30]

After the ships departed Boston, boys came running across the Boston neck to report that the "lobster backs" were gone. The patriot troops marched into Boston early that afternoon and Washington rode in the next day without ceremony. Washington did not speak ill of his New England soldiers after that. Of the loyalists, he said, "By all accounts a more miserable set of beings does not exist."[31]

Harvard bestowed an honorary degree on Washington, who was convinced that the British ships were headed for New York. On April 4, 1776, Washington left Boston and headed for New York.[32] Most of the patriot troops did not know where they were headed.

The British Give It Another Go at Long Island

Three weeks later, the British troops left Halifax and headed for New York. By the end of June, the first British ships appeared in New York Harbor. In fact, more than 100 ships arrived on the first day. They anchored at Staten Island, which the British used as a staging point for their attack.

---

[29] Ibid., pp. 25, 99–104.

[30] Ibid., pp. 59, 107–108; Puls, p. 45.

[31] McCullough, pp. 105–111.

[32] Ibid., pp. 107–109, 112.

General Howe then sat for a month waiting for reinforcements. In all, he brought more than 400 ships and 45,000 soldiers with him. It was the largest assemblage of ships and men that had ever been amassed by the British Empire. Howe hoped to end the war in a single decisive blow. Though Washington had no idea how many British soldiers there were, he wanted to attack them at Staten Island. His officers thought it too risky. By putting his army on Manhattan, however, Washington was vulnerable to being trapped and destroyed.[33]

In his typical grand style, Washington set up headquarters in a splendid townhouse at the southernmost tip of Manhattan. It featured a banquet hall, a grand stairway, and a long parlor, with a garden leading down to the Hudson River. There, he would attempt, as historian McCullough says, "to defend a city bounded by navigable rivers on two sides and a harbor of a size sufficient to accommodate the largest fleet imaginable."[34]

In front of Washington's headquarters stood a larger-than-life gilded statue of King George III on horseback. The marble pedestal upon which the horse and rider stood was 15 feet high. King George III had never been a soldier and he had never been to America. Inheriting the British throne at age 23 from his grandfather, King George III was now 37 years old and had married a princess whom he had never met before the day of their wedding. They would have 15 children during their marriage. George was socially awkward, preferring to walk around his Windsor farm wearing farm clothes. He also played the violin and piano and was interested in astronomy and the arts. George also suffered from episodes of insanity throughout his life. During those episodes, he talked nonstop until foam ran out of his mouth and he had convulsions. His attendants had to sit on him to keep him safe on the floor.[35]

George Washington was born into a wealthy Virginia family that had made money growing tobacco and speculating in land. He stood

---

[33] Ibid., pp. 117, 133–134, 148; Philbrick (2016), pp. 7–9.

[34] McCullough, pp. 117, 121.

[35] Ibid., pp. 5–6, 124; https:www.revolutionary-war.net/king-george-iii/ p. 2, accessed July 3, 2021; https://www.bbc.com/news/magazine-22122407, "What was the truth about the madness of George III?" April 15, 2013, accessed July 15, 2021.

at six feet two inches and weighed 190 pounds. By all accounts, he was physically quite strong and a superior horseman to boot. Washington had reddish-brown hair that was powdered white, as was customary at the time, and his personality was reserved. He had worked as a surveyor in Virginia and had fought with mixed success in the French and Indian War.[36]

George Washington had married Martha Custis 17 years earlier, receiving 6,000 acres in dowry. All told, he was one of the wealthiest men in Virginia, holding more than 50,000 acres of land. He had only seven or eight years of education and was self-conscious about it. Though not arrogant, Washington did carry himself in a way that set him off from others. He also wore false teeth, due to years of cracking walnuts with his real ones. But wood was never used to make his teeth. Instead, they were made of ivory, gold, lead, and even other human teeth. As to military matters, he felt that a leader should look and act like one. Washington had a certain dignified bearing that one observer claimed hyperbolically would set him apart as a general out of a crowd of 10,000 people.[37]

Living the life of an English country gentleman, Washington ordered his clothes from England and had his coach custom built in England. He was also a perfectionist, and a bit of a nerd, recording to the minute how long each fox hunt lasted. He had, however, never led an entire army in battle and he told Congress that he was not qualified for the job when it appointed him as commander of the patriot army. Yet, as McCullough puts it, "to lead an undisciplined, poorly armed volunteer force of farmers and tradesmen against the best-trained, best-equipped, most formidable military force on earth . . . was, in reality, more than any man was qualified for."[38]

On July 4 of 1776, the Continental Congress unanimously passed the Declaration of Independence. Washington received a copy of the text

---

[36] McCullough, pp. 48–49; Ferling (2002), p. 16; Chernow (2010), pp. 29–30, 123–125; Ford (1896), pp. 18–19; Unger (2019), pp. 100–101.

[37] Wiencek, pp. 9–10, 67–69, 80–81; https://www.mountvernon.org, accessed July 20, 2021; McCullough, pp. 42–44, 47; Ellis, pp. 41–42, 48; https://www.mountvernon.org/library/digitalhistory/digital-encyclopedia/article/wooden-teeth-myth, accessed July 21, 2021; Philbrick (2016), pp. 8–9.

[38] McCullough, pp. 46–50.

two days later. When it was read to the patriot troops and townspeople of New York, they tore down the gilded statue of King George III, hacked off its head, and mounted it on a spike outside a tavern.[39]

Britain soon signed a series of treaties with German states to supply soldiers for the war. Lord Sandwich in the House of Lords called the patriot soldiers "raw, undisciplined, cowardly men." As for the Declaration of Independence, one British writer proclaimed, "A more impudent, false, and atrocious proclamation was never fabricated by the hands of man."[40]

The colonies were not only engaged in a struggle with Britain. There was also conflict between patriots and loyalists. The split between patriots/loyalist/independents was somewhere between 33/33/33 and 40/20/40. New York City, with a population of 20,000, had a large number of loyalists. But by now roughly a third of the city population had fled in fear of the coming battle.[41]

On one side of Manhattan was the East River, a mile wide and notoriously hard to navigate with its fast, churning currents and tidal changes of up to six feet. On the other side was the Hudson River, more than two miles wide. The British of course wanted to control the Hudson River and thereby separate all of New England from the rest of the colonies. Washington placed cannon along the banks of the Hudson and at the mouth of the East River. He also placed several thousand troops on Long Island, across the East River from Manhattan.[42]

---

39 Ibid., p. 137.

40 Ibid., pp. 6, 141; Miller (1959), pp. 410–412.

41 Mays, pp. 2–3; Greene and Pole, p. 235; McCullough, pp. 119–123.

42 McCullough, pp. 118, 126–127.

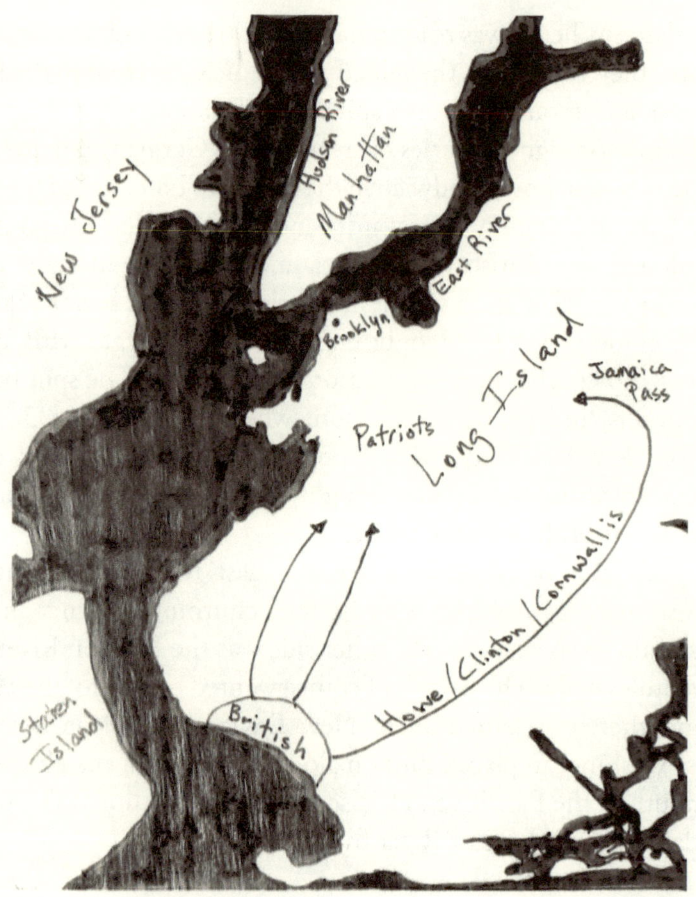

The Battle of Long Island, August 1776

In mid-July of 1776, the British sent ships up the Hudson, anchoring at Tarrytown 30 miles above Manhattan. More than 200 patriot cannon blasts had fired from shore at the ships, to no avail. From this it was evident that the British could place a large force north of Manhattan and trap Washington on the southern end. In the meantime, Washington was digging defenses on Long Island.[43]

More British ships kept arriving at Staten Island in late July. Yet Washington was hell-bent on making a stand in New York. He had 12,000 men and believed, due to inaccurate intelligence, that the British

[43] Ibid., pp. 139–143; Billias (1969), p. 51.

had only 8,000. For Washington, desertions were increasing daily and many of his men were sick. Meanwhile, Howe seemed to be in no hurry.[44]

Then Washington began to worry that a British attack on Long Island might simply be a feint, with the full attack on New York coming from some other direction. So, against one of the most basic rules of battle, he split his army into two parts, with one on Long Island and the other on Manhattan. By doing so, he figured that he could move the two forces back and forth, depending on what occurred.

The British ships that had gone up north on the Hudson River to Tarrytown suddenly headed south, sliding past Manhattan and rejoining the British fleet at Staten Island. Then a hellacious storm followed, with houses bursting into flame and ten patriots being killed by a single lightning flash near the East River. Elsewhere in town, three continental officers were killed by a single flash that caused the coins in their pockets and the tips of their swords to melt. It seemed like an omen. The British invasion of Long Island indeed began the next morning on August 22, 1776. It would be the biggest battle of the Revolutionary War.[45]

By noon, 15,000 British soldiers and 40 cannon had crossed the Verrazano Narrows of the Hudson River on barges. They arrived on the southwest tip of Long Island. More were on the way. Yet Washington was told that only 9,000 had arrived. He therefore incorrectly concluded that the Long Island landing was indeed a distraction and that the main attack would be elsewhere. He sent only a few more troops over to Long Island, where his total force became nearly 6,000 men. The British forces there soon totaled 20,000. Meanwhile, Washington sat on Manhattan with 6,000 men, awaiting an attack from elsewhere.[46]

With no cavalry and few spies, Washington had no idea where on Long Island the British were nor what they intended to do. He protected the three main approach roads on Long Island, but there was an unguarded fourth, the Jamaica Pass, coming in from his far left. At the

[44] Ellis, pp. 95–96; Chernow (2010), p. 244; McCullough, pp. 149–151.

[45] McCullough, pp. 152–153, 156; Burrows, p. 1.

[46] Philbrick (2016), p. 10; Fischer, p. 32; Billias (1969), pp. 51, 53; McCullough, pp. 157–161.

last moment, he decided to put five guys there to keep a lookout. This was his first ever command of a battlefield army.[47]

British General Henry Clinton (who had unsuccessfully urged Howe to take Dorchester Heights before the patriots did, and who had been sent off by Howe to the Carolinas) was now back. He had pushed for an invasion up the Hudson River, but Howe rejected it. Then a loyalist on Long Island told Clinton of the unguarded Jamaica Pass. Clinton in turn told Howe and proposed an attack. Surprisingly, Howe agreed.[48]

Henry Clinton was 46 years old. He had arrived in America on the same ship to Boston with Howe and he served under him. The two men did not get along. Clinton was difficult, overzealous, and touchy.[49] He had in fact grown up in New York. Clinton was short, fat, and pale and he could be shy and petulant. But he and Howe were among the best officers in the British army. They were well-educated aristocrats who disliked each other. As Philbrick says, "No one liked Henry Clinton, especially Clinton himself, who was, by his own account, a 'shy bitch' . . . he did what Clinton did best: act so obnoxiously that even when he proposed the most logical move, those he was attempting to convince felt compelled to do the opposite." But on Long Island, general Howe for some reason adopted Clinton's suggestion to go around the left side of the patriots.[50]

Under Clinton's Jamaica Pass plan, Clinton would march at night followed by Howe's main force. They would go around the left side of the patriots, while the rest of the British army distracted the patriots by a demonstration attack at their center and on their right. The total number of soldiers with Clinton and Howe would be 10,000. Howe was taking a huge risk by spreading out his army in the pitch dark in unfamiliar territory where it might be attacked during the nine-mile march.

At two in the morning on August 27, Clinton's men encountered the five guys guarding the Jamaica Pass. They captured them right away and confirmed from them that there was no one else guarding the place.

---

47 McCullough, p. 163.

48 Ibid., p. 165.

49 Hamilton, Vol 2, pp. 174–191; Ketchum (2014), p. 2; McCullough, pp. 164–165.

50 McCullough, p. 77; Philbrick (2016), p. 12.

Then at nine o'clock, the British attacked at the center, distracting the patriots. Soon after, Clinton's men attacked from the patriot's left rear side and the patriots scrambled backward. Washington sent more troops into the fray, finally convinced that Long Island was indeed the place of battle. But it was too little too late. The fighting lasted six hours and the defeated patriots retreated toward the East River. But Howe did not follow. Instead, he ordered his troops to stop for the day. The patriots waited all afternoon to be attacked, but nothing happened. They were pinned against the East River.[51]

On Long Island, 64 British soldiers died. The patriots lost 300. More than 1,000 patriots were captured and would be held in jails, churches, and prison ships. As one British officer declared at the end of the day, "This business is pretty near over."[52]

The next morning Washington sent over 1,200 more soldiers to Long Island, not seeming to understand how much trouble his troops were in. The 20,000-man British army was within a mile and a half of the 9,000 patriots and Howe was preparing to put the patriots under siege. However, the wind was blowing the wrong direction for Howe to send ships up the East River in order to trap the patriots from behind. When Washington realized the peril that he was in, he decided to get his men off Long Island. He ordered the immediate roundup of every boat that could be found. Boats of every kind were gathered frantically near what is presently the base of the Brooklyn Bridge.[53]

By the following night, the patriots were ready to move. They were told that they were preparing for a night attack, so that absolute secrecy could be maintained for their evacuation. Otherwise, the British would come crashing down upon them at the riverside. At 11 o'clock that evening, the wind finally died down enough for the crossing of the East River to begin. As one patriot officer said of Washington's retreat: "To move so large a body of troops, with all their necessary appendages,

---

[51] Gruber, pp. 111–112; McCullough, pp. 166–182.

[52] McCullough, pp. 178–182, 192; Lord Percy to his father, September, 1776, in Charles Knowles Bolton, ed., *Letters of Hugh Earl Percy from Boston and New York, 1774–1776*. Boston: Gregg Press (1972).

[53] McCullough, pp. 183–185; Philbrick (2016), p. 17.

across a river full a mile wide, with a rapid current, in face of a victorious well-disciplined army nearly three times as numerous as his own, and a fleet capable of stopping the navigation, so that not one boat could have passed over, seemed to present most formidable obstacles."[54]

The escape boats were loaded with troops, horses, and cannon silently in the dark. The patriots tended their campfires to maintain the illusion that they were remaining in place. No one was allowed to speak. Wagon wheels were muffled with rags. When one boat was overloaded with men, Washington grabbed a large stone and threatened to put a hole in the bottom of the boat if some of them did not get off.[55]

At daybreak on August 30, most of the patriots were still on the riverbank waiting to depart. Fortunately, a heavy fog rolled in, allowing them to escape. To the British, all 9,000 patriots had in essence vanished overnight. The British were stunned, much as they had been at Boston. While many Brits thought that the patriots had "behaved very ill as men," others saw it as a gutsy, perfectly executed maneuver.[56]

As McCullough observes, luck had played a large part in the escape, and well-performed retreats did not win wars. Nor did the escape undo the dead and the wounded, nor the 1,000 prisoners lost on Long Island. The battle of Long Island had been a "fiasco" and Washington had proven "indecisive and inept," not realizing from the outset that New York was indefensible and that he was setting his own trap there, whether attacked from the southwest tip of Long Island or from northerly upper Manhattan.[57]

Washington should have continued his retreat by getting the hell off of Manhattan Island. But he was still stuck on the idea of defending New York City, since Congress had insisted that it not be abandoned. He was aggressive by nature and he wanted to fight it out.[58]

---

[54] McCullough, pp. 186–187; Lord Percy to his father, September, 1776, in Charles Knowles Bolton, ed., *Letters of Hugh Earl Percy from Boston and New York, 1774–1776.* Boston: Gregg Press (1972).

[55] Philbrick (2016), p. 17; McCullough, p. 188.

[56] McCullough, pp. 190–192.

[57] Ibid., p. 193.

[58] Philbrick (2016), p. 19.

By assuming that the British would make a frontal assault on Long Island, and leaving the Jamaica Pass on his left side wide open, Washington had made a major blunder. As one of his lieutenants remarked, "Upon the whole, less generalship never was shown in any army since the art of war was understood." Meanwhile, Howe had blown his chance to finish off the patriots on Long Island and perhaps end the war there. Of course, Clinton had, to no avail, urged Howe to follow up immediately on his Long Island victory. As one patriot said, "General Howe is either our friend or no general."[59]

As Philbrick describes it, "Despite having at his command the largest army anyone had ever seen in America, General Howe . . . seemed reluctant to use it. George Washington, on the other hand, seemed determined to put his much weaker and disorganized army squarely in harm's way, first on Long Island and now on Manhattan." He suggests that Howe believed a brutal show of force would only alienate the colonies further, making peace negotiations more difficult. It is unclear to what degree Howe's aid to the patriots was intentional or subconscious. Nevertheless, King George III knighted him for his Long Island victory.[60]

William Howe came from an eminent British family. He was rich and accomplished. And though he had demonstrated valor and ability, Howe was in general a procrastinator, slow to move, and interested foremost in his own comfort. He was a calm man of few words. After entering the army at age 17, Howe had gained substantial military service and was widely regarded as one of the best officers in the British army. But he was sympathetic to the American colonies and had disagreed with British policy toward them. He was also a member of Parliament and had said that if he were offered a command, he would decline. Yet he took it when the time came. Howe had also declared back in England that, though he stood ready to serve, the British army could not defeat the patriots. All told, William Howe was one conflicted fellow.[61]

---

59 Ibid., pp. 15–19.

60 Ibid., pp. 21–22; McCullough, p. 196; Willcox, p. 107; Hadden, p. 375.

61 McCullough, pp. 7, 76; Gruber, p. 56; Fischer, pp. 70–71; Gruber, p. 58; Philbrick (2016), p. 12.

Whereas Howe had been trapped on the Boston peninsula with a clear escape by sea, Washington was now on Manhattan with an escape by land that could be blocked. One of Washington's officers described Manhattan as "this tongue of land, where we ought never to have been." His evacuated soldiers from Long Island were angry, roaming the Manhattan streets, breaking into houses and stealing things. Others just walked off, having had enough. They felt that they had been "sold out" and that Washington was a poor leader. Washington asked Congress whether he should burn the city if he had to evacuate it. He wanted to do so, but the answer was no.[62]

Hightailing It Out of Manhattan

Four days after Washington's men escaped from Long Island, a British ship towing flatboats made its way up the East River at night. More followed the next day. Then nothing happened, while general Howe met with Benjamin Franklin and others to discuss resolution of the war.

Meanwhile, Washington could not decide whether to abandon New York. He was under tremendous pressure and distracted himself by writing letters home to oversee improvements at Mount Vernon: "The chimney in the new room should be exactly in the middle of it—the doors and everything else to be exactly answerable and uniform—in short I would have the whole executed in a masterly manner." Finally, he decided to bail out. He would move his army 14 miles north to Harlem Heights, a rocky and more defensible position. So over the following two days, his troops gathered their supplies and began the march northward.[63]

---

[62] Joseph Reed to Esther Reed, September 2, 1776, New York Historical Society, New York, New York; McCullough, pp. 201–206.

[63] McCullough, pp. 203, 207–208; Philbrick (2016), pp. 20, 25.

Our daughter, Natalia, participated in dress-up day at school for the Revolutionary War. She went as Samuel Adams, signer of the Declaration of Independence. When asked why she chose him, she said that he was "the beer guy" and that he was the only person she recognized.

The British invasion of Manhattan began in mid-September of 1776, with General Clinton leading the way. Though he had also suggested maneuvers to trap Washington's retreating army, Howe had rejected them, naturally. So, while British ships moved up the Hudson River to create an impression that the attack would be there, Clinton and 4,000 men rode 80 flatboats up the East River to Kip's Bay (near modern-day East 30th Street). British ships on the East River fired their 80 cannon for two solid hours to loosen things up before Clinton went ashore on Manhattan.[64]

The 750 patriots who were there fled, though Washington, who was with them, tried to stop their retreat. He was in a lather, throwing his hat to the ground, swatting at the retreating men with his sword, firing his unloaded pistols in the air, and calling the retreat "disgraceful and dastardly conduct." Henry Knox narrowly avoided capture, being only 80 yards away from the British. But rather than race across Manhattan

[64] McCullough, p. 211; Philbrick (2016), p. 27.

to prevent the patriot escape to the north, the British troops had been ordered by Howe to await reinforcements. So they stayed put until another 9,000 British soldiers arrived that afternoon.[65]

Though Washington had fortified the hell out of Manhattan, he and his soldiers were now retreating north to Harlem Heights. When one of his scouting parties was attacked along the way, Washington ordered a counter-attack. Then the British and the patriots sat for several days. Meanwhile, patriot soldiers were deserting 30 or 40 at a time, with many going over to the British. Colonial army surgeons were accepting bribes to state that soldiers were too sick to serve.[66]

Fighting on Lake Champlain

On the same day that the British invaded Manhattan, Benedict Arnold was at Lake Champlain in upstate New York. The British were building a fleet to sail down the lake, which was the only way to attack from Canada, as there were no roads. The patriots were constructing ships as well in order to face off against them. As commander of the fleet, Arnold supervised more than 200 carpenters in the shipbuilding process. He was short and stocky, with tremendous energy and endurance.[67]

The British fleet from Canada intended to meet up with forces coming from the south in order to take control of the area. But they needed to do so before Lake Champlain froze in late November. Lake Champlain was 125 miles long and 14 miles wide at its widest point. Arnold was ordered by his commander, Horatio Gates at Fort Ticonderoga, not to wage an all-out attack on the British fleet and to take a defensive approach instead. Gates also told him not to take unnecessary

---

[65] Philbrick (2016), p. 30; Library of Congress, George Washington Papers, The American Revolution, A Timeline of George Washington's Military and Political Career During the American Revolution, 1774–1783, https://www.loc.gov/collections/george-washington-papers/articles-and-essays/timeline/the-american-revolution/#1775, p. 17, accessed September 13, 2021; Brooks (1900), pp. 54–67; McCullough, pp. 210–216.

[66] McCullough, pp. 218–219, 225–227.

[67] Philbrick (2016), pp. 32–39.

risks, but to do everything possible to combat the British, whatever that meant.[68]

Arnold knew that the British would wait until a favorable wind came up to set sail, so that the wind would be at their backs. That wind arrived on October 11, 1776, and the British set off. Arnold tucked his fleet in the bay between Valcour Island and the western shore of Lake Champlain, where he waited for the British fleet to pass by. When the British were nearly two miles south of him, Arnold sent one of his ships, *Royal Savage*, out into the river to notify the British of the patriot presence by firing cannon. The British turned about to face him, but they were now facing upwind. Arnold held the marine equivalent of high ground. He had 4 ships and 11 more vessels of various sorts and most of his 700 men had never been at sea. The British had 36 warships and 1,000 soldiers.[69]

Most of Arnold's fleet was still in the bay between Valcour Island and the shore. The British could have maneuvered back upstream to approach from both the south and the north end of the bay, trapping him, but Arnold did not care, saying he would fight them then and there in the bay, between the island and the shore, if need be. *Royal Savage* did not make it back to the bay before its mast and rigging were blown away by cannon from the gigantic British warship *Inflexible*. Arnold's 50 men jumped overboard and went ashore on the island.[70]

The *Inflexible* was unable, however, to sail upwind and was effectively taken out of the fight. Several other British boats were also unable to do so. As a result, the British had only 22 gunboats fighting against Arnold's 14 remaining vessels for the two hours that followed. One British ship came within a few hundred yards of the patriot vessels and then turned sideways to send a blast of cannon shots at them. The patriot vessels all focused on that ship and their cannon fire ripped through it, sinking it within an hour. Cannonballs skipped across the water, blowing holes in the hulls of the warring ships.[71]

---

[68] Ibid., pp. 34–41.

[69] Ibid., pp. 42–45.

[70] Ibid., pp. 45–46.

[71] Ibid., pp. 46–49.

At nightfall, the fighting stopped and the British set fire to the *Royal Savage*. By that time, Arnold had 60 soldiers dead and three fourths of his ammunition exhausted. He now needed a way to escape down the lake. The south end of the bay was blocked by British ships, and the sensible thing to do was to go out the north end of the bay and turn downstream. But Arnold refused to do that. Fog was rolling in and the *Royal Savage* was ablaze, rendering all of the surroundings dark as pitch. After several hours of cannon blasting earlier in the day, neither army could hear too well, so the chances of being heard were reduced. So Arnold and his men quietly escaped through the south end of the bay, passing perilously close to and between the unsuspecting British ships. Naturally, Arnold's ship was the last to pass through. As Philbrick says, he "always seemed to go for the most spectacular and dangerous stroke . . . With Arnold it was always difficult to draw the line between acceptable risk and self-serving derring-do . . . Was this Arnold's idea of a 'defensive war'?"[72]

The following morning was misty and it took some time for the British to realize that the patriots had escaped. Eventually, the British took off in hot pursuit. When they caught up with the patriots, one of Arnold's ships immediately surrendered. Arnold, however, took off down the lake, fighting it out alone for two hours until his ship was blown to pieces. He floated his busted ship to shore, where he destroyed it, naturally, before the British could seize it. Arnold and his men then marched south to Fort Ticonderoga. Surprisingly, the British, instead of attacking Fort Ticonderoga after winning the Battle of Valcour Island, headed back up Lake Champlain for the winter. Arnold had accomplished his goal of preventing British control of the area.[73]

---

[72] Ibid., pp. 50–52.

[73] Ibid., pp. 54–56.

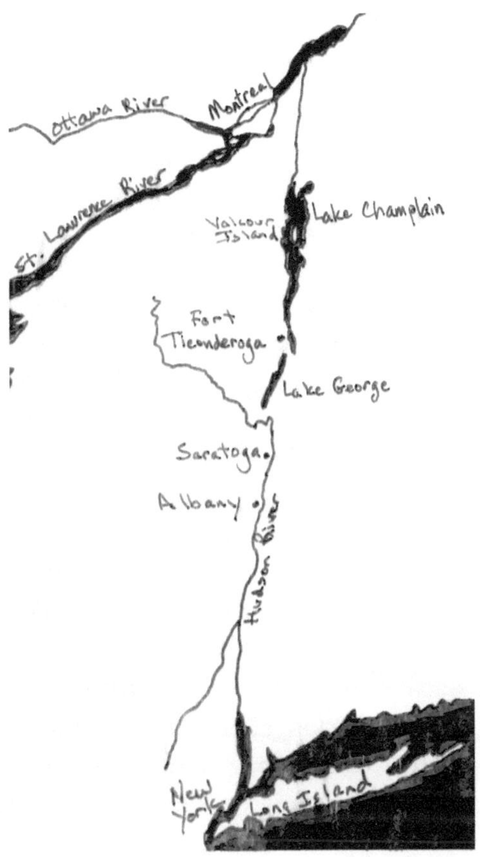

Upstate New York and Valcour Island on Lake Champlain

Benedict Arnold now hungered for a promotion to major general. Instead, Congress promoted five other officers past him. Even George Washington was shocked by this. And though Congress later promoted Arnold to major general, he remained junior to the others who had been promoted earlier. As John Adams described the wrangling among officers for stature, they scrambled for rank and pay "like apes for nuts."[74]

Arnold later appeared before Congress to plead his case for seniority. Though he was handsome and grand in his appearance, his speech was dull, ungrammatical, and vulgar. And instead of discussing matters, he shouted and pounded the table. As Philbrick describes him, he was

[74] Ibid., pp. 58, 90, 99, 103; Randall (1990), pp. 324–327, 332–334; Brandt, p. 118.

"emotionally obtuse" and aggressive. In making his case to Congress, he even tendered his resignation, but Congress refused to accept it. As an expression of gratitude for his valor at Valcour, Congress gave Arnold a horse.[75]

Bailing Out of New York State

Meanwhile, back in Manhattan, patriot Nathan Hale had been apprehended and hanged as a spy at the age of 21. After the British had invaded Manhattan, Washington needed to know their locations and strategies. He had sought a spy to go behind enemy lines and Hale was the only volunteer. But Hale was a poor choice for a spy. He knew nothing about spying. He had graduated from Yale with honors at age 18, become a teacher, and later joined the Connecticut militia. To do his spying, Hale posed as a Dutch schoolteacher looking for employment, but he did not travel under an assumed name and he even carried his Yale diploma with him. Two weeks into his job as a spy, he was recognized in a tavern by a Massachusetts loyalist who struck up a conversation with him, pretending to be a patriot. He lured Hale into betraying his own position and then turned him over to General Howe.[76]

On October 9, 1776, the gig on Manhattan Island was up. Three British warships came up the Hudson River and anchored again at Tarrytown, about 20 miles north of Harlem Heights. They had once again passed the patriot guns without difficulty. Then, a few days later, 150 British ships sailed up the East River all the way to Long Island Sound, landing at Pell's Point straight across from Harlem Heights on the other side of Manhattan Island.

Washington was once again in a trap. He moved north as soon as possible to White Plains, eighteen miles away. Yet he decided to try to

---

[75] Randall (1990), pp. 339–342; Philbrick (2016), pp. 59, 103, 106,143.

[76] "Capt. Nathan Hale (1755–1776) - Sons of the American Revolution, Connecticut - CTSSAR." www.connecticutsar.org.; "Nathan Hale: Yale 1773." Curator: Richard E. Mooney." www.library.yale.edu., p. 2. Retrieved January 16, 2016; McCullough, p. 224; Smith, Jr., John L. "9 Rules of Spying That Nathan Hale Failed to Follow." *Journal of the American Revolution*, May 21, 2015; "Captain Nathan Hale (1755 - 1776)."*Patriots*. The Connecticut Society of the Sons of the American Revolution.

hold on to Fort Washington, which stood 20 miles to the south, on the eastern bank of the Hudson River. He left some men at that fort and moved the rest of his army to White Plains. Instead of calling it a retreat, he called it an "alteration of our position."[77]

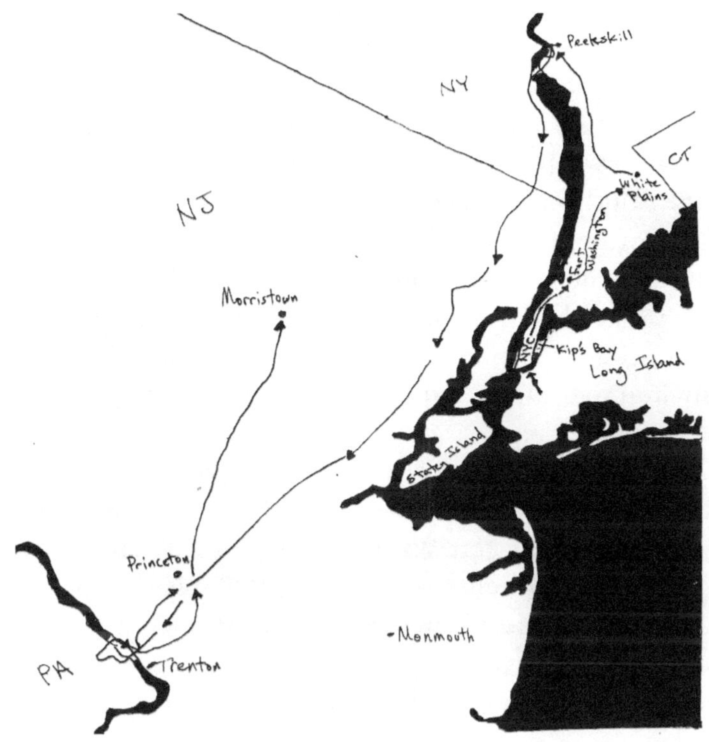

Washington's Retreat to New Jersey,
November 1776 to January 1777

At Pell's Point on Manhattan, 4,000 British soldiers went ashore, but their approach was slow and careful. Howe did not expect to cut off the patriot retreat. As always, he wanted to draw Washington into the open for one grand, decisive victory. And even after he reached White Plains, Howe took a few days to settle in before confronting the enemy.

[77] McCullough, pp. 229–231. Washington's characterization of the retreat as an "alteration of our position" is similar to McClellan's claim of a "change of base" during the Virginia Peninsula Campaign of the Civil War.

The British then charged uphill and the patriots ran, after inflicting heavy casualties upon Howe's men.[78]

Howe sat the next day, waiting for more reinforcements. The day after that it was pouring rain, so he did nothing. Finally, on November 1, Howe discovered that Washington had retreated overnight to a stronger position half a mile away across the Bronx River. The two armies sat and watched each other for two days.

Curiously, the entire British army then withdrew southward on the evening of November 3. Washington was bewildered, having no idea where the British were headed. Perhaps they were going south to attack Fort Washington. Or perhaps they were going to board ships on the Hudson River and head north in order to get above him again and attack him from the north. Or perhaps they were changing their plans altogether and heading for New Jersey or Philadelphia. This time Washington split his army into four pieces and took his piece, consisting of 2,000 men, toward Fort Washington.[79]

Howe was indeed headed to Fort Washington, where he delivered an ultimatum: surrender or be destroyed. Howe was told to go to hell, so the British attacked Fort Washington with 4,000 Hessians from the north, another 1,000 from the east, and 3,000 soldiers from the south. Two hours later, the fort surrendered all of its 2,837 soldiers and 146 cannon. The British changed the name of the place to Fort Knyphausen in honor of the Hessian general, Wilhelm von Knyphausen, who had led the attack.[80]

The Hessians were rented soldiers. Technically, they were "auxiliaries" to the British army and not "mercenaries," since they did not hire on directly with England as individuals. Instead, they were rented in units. More than half of them came from the Germanic state of Hesse, so the patriots just called them all *Hessians*. As auxiliaries, they wore their usual uniforms and had their own flag and officers. Nearly 30,000 of them

---

[78] Ibid., pp. 233–235.

[79] Ibid., pp. 234–235.

[80] Ibid., pp. 237, 239–243; https://www.mountvernon.org/library/digitalhistory/digital-encyclopedia/article/wilhelm-von-knyphausen, accessed July 14, 2022.

fought in the Revolutionary War and their mitre hats stood more than nine inches tall, making them look taller, meaner, and crazier.

The 1,000 patriot soldiers captured on Long Island had been bad enough. After the capture of Fort Washington, nearly 3,000 more men were prisoners. In all, George Washington lost 4,500 men to capture in the last three months of 1776, along with 250 cannon. Of those not captured, more than three-fourths of the soldiers under his direct command were gone due to death, injury, or desertion.[81]

Then, in late November of 1776, the British advanced on another patriot fort on the New Jersey side of the Hudson River. By the time they arrived, the fort had been abandoned, except for a dozen drunk patriots who had tapped the fort's rum supply. So Washington took off across New Jersey with 3,000 men. By now, the British held more patriots as prisoners than Washington had in his army.[82]

All Aboard: The Prisoners of New York

After taking only 30 prisoners at Bunker Hill, the British were confounded about where to put the 1,000 patriot prisoners after the Battle of Long Island. General Howe appointed loyalist Joshua Loring, the husband of Howe's mistress, as head of military prisoners. Loring thought that those who took up arms against Britain deserved no mercy, and he began transferring prisoners to ships in the New York harbor where they were tossed into the hold. One ship was a reeking cattle barge, where they lay on cow dung and drank bilge water.[83]

The invasion of Manhattan had yielded another 320 prisoners. With Manhattan in their possession, the British now had more places to house their prisoners. Only a few thousand New York City inhabitants remained in the city, so the captured patriot officers were assigned to housing. They were even allowed to find lodging on their own, if they could afford it. When Fort Washington surrendered, the 2,837 soldiers

---

81 Philbrick (2016), p. 61.

82 McCullough, pp. 245–246; https://www.historynet.com/british-prison-ships-a-season-in-hell.htm, p.3, accessed July 25, 2021.

83 Burrows, pp. 9–13.

captured there poured into the city as well. By November, every church on Manhattan, other than the Church of England, had been converted to a prison.[84]

Prisoners of war customarily received two-thirds rations—1,640 calories per day. As historian Edwin Burrows notes, a totally sedentary prisoner who weighed 160 pounds would lose one pound per week on these rations. When food ran short, prisoners received even less. Nearly 1,000 men were crammed into buildings on Manhattan, with up to 800 in the Old North Church. The rest went to sugar refineries, known as "sugar houses."[85]

Whether the so-called "rules of war" even applied to the insurrection in American was not clear. As Burrows puts it, "Unprotected by international agreement or by the code of honor that regulated the conduct of officers and gentlemen, the patriots were at the complete mercy of their enraged captors."[86] The British refused to call the patriots prisoners of war, as doing so might confer some rights upon them and give legitimacy to their claim of independence.

Though "honor" justified the release of prisoners who were officers, common soldiers were not considered to be gentlemen and were therefore seen as having no honor. Also in question was whether a plain person holding an officer's rank in the ragtag patriot army merited exchange with an aristocrat of equal rank in the British army, as if they were social equals. The British viewed the patriots as rebels and wanted them hauled off to England and tried for treason. Yet two of the patriot generals who were captured on Long Island soon dined with General William Howe aboard his ship before being exchanged, consistent with the aristocratic practice among officers at the time.[87]

In the British military system, commissions were bought and aristocrats were given preference. As Burrows explains, ". . . military rank in Britain remained intimately connected to inherited property and privilege. Only someone entitled by birth to the deference of others was

[84] Ibid., pp. 15–18, 48–50.

[85] Ibid., pp. 19, 23

[86] Ibid., p. 37.

[87] Ibid., pp. 28–32; McCullough, p. 180.

believed capable of leading men in war: gentility, not expertise, constituted the foundation of an officer's authority . . . army officers purchased their commission, typically at prices so steep . . . that the service essentially belonged to the few hundred wealthy families who ran the country." For example, the cost of becoming a colonel was around $900,000 in today's dollars. And roughly one out of every seven members of the House of Commons held a commission in the British army or navy.[88]

The New York prison ships were sometimes reduced to hulks, with the masts and rigging removed, so that they sat stationary in the water. The hulks were freezing in winter and sweltering in summer, serving to "incubate hosts of lice and diseases in the overcrowded conditions." While captured patriot General Charles Lee walked the streets of New York freely, enjoying a fire, food, and wine in his suite, where he received guests and had a servant, the ordinary soldier wasted away in bleak captivity.[89]

The prison ships were so overcrowded that the prisoners could not all lie down at once. There was stagnant air, wormy food, foul water, vermin, and smallpox aboard. Dead bodies were thrown overboard each morning. One prisoner said they were "treated worse than cattle and hogs."[90]

On land, imprisonment was not much better. Ethan Allen, himself a prisoner in various places for more than three years, described the filth in the churches that were used as prisons: "The floors were covered with excrements . . . I have seen in one of these churches seven dead, at the same time, lying among the excrements of their own bodies." Over time, he came to believe "that it was a premeditated and systemic plan of the British" to inflict "relentless and scientific barbarity" upon the patriots and to justify it by use of the word "rebels." On land, 20 to 30 died each day by December of 1776. On the ships, there were 10 to 12. In fact,

88 McCullough, p. 78; Burrows, pp. 27, 34.

89 https://www.historynet.com/british-prison-ships-a-season-in-hell.htm, pp. 6–7, accessed July 25, 2021.

90 Burrows, pp. 55–57.

half of those captured on Long Island in late August of 1776 were dead by the end of the year.[91]

Most Americans suspected that the deaths were not accidental. The prisoners were instead being "murdered by inches" in a preconceived system meant to punish them for having rebelled. The British Parliament then worsened matters in March of 1777, when it authorized the prosecution of colonial soldiers for treason. The British prime minister declared that trials for treason would occur "at the pleasure of the crown," meaning that the prisoners would be held as criminals to be dealt with whenever the crown got around to it.[92]

The British commanders in New York City meanwhile flatly denied that anything was wrong. One sugar house prisoner said he survived only by eating garbage that was thrown into the prison yard from a nearby home. Another said that "old shoes were bought and eaten with as good a relish as a pig or a turkey." To save themselves, some of the prisoners defected to the British army. A few then gained freedom by deserting after defecting.[93]

Bringing the War to New Jersey

British General Clinton wanted to enter New Jersey and decimate Washington's retreating army before winter set in. Clinton sought to destroy armies, whereas Howe sought to control territory. This time Howe sent Clinton to Newport, Rhode Island, to secure the British naval supply line, which was being disrupted by colonial privateers. Then Howe ordered Cornwallis to go with 10,000 men into New Jersey to chase down Washington. Yet he told Cornwallis to chase only as far as New Brunswick and then to await further orders. This is regarded as one of the greatest mistakes of the war. When Clinton learned of this, he suggested that his own troops land by boat in New Jersey to trap

---

[91] Ibid., pp. 62–64,103.

[92] Ibid., pp. 76, 80; https://www.historynet.com/british-prison-ships-a-season-in-hell.htm, pp. 1–2, accessed July 25, 2021,.

[93] Burrows, pp. 82, 91,111–112; https://www.historynet.com/british-prison-ships-a-season-in-hell.htm, p. 3, accessed July 25, 2021.

Washington. Howe, of course, refused, so Clinton sailed for Newport as ordered. It was late November of 1776.[94]

Howe had already blown it in New York, squandering his best opportunity to block the escape of Washington's army and destroy it. By the time the patriots were in New Jersey, Howe's gigantic army was spread too thin to keep possession of the territory it had conquered and also pursue war against Washington. The British were soon offering to pardon any American who would swear loyalty to the crown. As a result, large numbers of colonists poured into the British camps in New Jersey to sign their names. Congress meanwhile offered 50 acres of land to any Hessian who would defect, and for British officers it promised 50 to 800 acres, depending on rank. To make matters worse, the enlistments of 2,000 of Washington's men would expire on December 1. Only four months earlier, his army had consisted on 20,000 soldiers. Since then, he had lost three battles and surrendered two forts. Many of his soldiers were shoeless. Some lacked coats or even shirts.[95]

On the first day of December 1776, 2,000 of Washington's men indeed walked off the job at New Brunswick with the British only two hours away. Alexander Hamilton blasted cannon to hold the British off and, by the time they entered New Brunswick the next morning, Washington and his small remainder of an army were gone. They had marched overnight to Trenton, only 30 miles from Philadelphia. Meanwhile, Congress moved from Philadelphia to Baltimore for its own safety. Two of its members, however, joined the enemy.[96]

Cornwallis remained at New Brunswick, as ordered by Howe. He sat for six days awaiting further orders. Howe showed up on December 6 with more soldiers and ordered Cornwallis to go forward. The Brits and the Hessians plundered and destroyed houses along the way to Trenton.[97]

---

94 McCullough, pp. 246–253; Gruber, p. 135; Willcox, pp. 123–124; https://www.mountvernon.org/library/digitalhistory/digital-encycl...es-cornwallis-1st-marquess-and-2nd-earl-cornwallis-1738-1805, p. 3, accessed July 17, 2021.

95 Philbrick (2016), p. 63; "Liberty! The Hessians." www.pbs.org, retrieved June 24, 2020; Hurt, p. 80; McCullough, pp. 249, 254.

96 McCullough, pp. 256, 270.

97 Ibid., pp. 258–261.

Trenton sat near the east bank of the Delaware River, which separated New Jersey from Pennsylvania. Washington destroyed every boat in sight over a 60 mile stretch along the Trenton side of the river. He and his men then crossed the river in the few boats that they had saved for that purpose. He was now 90 miles west of Manhattan. Washington set up his headquarters straight across the Delaware River from Trenton in order to keep an eye on the enemy. The prospects for his army were grim. Supplies were scarce and a harsh winter was setting in.[98]

One week later, Howe decided to call everything off until the springtime. He left Trenton the following day and headed for New York City, leaving 1,500 Hessians behind to protect the newly gained ground. As McCullough says, "eighteenth-century professional armies and their gentlemen commanders did not subject themselves to the miseries of winter campaigns," so Howe returned to "the comforts and pleasures that so appealed to the general himself." Cornwallis went with him to catch a ship for England. In essence, the British believed the 1776 fighting season to be over. And though Washington was just across the river keeping an eye on them, he had no idea that Howe and Cornwallis were gone, nor that the fighting had been called off for the winter. Howe spent the winter in New York drinking and gambling.[99]

Washington Goes Fabian

Three days after Howe and Cornwallis hit the road, Washington moved ten miles upstream. More of his enlistments were expiring in two weeks (on New Year's Day) and he desperately needed new men. He wrote to his cousin, "If this fails, I think the game is pretty near up."[100] Within a few days, 2,000 patriot soldiers showed up from the regiment of an officer who had been captured. Another 600 came in with patriot general

---

[98] Ibid., pp. 263–264; Taylor, pp. 166–167, 169; Ketchum (1999), p. 235; Chernow (2010), p. 264.

[99] McCullough, p. 267; Philbrick (2016), p. 92.

[100] George Washington to Lund Washington, December 10–17, 1776, in The Papers of George Washington, *Revolutionary War Series, Vols. I–VIII,* W.W. Abbott, Philander D. Chase, and Dorothy Twohig, eds. Charlottesville, Virginia: University Press of Virginia, 1985–1988, VII, p 291; McCullough, p. 269.

Horatio Gates. Washington now had around 6,000 soldiers fit for duty. Henry Knox was by Washington's side and he was ready to rumble.[101]

On Christmas night, Washington's men boarded flat-bottomed boats that were 8 feet wide and more than 40 feet long. They stood, 40 men to a boat. Fifty horses and 18 cannon also went along. Young Henry Knox managed it all. They crossed the Delaware River, which had ice in it and a strong current. First it rained, then it hailed, then it snowed, and the sound of the winter storm muffled the noise that they made during the crossing. It was three in the morning by the time everything made it across the river. Two of the men then froze to death on the 12 mile march south to Trenton.[102]

Washington reached Trenton at eight in the morning and soon attacked, with the patriots firing at and trotting toward the Hessians guarding the town. When the shooting began, other Hessians poured into the streets and Henry Knox blasted away at them with cannonballs flying down the streets of Trenton. They were chased into an orchard on the edge of town, where they surrendered. The whole thing took 45 minutes. It was Washington's first attack as a field commander.[103]

At Trenton, 900 Hessians were captured and another 500 escaped. Another 21 were killed and 90 were wounded. In contrast, no patriot died and only four were wounded. The Hessian commander, who was killed during the battle, had been alerted on Christmas Day that an attack was imminent, but assumed that nothing would happen during the winter storm that was underway. He was playing cards that evening when he received a note from a loyalist warning him of the impending attack, but he put the note in his pocket and kept playing. After the battle, some of the patriots broke into the Hessian liquor supply and wore Hessian mitres while they drank.[104]

Washington's army returned to Pennsylvania across the Delaware River that night with their 900 Hessian prisoners. Knox was again in charge of the logistics for getting the patriot soldiers, horses, and cannon

---

[101] McCullough, pp. 269–270.

[102] Ibid., pp. 274–275; Philbrick (2016), p. 73.

[103] McCullough, pp. 277, 280.

[104] Ibid., p. 279; Philbrick (2016), p. 76.

back across the river, along with the hundreds of prisoners and captured supplies. Back in camp, Washington told his soldiers that they would receive cash in proportion to the total value of everything they had captured at Trenton—horses, guns, and cannon included. The Trenton news soon made Washington a hero. Meanwhile, Howe stayed in New York and ordered Cornwallis to return to New Jersey with 8,000 men in order to deal with their patriot rival.[105]

Though his soldiers fought at Trenton, patriot general Horatio Gates did not. In fact, he had recommended that Washington retreat rather than attack. When Washington decided to attack, Gates claimed illness and did not participate. Instead, Gates headed to Baltimore, where the Continental Congress was meeting. He complained that he, rather than Washington, should command the Continental army. Though Gates dressed like a slob, he was ambitious. But Washington's victory at Trenton shut him down. Gates was ordered to return to Fort Ticonderoga in upstate New York.[106]

The Battle of Trenton, with its night crossing of the Delaware River and capture of 900 Hessians, was a turning point in the war. Washington had begun using Fabian maneuvers to battle a larger enemy. This involved indirect assaults and attrition, rather than frontal assaults and pitched battles. Roman commander Fabius Maximus had successfully used such distraction in smaller skirmishes 2,000 years earlier to combat Hannibal on the Italian peninsula. He attacked Hannibal's supply line and his isolated outposts. Pitched battles were avoided, while small patrols and forage parties were captured, ultimately forcing Hannibal to attack fortified cities in an effort to conquer a port for supplies.[107]

---

[105] Ibid., p. 76; McCullough, pp. 281–284; https://en.wikipedia.org/wiki/American_Revolutionary_War, p. 4; Fischer, pp. 259–295; Wickwire (1970), p. 95.

[106] Philbrick (2016), p. 59; https://en.m.wikipedia.org/wiki/Horatio_Gates, p. 11, accessed July 22, 2021.

[107] McCullough, p. 290; https://en.m.wikipedia.org/wiki/Fabian_strategy, accessed July 22, 2021; https://www.mountvernon.org/library/digitalhistory/digital-encyclopedia/article/fabian-strategy, p. 2, accessed August 31, 2021.

Though Washington had no formal military education, he was familiar with the strategy of Fabius from his reading of classical history.[108] Of course, he would have preferred to defeat the British in one grand battle. But after getting creamed on Long Island and chased into New Jersey, he began to consider a defensive posture, putting the survival of his army ahead of the defense of any particular place. At Trenton, he used ambush and indirection to level the playing field.

New Jersey

Rather than going head-to-head against larger forces, Washington was now picking them apart in smaller pieces. "As had been demonstrated at Long Island and New York, Washington was not a good battlefield thinker. Howe (with the help of Henry Clinton) consistently outgeneraled him. Washington's gifts were more physical and improvisational,"

[108] https://www.mountvernon.org/library/digitalhistory/digital-encyclopedia/article/fabian-strategy, p. 2, accessed August 31, 2021.

Philbrick observes. Washington referred to his Fabian strategy as a "war of posts." When he explained the concept to Congress, they seemed to be unfamiliar with it.[109]

Three days later, on December 29, 1776, Washington was on the move once more, crossing the Delaware yet again. At Trenton the next day, he urged his men to stay with him, offering an extra ten dollars to any soldier who would stay on for another six months. Nobody took the deal. He asked them to stay on for just one more month. Many stepped forward. Washington then sent Arnold to defend Rhode Island after the British (under Clinton) seized Newport. Arnold, however, spent much of the winter socializing in Boston.[110]

Nipping at Their Heels

Cornwallis appeared in Trenton with 5,500 men on January 1, 1777. The patriots retreated west across the Assunpink Bridge, a narrow stone bridge that they could defend more easily. Cornwallis attacked at the bridge head-on. If he broke through, the war was likely over.[111]

Henry Knox bombarded the Brits with 20 cannon, preventing them from crossing. He drove Cornwallis back three times before Cornwallis took one final plunge, unsuccessfully. The patriots had 50 dead or wounded, while Cornwallis had 365 dead, wounded, or captured. As evening fell, Cornwallis deliberated whether to attack yet again. One of his officers commented that, given his tendencies, Washington would not be there in the morning. With that, Cornwallis retired for the day, saying he would "bag him" in the morning.[112]

In the morning, Washington was indeed gone. But instead of running away, he had sneaked around Cornwallis to attack the back end of his army at Princeton. Washington had wanted to stay put and fight it out, of course, but one of his officers had suggested that they sneak around instead. Washington liked that idea, since it avoided the appearance of

---

[109] Philbrick (2016), pp. 68, 100.

[110] McCullough, pp. 285–286; Randall (1990), pp. 324–327

[111] Philbrick (2016), pp. 79–81.

[112] McCullough, p. 287; Philbrick (2016), p. 83.

a retreat and gave him a chance to attack. He made Cornwallis believe that the patriots were still in front of him at Trenton by leaving some men behind to maintain campfires and make noise late into the night. Trenton and Princeton were only 12 miles apart as the crow flies. But Washington's arcing overnight march was 20 miles long, made by men with ragged clothing and broken shoes, if any. The next morning they attacked.[113]

The fighting at Princeton was furious, with Washington at the front of the battle line, but it only lasted 15 minutes. By then, the patriots had killed or captured 273 British soldiers and the rest of them were hauling ass toward Trenton. Washington had once again used Fabian strategy to antagonize the enemy. His men moved on before the main body of Cornwallis's army arrived. Washington also wanted to capture the British pay chest, which held 70,000 pounds ($12.6 million in today's dollars) at New Brunswick. It was only 18 miles away, but Knox and others talked him out of it.[114]

It was January 3, 1777, when Cornwallis went into winter quarters in New Brunswick, closer to New York City. Washington marched his men 37 miles to Morristown, New Jersey, where they stayed for the winter. The patriots were only 35 miles from Manhattan, but Morristown was nestled in the Watchung Mountains and provided a good defensible position for his troops. It was also close enough to New York for Washington to react to anything that Howe might try.[115]

During the winter encampment at Morristown, Washington had all of his soldiers inoculated against smallpox. Given that during the course of the war smallpox killed 17,000 soldiers (whereas battles killed 6,800) this decision was one of his best. In fact, most of the patriot smallpox deaths occurred on the British prison ships in New York Harbor.[116]

---

[113] Philbrick (2016), p. 84; McCullough, p. 288; Wickwire (1970), p. 97.

[114] Fischer, pp. 306–307; Ketchum (1999), p. 146; McCullough, p. 290.

[115] McCullough, pp. 289–290; Lengel, p. 208; Fischer, p. 343; Gruber, pp. 154–156; Martin (1993), p. 22; Philbrick (2016), p. 85.

[116] Brooks (1900), p. 87; Washington (*Writings*) v. 7, pp. 38, 130–131; Ellis, p. 87; Philbrick (2016), p. 103; https://www.historynet.com, "British Prison Ships: A Season in Hell," James E. Held, November 2006; accessed July 25, 2021.

The strength of the patriots lay in their will rather than in their control of New York, or the Hudson River, or any place for that matter. That strength, in turn, derived from Washington, who somehow held the army together. As McCullough so eloquently says of Washington: "He was not a brilliant strategist or tactician, not a gifted orator, not an intellectual. At several crucial moments he had shown marked indecisiveness. He had made serious mistakes in judgment. But . . . he learned steadily from experience. Above all, Washington never forgot what was at stake and he never gave up." By May of 1777, he had 9,000 soldiers.[117]

The British still desired to isolate New England from the rest of the country by taking control of the Hudson River. This would allow them to focus separately on the south, where they believed loyalist support was strong.[118]

Every Brit for Himself

British General John Burgoyne set out from Montreal on June 14, 1777. When his 8,000 men appeared on high ground above Fort Ticonderoga in New York on July 5, the 3,000 patriots in the fort retreated. The British retook the fort. From there, Burgoyne intended to attack Albany from the north while Howe attacked from the south. Like Howe, Burgoyne was one of the better officers in the British army. He was also a member of Parliament.

But Howe was determined to capture Philadelphia instead. Clinton told him bluntly of the problems associated with doing so, including the fact that it would leave Burgoyne stranded in upstate New York. Tired of dealing with Howe, Clinton had gone to England to resign, but King George III refused his request. To appease him, the king knighted him and then ordered him back to New York to continue working under Howe. Howe was competing with Burgoyne for glory. He did not even bother to tell Burgoyne of his change of plans. Howe decided to focus

---

[117] McCullough, p. 293; Philbrick (2016), p. 104.

[118] Ketchum (1997), pp. 79–80.

on his own triumph, and he refused to serve in a role subordinate to Burgoyne.[119]

Horatio Gates led the patriot retreat from Fort Ticonderoga. Washington soon sent some of his best soldiers to support Gates, including Benedict Arnold. Gates was 49 years old and had been born in England. After purchasing a military commission in the British army at the age of 18 with financial help from his parents, he sold it nine years later and then bought another one in New York. Gates had served with Washington during the French and Indian War, where he showed skill mostly in military administration. Though he had reached the rank of major in the British army, he lacked the money and connections he needed to gain a higher rank. So he again sold his British army commission at the age of 42 and moved from New York to Virginia. When the war broke out, Gates yearned for a field command and rushed to Mount Vernon to offer his services to Washington, who saw to it that he indeed became a Brigadier General.[120]

After capturing Fort Ticonderoga, the sensible route for Burgoyne was to use the well-established portage to Lake George and then proceed down the Hudson River. However, he unwisely pursued Gates and the retreating patriots. At the southernmost tip of Lake Champlain, the patriots ditched their boats and fled south through the woods. But rather than turn around and go over to Lake George, Burgoyne followed them into the mountains. While he waited to establish a supply line from Canada, the patriots cut down every tree they could put in his way and destroyed the bridges in his path. Burgoyne was 55 years old. He had been a member of the House of Commons for 16 years and would serve another 15. He was overconfident, viewing his mission as a walk in the woods that would make him a hero.[121]

---

[119] Wilcox, p.154; Stedman, vol. 1, pp. 317–319; Philbrick (2016), p. 93.

[120] Nickerson, p. 216; https///en.m.wikipedia.org/wiki/Battles_of_Saratoga, pp. 1–7. accessed July 22, 2021; Philbrick (2016), p. 124; https://en.m.wikipedia.org/wiki/Horatio_Gates, pp. 7–8, accessed July 22, 2021; Horgan, p. 32; Billias (1964), pp. 82, 85.

[121] Philbrick (2016), pp. 111–113, 118; https://en.m.wikipedia.org/wiki/John_Burgoyne, p. 8, accessed August 21, 2021.

Burgoyne also believed that Howe was still coming from the south to meet him near Albany for its capture. But Howe was preparing to sail his 267 ships and 18,000 men to Philadelphia, the largest city in the colonies, instead. Howe also continued to ignore Clinton, who tried three times to talk him out of Philadelphia. So Howe left New York on July 23, 1777, and took five weeks to reach the Chesapeake Bay, 50 miles west of Philadelphia. There, he hoped to lure Washington into a grand, open field battle. Howe was clearly not coming to the aid of Burgoyne.[122]

In London, John Burgoyne had cut quite a figure in high society and was known as "Gentleman Johnny" for his stylish uniforms and his luxurious lifestyle, which caused him to amass large debts. He was also a notorious gambler. Burgoyne was referred to as "General Swagger" by British writer Horace Walpole. In upstate New York, 500 Indians joined Burgoyne's forces and he allowed them to scalp dead patriot soldiers, but not wounded ones or prisoners. The patriots in New England were outraged about this and militiamen began pouring into the army. While wandering in the mountains south of Lake Champlain, Burgoyne sent out 1,400 men to find food and horses in the area. They were attacked by militiamen, who killed 207 of them and captured 700. Burgoyne had lost 15 percent of his army in a single blow.[123]

George Washington went to Philadelphia with 15,000 men in September of 1777 and placed himself between Howe and the city. Howe was apparently going to get his wish for a grand open field battle. He presented a demonstration attack at Washington's center, while leading the main part of his army around Washington's right side. Washington decided to attack the demonstration forces in front of him, thinking he would destroy them and then deal with Howe's main force. But Washington somehow soon concluded that Howe was not really trying to go around his right side and that, instead, Howe's whole army was in front of him. So Washington retreated, only to learn that Howe really was attacking on his right! As at Long Island, Howe had outflanked and outgeneraled George Washington, whose army fled in retreat. As usual,

[122] Philbrick (2016), pp. 119, 122, 136, 175; Chernow (2010), pp. 300–301.

[123] https://en.m.wikipedia.org/wiki/John_Burgoyne, p.3, accessed August 21, 2021; Philbrick (2016), pp. 111–115, 123, 133.

Howe allowed the patriots to retreat in good order, rather than pursuing them.[124] Fortunately, Washington's army did not get annihilated.

Having once again outfoxed Washington, Howe marched into Philadelphia unopposed. He left some soldiers at Germantown, eight miles north of Philadelphia, so Washington then decided to attack there. But as the attack got under way, Washington got sidetracked, with one group of his men marching down the wrong road and another group inadvertently alerting the British of the coming attack. In sum, Washington did not move forward in full force and thereby allowed the British to counter-attack and send the patriots scrambling in retreat again. His "war of posts" strategy was good in theory, but he abandoned it whenever his indecisiveness or his aggressive instincts kicked in. Washington decided to attack Philadelphia itself, but was talked out of it.[125]

Arnold Tolerates Gates, for a While

Though isolated and outnumbered, Burgoyne pushed on in the fall of 1777 toward Albany, rather than retreating to Fort Ticonderoga. He was running out of provisions and Gates wanted to wait him out. The patriot force was now nearly twice the size of Burgoyne's. Gates put Benedict Arnold in charge of the patriot left side. Unlike Gates, Arnold wanted to send out men to find out what Burgoyne was doing. So a scouting party was sent out from Arnold's left side and soon ran into Burgoyne's troops at Freeman's Farm. The patriots retreated. Gates wanted to sit and wait for Burgoyne's next move, but Arnold convinced him to send men into the left side to fight at Freeman's Farm in what became known as the First Battle of Saratoga. Arnold was in essence fighting a battle on the

---

[124] Chernow (2010), pp. 300–304; Randall (1997), pp. 340–341; Philbrick (2016), pp. 138–139, 169.

[125] Ward (1952), pp. 361–362; Library of Congress, George Washington Papers, The American Revolution, A Timeline of George Washington's Military and Political Career During the American Revolution, 1774–1783, https://www.loc.gov/collections/george-washington-papers/articles-and-essays/timeline/the-american-revolution/#1775, p. 27, accessed September 13, 2021.

left side while Gates stayed in his tent and the rest of the patriot army sat inactive.[126]

Gates soon insisted that Arnold stay in camp with him while the fighting was going on. Arnold finally reached the snapping point and, against orders, joined in the fighting. Burgoyne had 750 casualties compared to 150 for the patriots. The official account by Gates of the fighting, however, made no mention of Arnold. Arnold was furious about that and demanded a pass to Philadelphia, which Gates granted. But Arnold then decided to stick around on the eve of battle, so Gates removed Arnold from command and forbade him from entering headquarters.

Gates had never commanded an army in battle. When Burgoyne attacked the patriot left one more time in what became known as the Second Battle of Saratoga, Arnold told Gates that a strong force should be sent to meet the attack.

"General Arnold," Gates replied, "I have nothing for you to do. You have no business here."

Arnold stayed in camp, drinking. As Philbrick puts it, Arnold "lived in the messy and emotional moment." Disobeying orders, he soon mounted his horse, rode around the camp agitated and angry, and then headed into the fight. Astute at recognizing an enemy's weakness, Arnold noticed one British officer who seemed to be in charge of the troops on the patriot left. Arnold had a sharpshooter take him out and the British were soon retreating.[127]

Arnold then rode across the battlefield, followed by 15 patriot riflemen. They burst through the backside of a fortified Hessian position and captured, killed, and wounded many of the enemy soldiers inside. During the charge, a musket ball smashed into Arnold's left thigh bone, fracturing it into splinters. It was the second time in less than two years that he had been shot in the left leg.[128]

By mid-October, all hope of escape for Burgoyne at Saratoga had vanished. Persistent rainfall had turned his camp into a "squalid hell"

---

[126] Philbrick (2016), pp. 145–146, 156, 243.

[127] Ibid., pp. xvi, 143, 149–150, 154–157, 163, 165.

[128] Ibid., pp. 166–171.

of mud and starving cattle. His supplies were dangerously low, his men were on half rations, and many of his wounded were in agony. Howe had indeed left him hanging. Burgoyne surrendered his more than 6,000 soldiers, including 197 musicians, on October 17, 1777. He and his officers were paroled and returned to England right away, while his men remained prisoners of war in America. Though Burgoyne had negotiated a surrender that involved all of his men going home as well, the continental Congress reneged on the deal, likely as retaliation for the treatment received by patriot prisoners.[129]

Yearning for Glory

Horatio Gates never went to the battlefield at Saratoga. Instead, he remained at his headquarters, at one point discussing the merits of the war with an injured British officer who had been captured and was resting in his tent. Yet Gates was soon praised as the hero of Saratoga. The patriot victory at Saratoga convinced France to enter the war in support of the colonies. Congress did restore Arnold's seniority in late November, six weeks after the battle, but Washington did not tell him until two months later.[130]

Soon Gates began sending reports directly to Congress, rather than to his commanding officer, Washington, and he got himself appointed as president of the Board of War. This made him Washington's civilian superior, while Washington was his military superior. Some members of Congress even considered replacing Washington with Gates as commander in chief of the army, but when Washington learned of it, Gates apologized to him and resigned from the Board of War.[131]

Five days after Burgoyne surrendered at Saratoga, Howe was trying to get food and supplies into Philadelphia from his ships, which had moved to the Delaware River. The patriots had planted metal-spiked

---

[129] Ferling (*Almost a Miracle*), pp. 238–239; Mintz, p. 234; Trevelyan, p. 3; Burrows at p. 98 says that the total surrendered was 3,200; https://en.m.wikipedia.org/wiki/John_Burgoyne, pp. 2, 10, accessed August 21, 2021; Ketchum (1997), pp. 421–424.

[130] Ketchum (1997), pp. 446–447; Philbrick (2016), pp. 166, 173.

[131] Ward (1952), p. 560; Ferling (*Almost A Miracle*), p. 282.

timbers into the water about a mile south of the city to tear up the bottom of the British boats. They also had forts on either side of the river. Howe sent 2,000 men to attack one of the forts at Philadelphia to allow for his ships to pass through. His men were repulsed. Though two of his warships somehow squeezed through the metal-spiked timbers, they then ran aground. The patriots quickly descended on those ships and one of them exploded during the fighting. Howe wrote his resignation that day.[132] He would be replaced by Clinton many months later.

Nearly two weeks later, the British attacked the other fort on the other side of the river at Philadelphia. The fort contained 500 patriots and the British cannon pounded it for 12 days. Finally, in mid-November of 1777, the fort was abandoned after the British fired more than 1,000 cannonballs at it during one 20-minute period.[133] At last, Howe's supply ships pulled into the harbor at Philadelphia.

Then in early January of 1778, the patriots placed fifty kegs into the river at Philadelphia, upstream from where the British ships were anchored. Each keg contained gunpowder and was designed to explode upon contact with a ship. But before the kegs reached the ships, some curious fellow on a barge hauled one onto his boat where it exploded. British soldiers were soon firing on the kegs, causing them to explode without any harm to the ships. This became known as the Battle of the Kegs.[134]

While the British wintered in Philadelphia, Washington and his 12,000 men were at Valley Forge, only 20 miles away. His men had no blankets, little food, and 3,000 of them had no shoes. They also had no shelter until they built their own. By the end of February, 1,000 of them would die of starvation, cold, or disease. Without the power to tax, Congress could not raise enough money to provide for them. Washington urged Congress in a lengthy, detailed letter to reorganize the army and

---

[132] Philbrick (2016), pp. 174–176.

[133] Ibid., p. 182.

[134] Ibid., p. 195.

to provide a regular flow of food and clothing. He stayed in a fieldstone summerhouse where his wife, Martha, joined him in early February.[135]

In Philadelphia, Howe socialized with the loyalist aristocracy and left Washington to his own devices in Valley Forge. Howe resided in a home that would later be occupied by George Washington and John Adams during their presidencies. Though Valley Forge was nearby, Howe made no effort to attack. Some say that doing so could have ended the war.[136]

Who Wants What?

France saw the war as a way to create an America that was economically and militarily dependent on it, rather than on Britain. It also viewed it as an opportunity to weaken its enemy, Britain. Many Americans opposed a French alliance, however, fearing the exchange of "one tyranny for another." France also wanted to protect the French West Indies from American expansion. The West Indies were extremely valuable, with the value of sugar and coffee produced solely by the island of Hispaniola (now Haiti and the Dominican Republic, covering 8,320 square miles) exceeding the value of *all* American exports from the thirteen colonies *combined* (covering 338,456 square miles, which is 40 times bigger).[137]

In February of 1778, France and the colonies entered into a military alliance against Britain. France guaranteed American independence. In turn, Congress agreed to defend French interests in the West Indies. The colonies also promised promotions and command positions for any French soldier who fought in the war. Many who joined were incompetent. Lafayette, who had already gotten involved eight months

[135] Taylor, p. 188; https://www.battlefields.org/learn/articles/winter-valley-forge, pp. 2–3, accessed July 21, 2021; Chernow (2010), pp. 327–328; Philbrick (2016), pp. 186–187, 191–192, 197.

[136] https://www.battlefields.org/learn/biographies/william-howe, accessed July 11, 2021; Cadwalader, p. 22; Risch, pp. 322, 417–418.

[137] https://en.wikipedia.org/wiki/American_Revolutionary_War, p. 16, accessed July 2, 2021; Eclov, pp. 23–24; Yes, I did look up the total area of each state that comprised the thirteen colonies, then computed the grand total, and compared that to the total area of the island of Haiti/Dominican Republic.

earlier at the age of 19, was an exception and served as a major general. As an ally of France, Spain later joined in against their common enemy, Britain. Spain controlled Louisiana and allowed the patriots to import munitions and supplies through New Orleans and then ship them to Pittsburgh, thereby getting around the British blockade on the Atlantic coast.[138]

Washington learned that France had entered the war while he was at Valley Forge. Lafayette was there. He was idealistic, wealthy, confident, and charming and the soldiers liked him. Benedict Arnold, after recovering from his second leg wound, was on the way. Arnold was 37 years old and the men who had served under him at Saratoga cheered upon his arrival. At Valley Forge, Arnold swore allegiance to the patriot cause, with Henry Knox administering the oath. The French navy would soon set sail for the colonies.[139]

Then, in early May of 1778, the British were ordered by London to abandon Philadelphia and return to New York City. Henry Clinton had by then replaced Howe as commander of the British army. Howe had sailed to London from New York City, after a grand parade with fireworks. The British had occupied Philadelphia for only eight months—after Howe had spent nearly six months capturing it. Some Brits questioned whether Howe had undermined the war effort due to his underlying sympathy for the patriots. More specifically, he was accused of having squandered several opportunities to defeat and capture Washington at Valley Forge by spending his time socializing in Philadelphia instead.[140]

---

[138] Ferling (*Almost A Miracle*), p. 283; Library of Congress, George Washington Papers, The American Revolution, A Timeline of George Washington's Military and Political Career During the American Revolution, 1774–1783, https://www.loc.gov/collections/george-washington-papers/articles-and-essays/timeline/the-american-revolution/#1775, p. 23, accessed September 13, 2021; https://en.wikipedia.org/wiki/American_Revolutionary_War, p. 21, accessed July 25, 2021; "The Little-Remembered Ally Who Helped America Win the Revolution" https://www.smithsonian.mag.com, Erick Trickey, January 13, 2017, accessed July 25, 2021.

[139] Taylor, p. 188; https://www.battlefields.org/learn/articles/winter-valley-forge, pp. 2–3, accessed July 21, 2021; Philbrick (2016) pp. xvi, 198–199, 203; Brandt, pp. 141–147.

[140] Philbrick (2016), p. 201; Martin (1993), p. 181, 198; https://www.battlefields.org/learn/biographies/william-howe, accessed July 11, 2021.

Before the British departed Philadelphia in mid-June, British captain John Andre organized a grand party in Philadelphia with a regatta on the Delaware River, followed by a dance, a sumptuous dinner, fireworks, and jousting. Andre had been captured in the war some two and a half years earlier and was exchanged shortly after meeting Henry Knox, who was en route to Fort Ticonderoga to get cannon for Boston.

With France now in the war, the new British strategy was to strengthen areas under British control and conduct raids into enemy territory. Though Clinton was ordered by London to evacuate Philadelphia by sea, he instead marched his army to New York City in June of 1778 with his 17,600 soldiers and their 1,500 wagons stretched out over 12 miles. His army marched in three groups, each large enough to stave off an attack until the other groups arrived.[141] If the French had not taken a leisurely 87 days to cross the Atlantic, they might have trapped the British army and navy at Philadelphia, forcing a surrender. The French had 850 cannon, whereas the British only had 534.[142]

At Monmouth, New Jersey, Washington was back in Fabian mode, attacking the rear guard of Clinton's army as it marched toward New York City. Benedict Arnold led the attack and Henry Knox handled the artillery. The Brits counter-attacked, putting up enough resistance to stop the patriots. Though the battle was inconclusive, it boosted patriot morale by inflicting more casualties than sustained and by holding the field at the end of the day.[143]

At midnight, Clinton's army slinked into New York City. After that, he and Washington stared at each other for months as the 1778 fighting

[141] Willcox, pp. 222–223; Higginbotham, pp. 175–188; https://en.wikipedia.org/Battle_of_Monmouth, accessed August 22, 2021.

[142] Philbrick (2016), pp. 216–217.

[143] Library of Congress, George Washington Papers, The American Revolution, A Timeline of George Washington's Military and Political Career During the American Revolution, 1774–1783, https://www.loc.gov/collections/george-washington-papers/articles-and-essays/timeline/the-american-revolution/#1775, p. 34, accessed September 13, 2021; Wickwire (1970), pp. 110–112; Willcox, pp. 227, 233–237; https://en.wikipedia.org/wiki/American_Revolutionary_War, p. 18, accessed July 3, 2021; https://en.wikipedia.org/Battle_of_Monmouth, accessed August 22, 2021; Philbrick (2016), p. 213.

season came to a close. Over the winter, Henry Knox established the army's first school for artillery and officer training. It was the predecessor to the military academy later housed at the fort at West Point. The Battle of Monmouth would be Washington's last battlefield command for three years.[144]

The French navy began blocking British provisions by sea, so New York City was running out of food. William Franklin, the estranged loyalist son of Benjamin Franklin, was by now urging loyalists to conduct a "predatory war" against patriot civilians. This brought 600 civilian prisoners into New York.[145]

Living High on the Hog in Philadelphia

After the British left Philadelphia, Washington put Benedict Arnold in command of the city. As historian John Shy notes: "Washington then made one of the worst decisions of his career, appointing Arnold as military governor of the rich, politically divided city. No one could have been less qualified for the position. Arnold had amply demonstrated his tendency to become embroiled in disputes, as well as his lack of political sense. Above all, he needed tact, patience, and fairness in dealing with a people deeply marked by months of enemy occupation."[146]

In Philadelphia, Arnold sought personal financial gain, arranging business deals in which he profited from wartime supplies. He lived extravagantly, socializing with loyalists and soon meeting Peggy Shippen. She was young and beautiful and had attended all of the Philadelphia social events hosted by the occupying British soldiers. In fact, her brother had joined the British army in New Jersey and her father was a loyalist. John Andre, the exchanged British officer, was charming and handsome and had paid attention to Peggy Shippen during the British occupation. Andre had occupied the house of Benjamin Franklin, who was away, and

---

[144] Chernow (2010), p. 343.; Alden (1996), pp. 176–77; Ferling (2002), pp. 195–198; Philbrick (2016), p. 214.

[145] Burrows, pp. 136, 142.

[146] Brandt, p. 146; see generally Shy.

he stole china and musical instruments from the home when he left for New York.[147]

Arnold was handsome and charismatic, with black hair, gray eyes, and an athletic gait. He came from a respected Rhode Island family. His father had moved the family to Connecticut before becoming a drunkard. Arnold was hypersensitive to any slight, obsessed with honor, and abrupt and impatient. He criticized and ridiculed anyone who disagreed with him. As a sea captain, he had traveled the Caribbean and had sailed north as far as Quebec City.[148]

Benedict Arnold had several enemies within the Continental army. One officer said of him, "Money is this man's God, and to get enough of it he would sacrifice his country." Arnold was by now determined to take whatever he could as repayment for his valor and war injuries, and he began concocting inside deals to get a cut of the commerce in Philadelphia.[149]

Philadelphia was a wreck. The State House had been used as a prison by the British. Houses had been used for stables, with holes cut in the floor for shoveling horse manure. Arnold entertained in high style at his new home, which Howe had previously occupied. Arnold even appeared at a ball wearing a red uniform. As Philbrick describes it, Arnold was "glorious in his epaulets and sword . . . As Peggy Shippen could no doubt attest, the battle-scarred Benedict Arnold was sexy." Her father, however, refused to accept Arnold. But Peggy was remarkably high strung and known for her histrionics. Her father eventually gave his consent for her to marry Arnold.[150]

Washington stayed in White Plains, New York, while the British sat in New York City. He then went into winter quarters at Middlebrook, New Jersey.[151]

---

[147] Brandt, p. 148–149; Philbrick (2016), pp. 202, 207.

[148] Philbrick (2016), pp. 35–36.

[149] Howe, pp. 4–6; Philbrick (2016), pp. 204–206.

[150] Philbrick (2016), pp. 215–225.

[151] Ibid., p. 219.

Entanglement

In January of 1779, George Washington went to Philadelphia to discuss plans for the war. He disapproved of Arnold's lifestyle there, but refused to take sides. By February, however, Congress was looking into Arnold's dealings in Philadelphia. It ultimately ruled in Arnold's favor due to lack of evidence being presented by his accusers. However, Arnold was also being court martialed for his activities and his primary accuser was dragging that out as long as possible in order to gather more evidence.[152]

Benedict Arnold married Peggy Shippen in April of 1779. She was nearly twenty years younger than Arnold and had courted British officer John Andre during the British occupation of Philadelphia. Andre was now the head of the British spy system in New York City.[153] Before marrying Peggy, Arnold had borrowed 12,000 pounds (over $2 million in today's dollars) in order to buy a house for her and impress her father. They did not live in it, however, because Arnold needed rent money from that house in order to pay off the mortgage. Instead, he and Peggy moved into a house owned by her father.

It is unknown whether the decision to become a traitor originated with Arnold or with his wife. But he began putting out feelers to the British in May of 1779. As Philbrick observes: "Like Robert E. Lee at the beginning of the American Civil War, Arnold could have declared his change of heart and simply shifted sides. But as he was about to make clear, he was doing this first and foremost for the money." By July, Arnold was negotiating compensation with the British, while providing them with patriot troop strengths, locations, and supply information. He was also still under court martial by the patriots for his profiteering in Philadelphia.[154]

John Andre and Benedict Arnold communicated through written, coded correspondence that passed back and forth through Peggy and others. Each coded word consisted of three numbers that represented, in

---

152 Ibid., pp. 229–230, 232–235.

153 Randall & Nahra (1999), p. 81; Allen (2010), p. 241.

154 Philbrick (2016), p. 238, 241; McCullough, pp. 239–240; Randall (1990), pp. 456–457.

order, the page, line, and word appearing in *Bailey's Universal Etymological English Dictionary*. They also occasionally used invisible ink that could be revealed by the use of chemicals or heat. According to Philbrick, "The same narcissistic arrogance that enabled him to face the gravest danger on the battlefield without a trace of fear had equipped him to be a first-rate traitor . . . Guilt was simply not a part of his makeup since everything he did was, to his own mind, at least, justifiable . . . Whatever was best for him was, by definition, best for everyone else . . . For Arnold, rules were made to be broken . . . What made Arnold unique was the god-like inviolability he attached to his actions."[155]

The British wanted to capture West Point so that they could control the Hudson River and shut down the patriot supply route that ran both down and across it. In May of 1779, Clinton sent 6,000 men and more than 200 ships up the Hudson River and captured a fort 11 miles south of West Point. He then waited for more soldiers to arrive in order to attack. But by July of 1779, Clinton's reinforcements still had not arrived.[156]

Meanwhile, in Philadelphia, things got personal. Militiamen rounded up the wives and children of exiled loyalists and expelled them from the city. They hurled rocks at Arnold's fancy carriage, identifying him with the upper class that largely sided with the British.[157]

By December of 1779, Washington was in winter quarters in Morristown, New Jersey. That winter was far colder than the one at Valley Forge and the hardships were even greater. Morale was poor, public support had fallen off for the protracted war, the Continental dollar was virtually worthless, the army was plagued with supply problems, and desertion was common. Within a month, there would be four feet of snow on the ground during the coldest winter on record. The Delaware River stayed frozen for 75 days. In New York City, the harbor was frozen for five weeks, with people going from Brooklyn to Staten Island by foot or sleigh. Washington's men built 1,100 huts for the winter and one

[155] Philbrick (2016), pp. 244, 246.

[156] Ibid., pp. 250–251.

[157] Ibid., pp. 237, 254.

soldier said it was "cold enough to cut a man in two." He added, "I saw several of the men roast their old shoes and eat them."[158]

The water all around New York City was frozen solid during that particularly harsh winter, yet the British declared that their prisoners on ships were "comfortable." On one ship only 40 percent would survive until spring. A massive prisoner exchange took place, at least until the patriots ran out of British prisoners to release. Meanwhile, William Franklin continued his "predatory war" against patriot civilians, even going over General Clinton's head and getting the approval of King George III to do so. He and his several hundred followers continued to supply a steady stream of prisoners into New York City. Benjamin Franklin and his son never spoke again.[159]

The Plot Thickens

Arnold was cleared in January of 1780 of all but two minor charges relating to his profiteering in Philadelphia. However, he was mad as a hornet that he had not been cleared of all. In March, he went to West Point and sent a detailed report about it to the British. He then arranged the sale of his home in Connecticut and began transferring assets to London through British middlemen in New York City.[160]

In April of 1780, Washington issued the required reprimand to Arnold related to the court martial. However, he also wrote a private letter to Arnold saying, "I will myself furnish you, as far as it may be in my power, with the opportunities for regaining the esteems of your country." Arnold decided that he would make good on this by obtaining the command of West Point. He resigned his command of Philadelphia in April of 1780, but remained in the army. Arnold was deeply bitter.

---

[158] Philbrick (2016), pp. 256–257; "How George Washington's Savvy Won the Day: Despite His Share of Errors, the Commander in Chief Prevailed as a Strategist and a Politician." Jay Tolson, June 27, 2008, https://www.usnews.com, accessed September 29, 2020; Chandler, pp. 363–380.

[159] Burrows, pp. 150–159.

[160] Philbrick (2016), p. 259; Randall (1990), pp. 486–497, 503–504.

He was also ambitious and jealous, unhappy with the injustices that he believed he had suffered.[161]

Dealing with the Rebels Down South

Cornwallis, who had been sent south after the battle of Princeton, captured Charleston in May of 1780. There his 14,000 men inflicted the most serious patriot defeat of the war. Over 5,000 patriot prisoners were taken and the Continental army in the South was effectively destroyed. Cornwallis, age 40, was reinforced at Charleston by Clinton, who then returned to New York, leaving Cornwallis in the Carolinas. But Clinton insisted on overseeing the Cornwallis campaign through the remainder of the war. And despite their success, the two men were barely on speaking terms.[162] There were now two principal campaign theaters: Northern and Southern.

Clinton told Cornwallis to keep Charleston and also to move into Virginia, but he only provided 8,300 men to accomplish that. He expected Cornwallis to recruit Southern loyalists to fill his troops. The British strategy for the Southern campaign assumed strong local loyalist support, but Cornwallis soon realized that this assumption was wildly optimistic. So captured patriot soldiers, who previously would have been sent home under an "exchange" after swearing not to take up arms against Britain, were instead forced to fight against their former comrades. And when Cornwallis resorted to coercion and brutality to recruit loyalist civilians, many changed sides.[163]

---

[161] Philbrick (2016), pp. 260–262; "On The Trail Of Benedict Arnold." W. D. Wetherell, *American Heritage.* 58, 2 April/May 2007; Randall (1990), pp. 497–499.

[162] Borick, pp. 127–128, 235–239; Wickwire (1970), p. 133; see "Sir Henry Clinton: A Psychological Exploration in History." F. Wyatt, William and Mary Quarterly, January 1959. 16 (1): 4–26. doi:10.2307/1918848. JSTOR 1918848, suggesting that Clinton was mildly neurotic and unable to work with others whom he considered equal.

[163] https://www.mountvernon.org/library/digitalhistory/digital-encycl...es-cornwallis-1st-marquess-and-2nd-earl-cornwallis-1738–1805/p. 4, accessed July 17, 2021; Wickwire (1970), pp. 135–137; Gordon and Keegan, pp. 101–102.

Charles Cornwallis was born into an aristocratic family. He attended school at Eton and Cambridge. His uncle Edward had founded Halifax, Nova Scotia. After joining the army at age 19, he served in the House of Commons for two years before inheriting his father's position in the House of Lords at the age of 24. Cornwallis sympathized with the colonists during the lead-up to the war. But when the war broke out, he sought active service in the British army. He was "enterprising and aggressive." He was also tall, overweight, and the most popular British general in America.[164]

After France entered the war, Dutch merchants made a lot of money shipping French-supplied munitions to the patriots around the British blockade. So Britain declared war on the Dutch, ending that activity and wrecking the Dutch economy. But Britain had underestimated the American merchant marine, as well as the support from other European countries, so the colonies continued to import munitions successfully.[165]

Historian Terry Mays identifies three separate levels of warfare that were taking place. First, there was the obvious conflict between the colonies and Britain. Secondly, a civil war was taking place between the patriots and the loyalists. In fact, many battles in the South were fought between these camps with no British involvement. Thirdly, a broader war was underway between America, France, Spain, the Dutch Republic, and Britain, with America being one of several different theaters.[166]

Arnold Plays His Hand

In July of 1780, Clinton gave up on the idea of capturing West Point before the snow fell. Instead he sent 6,000 men to stir up trouble in Connecticut. Predictably (and unrealistically) Washington was chomping at the bit to attack New York City while some of the British troops were away.[167]

---

[164] Cornwallis (Ross ed.), pp. 4–11; Bicheno, p. 168; Weintraub, p. 34; Wickwire (1970), pp. 79–80; McCullough, pp. 252–253.

[165] Scott, pp. 572–573.

[166] Buchanan (1997), p. 241; Mays, pp. 2–3.

[167] Philbrick (2016), pp. 251–252.

Arnold, who had somehow just convinced Congress to give him a $25,000 advance, met Washington on the Hudson River on the last day of July 1780. Washington was busy transporting his men across the river in preparation for his attack on New York City. He told Arnold that he wanted him to lead the left wing of that attack in a "post of honor." Arnold did not say a word. Later in the day, Arnold claimed that his leg would not enable him to execute the assignment, but Washington insisted. Rather than suspect Arnold's motives, Washington saw Arnold as a broken man who lacked the confidence to perform the job. Washington soon gave up on attacking New York, after learning that Clinton had called his troops back.[168]

Arnold requested and was given command of West Point in August of 1780. Soon Peggy and their infant child joined him at a home on the Hudson River, two miles south of West Point. The British had suggested they would pay him 20,000 pounds to deliver West Point to them (the equivalent of $3.6 million in today's dollars). So he began weakening its defenses and squandering its supplies. His subordinates thought that he was selling them on the market for personal gain.[169]

Chasing Swamp Fox in South Carolina

Congress appointed Arnold's old pal, Horatio Gates, as commander in the South after the fall of Charleston. But Gates was soundly defeated only three weeks later by Cornwallis in Camden, South Carolina. There, 900 of his men were killed or wounded and nearly 1,000 were captured along with supplies and artillery. Gates had overestimated the ability of his soldiers. He had also failed to arrange for an organized retreat in case one was needed. So he fled the battlefield in a panic, putting 180 miles between himself and the British before stopping. The defeat of Gates at Camden destroyed his military reputation and he was never again placed in field command.[170]

---

[168] Ibid., pp. 253, 263–273.

[169] Philbrick (2016), p. 275, 280–282; Chernow (2010), pp. 378, 380–381; Lengel, p. 322; Adams (1928), p. 366; Randall (1990), pp. 522–523.

[170] Ward (1952), p. 717; Philbrick (2016), pp. 266, 270, 280; https://en.m.wikipedia.org/wiki/Horatio_Gates, p. 15, accessed July 22, 2021; Nickerson, p. 216.

With Gates out of the way, Cornwallis was now free to enter North Carolina. He soon became a hero in London, though his victory at Camden was due as much to the embarrassingly rapid retreat of Gates as it was to his own skill. Washington soon replaced Gates with Nathanael Greene, age 38. Greene, a self-taught military strategist, had encouraged Washington to use Fabian strategy earlier in the war. He now used it successfully against Cornwallis, who exhausted his men and supplies chasing Greene around, but never caught him.[171]

The most persistent antagonist of Cornwallis, however, was 48-year-old Francis Marion, also known as the Swamp Fox. Marion was a wild ass and a true Fabian if there ever was one, much more so than Washington or Greene. At age 15, he had hired on with a ship to the West Indies. It sank on the return leg of his first voyage and he spent a week at sea in a lifeboat with the seven crew members, two of whom died before reaching land. Marion was a South Carolina planter who had served in the French and Indian War. When the Revolutionary War broke out, he enlisted in the South Carolina militia, becoming a colonel in 1776.[172]

Marion had not been captured when the British took Charleston because he was outside of the city recuperating from a broken ankle. Marion had been at a dinner party at the home of a fellow officer who, as was customary, had locked all the doors while toasting to the patriot cause. The toasts went on and on and Marion, who was not a drinker, felt trapped. He departed by jumping out a second-story window, breaking his ankle in the process.[173]

After Charleston fell, Marion formed a fighting unit of 50 men, who served without pay and supplied their own horses, arms, and food. They moved north and met with Horatio Gates before he got creamed at Camden. Upon seeing Marion hobbling on his broken ankle and his men poorly equipped and ragged, Gates had ordered them to the interior

---

[171] Piecuch, pp. 102–114; Wickwire (1970), p. 165; Buchanan (1997), p. 275; see https://www.mountvernon.org/library/digitalhistory/digital-encyclopedia/article/fabian-strategy, note 3, accessed August 31, 2021, as to historians' debate regarding whether and to what extent Washington used Fabian strategy.

[172] "The Swamp Fox." Amy Crawford, *Smithsonian*, June 30, 2007, https://www.SmithsonianMag.com, accessed July 12, 2021.

[173] Ibid.

of South Carolina, purportedly to scout enemy movements. In reality, Gates was just trying to get rid of the guy and his ragtag crew.[174]

Marion had the only fighting force left in South Carolina after Gates was routed at Camden. It was an efficient, hard-hitting, guerilla group that could evaporate into the swamps when threatened. Using Fabian strategy, Marion fought a war of attrition to wear down the superior British forces, attacking when the situation favored him. When it did not, he lured the British into the swamps, where he was uncatchable. Hiding in dense foliage, Swamp Fox attacked a British camp from behind and rescued a patriot regiment that had been captured at Camden. He disrupted supply lines and communications, menacing the British and slowing their movement into North Carolina. One subordinate described him as an "ugly, cross, knock kneed, hook-nosed son of a bitch."[175]

The British never knew where the Swamp Fox was or where he might strike. So whenever they divided their forces, he struck one of the weaker units. He rarely attacked frontally, instead using superior intelligence gathering, surprise attacks, and sudden withdrawals to inflict damage. The British despised him. At one point, they sent a colonel to capture or kill him. But after pursuing him for more than 25 miles through swampland, he gave up the chase, calling Marion the "old swamp fox." As historian Sean Busick puts it, Marion "helped make South Carolina an inhospitable place for the British."[176]

---

[174] "Up from the swamp: Francis Marion turned South Carolina's Low Country into a quagmire for the British and became one of history's greatest guerrilla leaders." Jefferson, Gray, *MHQ: The Quarterly Journal of Military History*. Autumn, 2011. 24 (1): pp. 60, 56–65; "Francis Marion: The Swamp Fox." *History on the Net*. https://www.historyonthenet.com/founding-fathers-francis-marion; accessed July 23, 2021.

[175] Library of Congress, George Washington Papers, The American Revolution, A Timeline of George Washington's Military and Political Career During the American Revolution, 1774–1783, https://www.loc.gov/collections/george-washington-papers/articles-and-essays/timeline/the-american-revolution/#1775, p. 49, accessed September 13, 2021; "Francis Marion: The Swamp Fox." *History on the Net*. https://www.historyonthenet.com/founding-fathers-francis-marion; accessed July 23, 2021.

[176] "The Swamp Fox." Amy Crawford, *Smithsonian*, June 30, 2007, quoting Busick, https://www.SmithsonianMag.com, accessed July 12, 2021; https://www.britannica.com, "Francis Marion, United States Military Officer." June 13, 2021, accessed July 12, 2021.

Andre Struts His Stuff

Arnold's home was across the Hudson from West Point and more than a mile downriver. He no longer needed a cane to walk but he now wore a special red shoe with a high heel. Arnold could ride his horse down to his dock on the river and then travel to West Point by boat. He had soon collected a large quantity of government supplies at his headquarters, keeping them in a locked room and converting them to cash from time to time. In late August of 1780, Arnold received a letter from Andre through Peggy. It confirmed that the British had agreed to the terms for turning over West Point, so long as Arnold delivered 3,000 patriots as prisoners during its capture.[177]

Andre and Arnold needed to meet to discuss the West Point plan. Arnold suggested that Andre pose as a patriot named John Anderson. But Andre had been imprisoned in Pennsylvania earlier in the war, before being exchanged; he had also met many patriot officers who had been British prisoners in New York. The risk of his being recognized was too high. General Clinton insisted instead that Andre come under a truce flag to Arnold while dressed as a British officer.[178]

So Andre arrived at night in mid-September of 1780 aboard the *Vulture*, a British warship. It anchored 15 miles south of West Point near the Smith house. Joshua Hett Smith had agreed to let Arnold and Andre meet there, apparently not knowing the nature of their meeting. As Philbrick exclaims, "one had to wonder how a man who styled himself a lawyer could be either so dimwitted or so gullible that his suspicions were not aroused . . ."[179]

As it turned out, Washington was on his way to Connecticut and had arrived at West Point at the same time. Arnold met with him for the last time and, after Washington headed on, Arnold told the British either to attack before Washington came back through one week later or, if they

---

[177] Philbrick (2016), pp. 277–279.

[178] Ibid., p. 283.

[179] Randall (1990), pp. 517–518; Philbrick (2016), p. 285.

wanted to capture Washington himself during the taking of West Point, to do so in one week.[180]

Smith, Arnold, and two other men rowed in darkness to the *Vulture*, retrieved Andre, and came ashore around one in the morning. Andre's red officer's coat was covered by a blue cloak. Arnold and Andre talked for three hours in the woods, during which time Arnold inquired what he would be paid if he failed to deliver West Point. As dawn approached, they still had a lot to discuss, so Andre went to Smith's house to stay until the following night when he could return to the *Vulture*. But when the sun came up, the patriots saw the British ship and fired upon it. With a tidal change underway and no wind, the *Vulture* stood still for two hours while patriot cannon blasted the sails and the rigging. Then it fled south out of range.[181]

When Smith next saw him in the morning, Andre was walking around Smith's house in his British uniform. Smith expressed his surprise to Arnold, who explained that Andre was really a patriot who had borrowed the uniform from a British officer who was an acquaintance of his. This made no sense, but Smith apparently bought it.

Now that the *Vulture* had disappeared to the south, Arnold suggested that Andre might have to return to New York by land. Andre did not like it, because he would have to change out of his British uniform and, if captured, would be treated as a spy rather than as a combatant officer. Arnold could not have cared less. He ultimately convinced Andre to go by land. So Andre stuffed the plans for taking West Point in his boot and soon Smith was escorting him southward on horseback, enthralled by the mystique of accompanying someone so important to the patriot cause. Even after Andre told Smith along the way that he was a British officer, Smith showed no misgivings.

On the whole, Philbrick is right about Smith. But there is more to this. Smith was a member of the patriot militia, but he was also the head of the secret service for West Point. When Arnold took over at West Point, he asked Smith to continue in that position. So Smith "unwittingly" became involved in Arnold's scheme. He was tried by a

---

[180] Philbrick (2016), p. 287.

[181] Sheinkin, p. 259; Philbrick (2016), pp. 289–292.

military court and acquitted for lack of evidence, which is not surprising since by then Arnold had escaped, Andre was dead, and the two men who had rowed the boat likely knew nothing of the plot—or at least claimed as much. Then Smith was arrested by the civil authorities and jailed, but he escaped and made his way to New York disguised as a woman. After the war he would sail to England with the British army, later returning to New York for the rest of his life.[182]

Treason on the Hudson

After Smith and Andre parted ways, Andre came across a man in a Hessian coat who told him to halt. He was only fifteen miles from the crossing into Manhattan. Two other men soon appeared.

"I am a British officer," Andre declared.

"We are Americans," replied the man, a patriot who had escaped only a few days earlier from a British prison in New York City using the Hessian coat as a disguise.

Andre then showed them his pass issued by Benedict Arnold. All was well until they decided to search him and found the West Point plans in his boots. Andre then tried to bribe them. They decided to deliver Andre to Arnold and the plans to Washington; then they decided instead to hold Andre. At that point, Andre wrote to Washington claiming that, rather than being a spy, he was an honorable British soldier who, like others, had been betrayed by Benedict Arnold.

"I was involuntarily an imposter," the slippery worm wrote.[183]

Two days later, Washington was on his way back from Connecticut and was going to have breakfast with Arnold at his headquarters. Henry Knox, Lafayette, and Alexander Hamilton were traveling with him. Neither Washington nor Arnold yet knew of Andre's capture. Washington was running late to breakfast and, meanwhile, Arnold received a hand-

---

[182] Philbrick (2016), pp. 293–294, 298; https://en.wikipedia.org/wiki/Joshua_Hett_Smith_House, accessed June 23, 2022; Randall (1990), pp. 517–518; see generally Van Doren.

[183] Lossing, pp. 151–156, 187–189; Philbrick (2016), pp. 300, 302–306.

delivered message reporting Andre's capture and advising him that the treasonous papers found on Andre had been sent to Washington.[184]

Benedict Arnold raced upstairs to tell Peggy of the turn of events. He then instructed an assistant to saddle his horse and to tell Washington, when he arrived, that Arnold was at West Point and would return in an hour. Arnold rode to his dock, scrambled into a boat, and ordered his men to row as fast as possible under a truce flag to the *Vulture*, telling them falsely that he needed to get there and back quickly in order to meet Washington on time.[185]

Washington showed up thirty minutes later, ate a quick breakfast, and then went to West Point, where he learned that Arnold had not been there for two days. He nevertheless conducted an inspection of West Point and returned to Arnold's headquarters around four in the afternoon. The documents describing Andre's capture and the treasonous West Point plans found on him were there when Washington returned. As soon as Washington read the papers, Alexander Hamilton tore off on horseback in an unsuccessful attempt to stop the southbound rowboat before Arnold escaped.

That is when Peggy Arnold put on her show. She came downstairs scantily clad with her hair disheveled and she acted stark raving mad, claiming that there was a hot iron on her head and that nobody but Washington could remove it. She pretended that her husband's treachery had caused her to lose all reason. This bought extra time for Arnold to escape. It also helped her to avoid questions. Arnold had now been gone six hours and was aboard the *Vulture*, fleeing to New York City.[186]

Washington was taken in by Peggy's performance. The next day, he asked her whether she wanted to go to Arnold in New York City or to her family in Philadelphia. She chose Philadelphia, where she continued to proclaim her innocence until authorities found a letter to her from Andre showing her complicity. Peggy was banished from Philadelphia and her father escorted her to the Hudson river, where she and her child boarded a boat to join Arnold in New York City.[187]

---

184 Philbrick (2016), pp. 308, 311.

185 Stuart, pp. 94–96; Philbrick (2016), p. 309.

186 Philbrick (2016), pp. 311–312; Lossing, p. 159.

187 Philbrick (2016), pp. 310–311; Stuart, p. 112; Brandt, pp. 234–238.

A letter from Arnold to Washington soon arrived saying: "The same principle of love to my country actuates my present conduct, however it may appear inconsistent to the world, who very seldom judge right of any man's actions." He went on to claim that Peggy Arnold was "as good and innocent as an angel." Washington tried to exchange Andre for Arnold, but General Clinton refused. John Andre was hanged in early October of 1780.[188]

In New York City, Benedict Arnold soon became a brigadier general in the British army. Meanwhile, in Philadelphia, his effigy sat on a horse-pulled cart. It had a two-faced, rotating head and, above the head, the devil appeared, holding a bag of gold and a pitchfork. Militiamen put candles in the muzzles of their muskets and set him ablaze at the end of night.[189]

Washington tried to kidnap Benedict Arnold in New York City. He sent men undercover there to capture him, but Arnold had changed living quarters. By the time they arrived at his new place, Arnold had sailed to Virginia to fight for the British, unknowingly giving them the slip. Arnold did not receive his 20,000 pounds for West Point, since the plot had failed. As a British officer, he captured Richmond, Virginia, in December of 1780, destroying supply houses, foundries, and mills.[190] Ironically, his treason spurred the colonies, at long last, to provide the support that Washington needed to fight the war.

Finishing the Job

By the fall of 1780, the British ship *Jersey* held 1,100 prisoners in New York, though it had been built to carry only 400 men. It was anchored 300 yards from shore, so escapes were few. In an effort to persuade prisoners to defect, the British cut their rations to one pint of water and eight ounces of bread per day. They also received eight ounces of meat per week. One prisoner described it as "one of the greatest scenes of

---

188 Arnold to Washington, 25 September 1780; Philbrick (2016), pp. 313–315.

189 Philbrick (2016), p. 321.

190 Ibid., p. 325; Lossing, pp. 160, 197–210; Randall (1990), pp. 582–583.

human distress and misery ever beheld." Hundreds of prisoners enlisted in the British navy in order to save themselves.[191]

In January of 1781, Washington asked that an American be allowed to inspect the *Jersey*. His request was denied. Instead, four British officers inspected the ship and found that every prisoner "was made at all times as comfortable as possible, and that they were in no instance oppressed or ill treated." One prisoner was so hungry that he ate the lice from his shirt.[192]

While chasing after Nathanael Greene in South Carolina, Cornwallis sustained heavy casualties and his supply line was stretched thin, so he retreated to Wilmington, North Carolina, for supplies and reinforcements. Then he went back to Charleston where he had started.[193] Cornwallis then learned that British troops under Benedict Arnold were in Virginia, so he developed an aggressive plan for a Virginia campaign. Meanwhile, Clinton was in New York City, still trying to figure out a coherent operational strategy for the war.[194]

Arnold remained in command as a British officer in Virginia until April of 1781 when Cornwallis took over. Arnold then went to New England, where he burned most of New London, Connecticut, to the ground in September and killed patriot soldiers even after they had surrendered in nearby Groton. All of this occurred only a few miles from where he had grown up.[195]

The Big Showdown

Washington was still itching to attack New York. But the French wanted to attack Virginia, where the smaller force under Cornwallis was easier to defeat. Washington agreed. Misreading the enemy, Clinton believed that a patriot attack on New York City was imminent. He ordered Cornwallis to establish a fortified sea base in Virginia where his troops could be

191 https://www.historynet.com/british-prison-ships-a-season-in-hell.htm, p. 7, accessed July 25, 2021; Burrows, pp. 167–168.

192 Burrows, pp. 176, 178.

193 Pancake, pp. 118–120, 133–138; Buchanan (1997), p. 24; Pancake, p. 221.

194 Ketchum (2014), pp. 423, 520; Ferling (*Almost A Miracle*), p. 444; Johnston (1881), pp. 26–28.

195 Randall (1990), pp. 585-591.

quickly evacuated by the British navy to come to the aid of New York. Cornwallis complied, moving to Yorktown, Virginia, where he built defenses and awaited evacuation to New York City.[196]

The patriots under Lafayette marched toward Virginia, with the French navy moving to support him as he made his way down the Virginia Peninsula toward Cornwallis. Then Washington feinted toward Clinton at New York City before marching south as well. At Yorktown, Washington might finally satisfy his urge to attack head-on. All told, the patriots had more than 16,000 soldiers for the march to Yorktown. Cornwallis had 7,000.[197]

Though his subordinate officers repeatedly urged Cornwallis to fight Lafayette, he made no attempt to do so before Lafayette placed him under siege. All along, Cornwallis had expected to escape to New York on British ships. Accordingly, he had also abandoned his outer defenses, which Lafayette promptly occupied.[198]

The British fleet indeed left New York and headed for Yorktown. But the French navy intercepted it, forcing it to retreat and leaving Cornwallis isolated and short on supplies. After a three-week patriot siege under a steady barrage of cannon fire from Henry Knox, Cornwallis surrendered on October 17, 1781, and the fighting in the war ended. Cornwallis sought generous surrender terms. Washington demanded total surrender.[199]

---

[196] Ketchum (2014), p. 139; Grainger, pp. 43–44; Taylor, pp. 293–295.

[197] Ferling (*Almost A Miracle*), p. 444; Dull, pp. 247–248; Alden (1996), pp. 198–201; Chernow (2010), pp. 372–373, 403–404, 418; https://www.mountvernon.org/library/digitalhistory/digital-encycl...es-cornwallis-1st-marquess-and-2nd-earl-cornwallis-1738-1805, p. 5, accessed July 17, 2021.

[198] Ketchum (2014), p. 205; Lengel, p. 337.

[199] Middleton (2014), pp. 29–43; Black (1992), p. 110; Unger (2003), pp. 158–159; Ferling (*Almost A Miracle*), pp. 534–535; https://www.mountvernon.org/library/digitalhistory/digital-encycl...es-cornwallis-1st-marquess-and-2nd-earl-cornwallis-1738–1805, pp. 5–6, accessed July 17, 2021.

After the Shooting Stopped

Charles Cornwallis was paroled and returned to Britain in January of 1782, riding on the same ship with Benedict Arnold. General Clinton tried to blame him for the failures in the Southern campaign and fierce public debate ensued between them in England over who was at fault. Cornwallis pushed back hard and managed to retain the confidence of King George III. Despite his defeat at Yorktown, Cornwallis was knighted in 1786. He was appointed governor general of India and later commander in chief of Ireland. After being reappointed to India, he died there at the age of 66, soon after his arrival. Cornwallis is buried overlooking the Ganges River.[200]

[200] Wickwire (1980), p. 4, 7–8, 17–18, 265–267; Middleton (2013), pp. 371–389; Ross, p. 16.

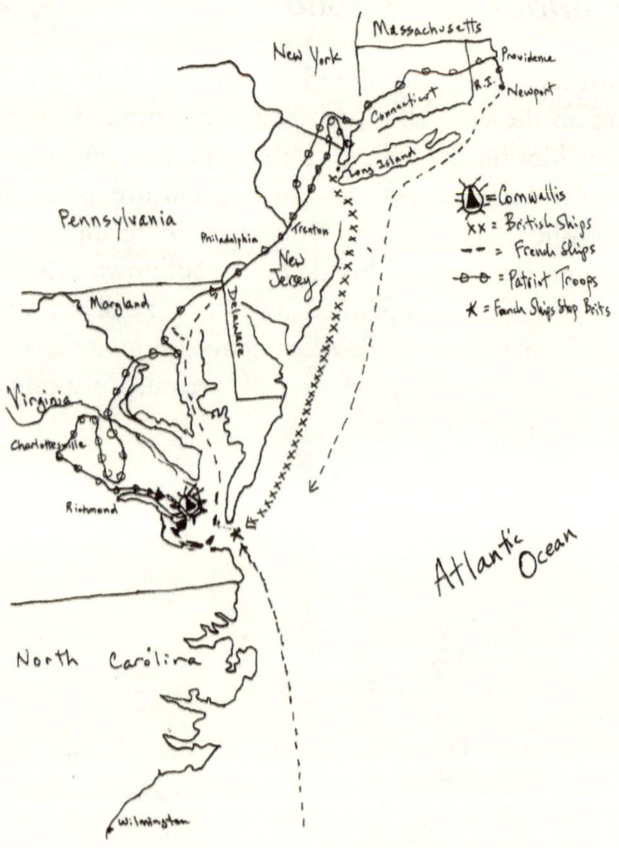

Cornwallis is hemmed in by land and by sea at Yorktown.
If this map makes sense to you, please let me know.

Henry Clinton took most of the blame for Yorktown. Though historian Piers Mackesy says that he was a "very capable general in the field," others say that Clinton was vain, open to flattery, and "crippled by self-distrust." One officer even described him as being "fool enough to command an army when he is incapable of commanding a troop of horse." After the war, Clinton served in the House of Commons for seventeen years. Shortly after being appointed governor of Gibraltar, he died in London in 1795 at the age of 65. He is buried at Windsor Castle.[201]

Henry Knox became the head of West Point in 1782 and commander in chief of the Continental army when Washington retired in 1783. Knox moved to Dorchester, Massachusetts, in 1784 and acquired several million acres of land in Maine, some of which had been confiscated by the patriots from his wife's loyalist parents. The following year, he was appointed secretary of war by president Washington and served for ten years. During that time, he created the United States Navy.[202]

Knox, who now weighed 300 pounds, then retired at the ripe old age of 45 and moved to Maine, where he engaged in cattle farming, shipbuilding, brick making, and real estate speculation. But his businesses, which had been built on borrowed money, ultimately failed and he sold off vast tracks of his land to pay his debts. Knox died bankrupt at the age of 56 after a chicken bone got lodged in his throat, causing a fatal infection. Fort Knox is named after him. So is Knoxville, Tennessee.[203]

As for the war, the fighting had lasted for six and a half years. It then took another two years to reach the Treaty of Paris, which officially ended it in 1783. Nearly 63,000 soldiers had fought for the colonies (40,000 patriots, 10,800 French, and 12,000 Spanish). The British had 116,000 (48,000 British, 25,000 loyalists, 29,875 Germans, and 13,000 Indians). The United States Constitution did not go into effect until March 4, 1789, more than seven years after the fighting ended. Until then, the colonies operated under the Articles of Confederation, which went into force shortly before Cornwallis surrendered.[204]

---

201 Middleton (2014), pp. 370–372; Willcox, pp. 29, 474; Mackesy, p. 213; *Oxford Dictionary of National Biography*: "Clinton, Sir Henry (1730–1795)." Ira D. Gruber. https://www. oxforddnb.com, accessed June 8, 2022.

202 Brooks (1900), p. 134; Puls, pp. 172, 184–186, 214–216; https://en.wikipedia.org/wiki/Henry_Knox, p. 6, accessed July 3, 2021; Chernow (2010), pp. 446, 448–449, 451; Ferling (*The Ascent*), pp. 281–282; Cooke, pp. 4–5.

203 https://en.wikipedia.org/wiki/Henry_Knox, p. 1, accessed July 3, 2021; Bell, p. 54; Puls, pp. 214–216, 249–250; Callahan, p. 380; McCullough, David (2001). *John Adams*. New York, New York: Simon & Schuster, p. 415. ISBN 0–684–81363–7.

204 https://en.wikipedia.org/wiki/American_Revolutionary_War, pp. 1, 3, 30, accessed July 3, 2021; Smith (1907), p. 86; Seineke, p. 36 footnote; Savas and Dameron, p. xli.

The protracted war worked in favor of the patriots, who depended on locally produced food and supplies, rather than on imports from more than 3,000 miles away. So the colonial economy was able to survive. With most American farms being far from seaports, British control of the ports did not mean British control inland. In all, a protracted war on home soil with fighting spread out along the eastern seaboard favored the colonists, particularly with regard to the Fabian strategy that Washington, Greene, and Swamp Fox began to use as the war went on.[205]

The patriots lost most of the pitched battles during the war. Their successes at Boston, Saratoga, and Yorktown came by amassing a greater number of troops to trap the British far from a support base. In general, the better-trained British officers utilized superior tactics and maneuvers, but the Revolutionary War required them to send and maintain large armies over great distances. And with ships taking up to three months to cross the Atlantic, orders from London were often obsolete by the time they arrived.[206]

Seven months after the fighting stopped, 800 patriot prisoners were released in England and sent home. Two months after that, King George III recognized the United States as an independent nation. Yet somewhere between 700 and 1,100 prisoners still remained on the *Jersey* in New York. At one point, the British reported that the prisoners were "in wholesome clean ships . . . every man furnished with a trade, bed, and sheets made of good Russia linen to lie in; the best of fresh provisions, vegetables, wine, rice, barley, etc."[207]

Finally, in November of 1782, thirteen months after the fighting had stopped, it was all over. A preliminary peace treaty was signed by Great Britain and the United States and all remaining prisoners were released. Parliament would not acknowledge that there had been prisoners of war, however, for another seven years. More than 11,000 men had died on the prison ships in New York. Another 4,000 to 7,000 had died in prisons on Manhattan. Whereas the mortality rate for patriot prisoners held in England was 5 percent, it was between 50 and 70 percent for

---

205 Greene and Pole, pp. 36–39, 42, 48; Clode vol. 1, p. 268.

206 Higginbotham, Chapter 3; Greene and Pole, pp. 298, 306.

207 Burrows, pp. 180, 185; Philbrick (2016), p. 181; Ferling (*Almost A Miracle*), p. 117.

patriot prisoners in New York. In battle, 6,824 patriots had died; 10,000 had died in camp due to wounds or disease. All told, roughly half of all patriots who died in the war did so as prisoners in New York.[208]

By then, at least 34,000 colonists had departed from New York to sail for England. William Franklin was among them. New York City was a mess, with many homes unfit for occupation. Streets were blocked by trenches and wharves were crumbling. On Long Island, the beaches at Wallabout Bay on the East River were scattered with the bones of soldiers who had died on the prison ships, with one resident describing skulls "lying about as thick as pumpkins in an autumn cornfield." As Burrows observes: ". . . the thousands of Americans who perished . . . were the victims of something well beyond the usual brutalities and misfortunes of war, even eighteenth-century war—a lethal convergence, as it were, of obstinacy, condescension, corruption, mendacity, and indifference. Although the British did not deliberately kill American prisoners, they might as well have."[209]

As time passed, some even began to deny the reality of the prison ships, calling the whole thing a "farce." Burrows again observes: "By the end of the nineteenth century, public opinion also began tilting in favor of the idea that nursing a hundred-year-old grudge against Great Britain no longer served any productive purpose." Decade after decade went by until, finally, more than one hundred years later, the Prison Ship Martyr's Monument was dedicated in 1908 for the remains of the patriot prisoners.[210]

Loyalists who were captured were treated harshly as well, and often executed. They were held in ships in New London, Connecticut, and in Connecticut copper mines. The Hessians who were captured at Trenton, Saratoga, and Yorktown were loosely confined in German settlements and often hired themselves out as laborers to local farmers and foundries.

---

[208] Burrows, pp. 199–201.

[209] Ibid., pp. xi, 204, 208–210.

[210] Ibid., pp. 219, 238, 242.

When the war was over, 10,000 Hessians and British soldiers decided to stay in America.[211]

King George III lived for 38 more years after the war. During that time, he presided over the War of 1812, when Britain and America were back at it again, and the Battle of Waterloo in 1815, when Wellington took down Napoleon. He died at the age of 81, having sat on the throne for 59 years. George spent his last decade blind and insane. He was also deaf by the time of his passing. Some say that his insanity was the result of a liver disorder known as porphyria. Others say it was purely psychological. A recent hair sample analysis suggests, however, that arsenic from his medicines may have been the cause.[212]

Though John Burgoyne was initially blamed for the defeat at Saratoga, over the years the responsibility has shifted to Howe for leaving him stranded in upstate New York. Burgyone became commander in chief of Ireland in 1782 and died ten years later. He is buried in Westminster Abbey.[213]

William Howe's responsibility for losing the war is still debated. After Bunker Hill, he seemed to have lost self-confidence, often failing to follow up on opportunities. He frequently blamed supply problems for his failure to pursue the enemy, such as his failure to pursue the patriots on Long Island and his allowing Washington's beaten army to escape into New Jersey. Why was he not more proactive during the war? Was it arrogance on his part? Laziness? Fear? Sympathy for the patriots? Though William Howe served in several administrative military positions after the war, he never again saw fighting action. He died in England more than 30 years after the war at the age of 84. As Philbrick notes, rather than being the "aristocratic buffoons"as they were later portrayed, the

---

211 https://www.historynet.com/british-prison-ships-a-season-in-hell.htm, pp. 9–10, accessed July 25, 2021.

212 https://www.history.com/topics/british-history/george-iii, George III, p. 3., accessed July 3, 2021.

213 https://en.m.wikipedia.org/wiki/John_Burgoyne, pp. 11–12, accessed August 21, 2021; Stanley, pp. 238–239.

British generals were "bright, ambitious, and conflicted men forced to fight a people whom they considered to be their countrymen."[214]

Francis Marion served for several years in the South Carolina senate after the war. At the age of 63, the Swamp Fox died at home.[215] Disney ran a television miniseries in 1959 with Leslie Nielsen playing Swamp Fox. As a kid, I was smitten with the idea of Swamp Fox and I talked about him and pretended to be him whenever possible. All of the kids and their parents in my neighborhood called me Swamp Fox. They still do. I especially liked the theme song:

> Swamp Fox, Swamp Fox, tail on his hat,
> Nobody knows where the Swamp Fox is at,
> Swamp Fox, Swamp Fox, hiding in the glen,
> He runs away to fight again.
> Got no cornpone, got no honey,
> All we got is Continental money,
> Won't buy bacon, hominy, or grits,
> Rodent ears and possum is all we get!

Apparently, a fellow named Parson Weems made it his mission in 1807 to create legendary status for Francis Marion, embellishing the life and times of Swamp Fox in a biography. (Weems also invented the tale about George Washington and the cherry tree.) In contrast, one British author described Swamp Fox as "a thoroughly unpleasant dude who was, basically, a terrorist." Another referred to him as being "very active in the persecution of the Cherokee Indians and not at all the sort of chap who should be celebrated as a hero." At Myrtle Beach, South Carolina, the wooden roller coaster is named *The Swamp Fox*.[216]

---

214 Fleming, p. 44; Davies, vol. 12–1776, 5:93, "Howe to Germain, June 7, 1776 and July 7, 1776."; https://www.battlefields.org/learn/biographies/william-howe, accessed July 11, 2021; Philbrick (2016), p. xiv.

215 https://www.tripadvisor.com/LocationPhotoDirectLink-g54394-d4105287-i63860148-Francis_Marion_gravesite-Pineville_South_Carolina.html.

216 "The Swamp Fox." Amy Crawford, *Smithsonian*, June 30, 2007, https://www.SmithsonianMag.com, accessed July 12, 2021; "Bookend; Life, Literature and the

Horatio Gates, one of the most controversial figures of the Revolutionary War, eventually moved to Manhattan, where he served one term in the New York state legislature. He died nearly 25 years after the war at the age of 78 in New York City.[217]

When the last British soldier left New York City in November of 1783, George Washington resigned from the military and went home to Mount Vernon to retire. As historian Philbrick observes: "That Washington resisted the temptation to resign in disgust or, at the other extreme, proclaim himself, like Napoleon, emperor, is a testament to his judgment and almost unbelievable patience."[218]

Washington served as chancellor of the College of William and Mary for 11 years beginning in April 1788. He was apolitical and opposed the formation of political parties. George Washington died of a throat infection at the age of 67 on December 14, 1799. Though he lost more battles than he won during the war, he never surrendered his troops. It was his resolve, rather than his military skill, that had carried him through the war.[219]

Upon his return to England in 1782, Benedict Arnold unsuccessfully encouraged King George III to renew the war against the patriots. He also sought several government positions in England, all unsuccessfully. However, his wife Peggy did receive payment from the king for her "meritorious" services. Over time, Arnold began claiming that he committed treason because the American cause had become hopeless and he did so to save bloodshed.[220] As Philbrick says, "[a]lthough it later became convenient to portray Benedict Arnold as a conniving Satan from

---

Pursuit of Happiness." Andrew Delbanco, *New York Times*, July 4, 1999; "Mel's Vendetta Against England. Neil Norman, *Evening Standard* online, June 19, 2000.

[217] Billias (1964), pp. 80, 103–104; Tuchman, p.192; "What remains of Manhattan's Rose Hill Enclave." *Ephemeral New York,* September 3, 2018; "Horatio Gates." Brandow, Rev. John H. Proceedings of the New York State Historical Association (1903). 3: 17–18. JSTOR 42889819. OCLC 862849155; accessed July 22, 2021; https://en.m.wikipedia.org/wiki/Horatio_Gates, p. 1, accessed July 22, 2021.

[218] Fleming, p. 312; Ferling (2003), pp. 378–379; Philbrick (2016), p. xvi.

[219] Gordon and Keegan, pp. 88–92; Buchanan (1997), p. 241; Dull, pp. 247–248; Rose, pp. 258–261.

[220] Brandt, pp. 257–259; Stuart, pp. 112, 135; Philbrick (2016), p. 267.

the start, the truth is more complex and, ultimately, more disturbing." He notes that it was his debilitating injury at Saratoga that was the "turning point that set him on the path to treason" and that he "lacked the ability to rise above petty and unjustified criticism" and "his need for money helped fuel his gradual creep toward treason."[221]

Philbrick further notes that Arnold was a skilled mariner and his abruptness and demanding personality were assumed qualities for a ship's captain. In fact, Arnold wrote several letters to Washington asking for a naval command. In addition, a patriot ship's crew received half the total value of any captured British merchant ship and the full value of a warship, with most of those proceeds going to the captain. Under such an arrangement, Arnold might have thrived at sea and never turned his back on the patriots.[222]

Benedict Arnold moved from England to New Brunswick, Canada, in 1784 and lived there for six years. But he was unwelcome, making bad business deals and filing petty lawsuits. During that time, Peggy even had the gall to return to Philadelphia to visit her family. After she came back to New Brunswick, the townspeople gathered in front of the Arnold home, calling them traitors and burning Benedict Arnold in effigy as Peggy and the kids watched. Soon they returned to England, where Arnold died nine years later at the age of 60. Peggy died three years after, at the age of 44.[223]

---

221 Philbrick (2016), pp. xv-xvi.

222 Ibid., pp. 90, 260.

223 "Benedict Arnold and Monson Hayt fonds." UNB Archives. Fredericton, New Brunswick, Canada: University of New Brunswick, 26 September 2001, https://web.lib.unb.ca, accessed June 8, 2022; Brandt, p. 263; Randall & Nahra (1999), p. 102.

Chapter 3

Remember the Alamo?

I remember the Alamo. My family pulled up to it in our station wagon in July of 1965. We stayed in a hotel next door and at the age of eight I was bursting at the seams to get inside the place. We had driven 1,000 miles to get there from Atlanta and all I could think about was Davy Crockett and Jim Bowie fighting with his famous knife to the death against Santa Anna's huge army. I had seen the whole thing on Disney's *Davy Crockett: King of the Wild Frontier*, starring Fess Parker and Buddy Ebsen.

We took a tour of the Alamo the next morning and learned about the brave men who died inside. It was a sad but glorious place. I left the Alamo in awe, and wore my coonskin cap for the next 3,000 miles as we drove all over the western United States before returning home to Georgia seven weeks later. Whenever I took off my cap in the car, I laid it out just so on top of the luggage behind my head. The tail laid out straight. If Walt or Anna wanted to perturb me, they touched the coonskin. That incensed me and I reported them to the front seat immediately. Whenever the miles got to be too much for me, I got into the back of the station wagon and held my hands over the top of the back seat so that Walt or Anna could tie me up with rope like a prisoner. Then I rolled around in the back of the station wagon, fighting to free myself as the mesas rolled by.

Now, nearly 60 years later, I still remember the Alamo clear as day. But I have never been clear on the bigger picture. What was the Alamo all about and what am I *supposed* to remember about it?

Wearing my coonskin, 1965

Trouble Brewing

The Spanish owned Mexico for 300 years and had tried for decades, without success, to settle its northern region. In an effort to populate the area, Spain invited foreigners to settle in the area in the 1780s.[224]

Then, in 1803, Napoleon sold more than 529 million acres of land to Thomas Jefferson under the Louisiana Purchase in order to raise money for his ongoing battles in Europe. This extended the United States westward to the Rocky Mountains, more than doubling the size of the country.[225] Jefferson thought that he had bought the northeastern part of Mexico known as Texas from France as part of the Louisiana Purchase, declaring that it would become the richest state in the Union.

---

[224] McNeese, p. 16.

[225] Ibid., p. 10.

But the border between Spanish-owned Mexico and the United States was unclear.[226]

This map shows the Nueces River and the Rio Grande River. Mexico asserted that its land extended to the Nueces River, rather than the Rio Grande.

Stephen Austin

Shortly before Mexico gained its independence from Spain in 1821, Spain granted 200,000 acres of Texas land to a Missouri banker named Moses Austin. This would help to populate the area and to reduce Indian raids.[227] Moses Austin died one month later, so his 27-year-old son, Stephen Austin, moved ahead with the plan to populate Texas. Stephen

---

[226] Kilmeade, p. 8; https://en.m.wikipedia.org/wiki/Mexican-American_War, p. 9, accessed March 27, 2022; McNeese, p. 17; Levy, p. 5.

[227] https://en.m.wikipedia.org/wiki/Mexican-American_War, p. 19, accessed March 27, 2022; Levy, p. 13; McNeese, pp. 26–27; Burrough, p. 11.

Austin had been a newspaper editor and a judge before becoming a land speculator. Under the Austin plan, each settler would receive 640 acres of land, along with an additional 160 acres for his wife and another 160 for each child.[228]

But with Mexico now independent, the Spanish land grants to Moses Austin were suddenly no good. Stephen Austin spent the next nine months straightening things out. Mexico needed the Texas area settled, so a deal was struck: Americans could bring their slaves, but could not engage in slave trading, and the children of slaves would become free at age 14.[229] Before the deal was made, Mexico had wanted to free all slaves within ten years, whereas Austin sought instead to "make them slaves for life and their children free at 21 . . ."[230] The government of Mexico would not, however, protect the settlers. They had to defend themselves. So Austin soon created what later became known as the Texas Rangers in order to protect his settlers from Indian attacks.[231]

The Mexican emperor was overthrown in 1824; the Mexican people now had a constitution, with a two-house legislature and an elected president. Once again, the validity of Austin's land grants fell into question. Austin got that squared away with the new Mexican Congress. It granted far more land than before: each settler received seven times more and Austin got 100,000 acres for his personal use.[232]

One year later, in 1825, the United States offered Mexico $1 million for Texas.[233] Mexico refused. Mexico also outlawed "commerce and traffic in slaves," declaring that any enslaved person became free as soon as they stepped onto Mexican soil. Yet, in its Constitution of 1827 Mexico stayed silent on slavery, instead leaving the issue to the individual

---

[228] McNeese, pp. 27–28; Burrough, p. 18; Note, however, that Hoyt at p. 16 says it was 640 acres, plus 320 for each family member and 80 for each slave, and that Kilmeade at p. 20 says it was 320 for the spouse and 160 for each child.

[229] McNeese, pp. 30–31; Burrough, p. 22.

[230] Burrough, p. 22.

[231] Hoyt, pp. 14, 16.

[232] McNeese, pp. 20–21, 32.

[233] Burrough, p. 73.

Mexican states. The Texas settlers were angry. Stephen Austin said, "Fathers tell me that I have reduced their children to a life of poverty."[234]

By 1828, Stephen Austin was relabeling each incoming slave as an "indentured servant." That term had been applied earlier to English settlers who had signed on to provide labor for a fixed period of time, often in exchange for the cost of transportation to the colonies. In contrast, each slave under Austin's plan was required to sign an employment contract with their owner under which they were paid $20 a year. They could buy their freedom for $1,200. But they had to pay for their food and housing. Surprisingly, the Mexican state approved this arrangement. Austin knew how to work the Mexican bureaucracy like nobody's business. And though Austin personally owned a vast tract of land, he himself lived in a dog-trot cabin.[235]

"Texas must be a slave country," he wrote to a friend. The Texans called the workers "indentures." A similar arrangement would arise in the United States after the American Civil War, with the workers being called "sharecroppers."[236]

Land in Texas was cheap: 12.5 cents an acre ($2.98 today) compared to U.S. land at $1.25 an acre ($29.80 today). The land was beautiful and settlers were exempt from taxes for their first seven years. Cotton and corn were the primary crops. Austin chose rich bottomlands for his settlers and Americans in Louisiana and Mississippi wanted to grow crops on that Texas land. They were supposed to swear allegiance to Mexico and convert to Catholicism. Most of them did so, if only in name. Austin was also responsible for controlling immigration into the area, setting up the legal system, overseeing the building of roads and schools, and representing the settlers' interests to the Mexican government. The settlers began referring to themselves as "Texians," with the *i* being pronounced as a *y*.[237]

Spain attempted to reconquer Mexico in 1829, but Santa Anna defeated them, becoming a national hero and referring to himself as

---

[234] Ibid., p. 24–26.

[235] Hoyt, p. 11; McNeese, pp. 33–42; Burrough, p. 36.

[236] Burrough, p. 30, 34–35, 41.

[237] McNeese, pp. 29–30, 37; Levy, p. 16; Hoyt, pp. 16, 18; Kilmeade, p. 20.

"The Savior of the Motherland."[238] By 1830, families in the American South had caught "Texas fever." They scrawled *GTT* on their front doors, indicating they had *Gone to Texas*. Many had been lured by handbills advertising the "smiling prairies" that "invite the plough."

Austin was careful. He declared that "no frontiersman who has no other occupation than that of hunter will be received—no drunkard, no gambler, no profane swearer, no idler." As a result, most of the settlers were farmers who could read and write. Other land agents were not so careful.

Between 1821 and 1830, the population of Texas had increased five fold and Americans now outnumbered Mexicans in Texas by a ratio of ten to one. As historian Bryan Burrough observes, during the first ten years of Mexico's independence after 1821, Mexican politics was a "blur of elections, coups, and revolts in which emperors, presidents, and generals took turns stumbling through the door of power."[239]

In Texas, nobody paid any attention to what was said and done in Mexico City, even though it was the richest city in the western hemisphere. It was also the largest, with 150,000 inhabitants compared to the 120,000 in New York City. Many of the settlers resisted speaking Spanish and insisted on having slaves, though prohibited by law.[240]

The president of Mexico was overthrown in 1830 and replaced by Santa Anna. New taxes were soon imposed on cotton, and immigration from America was banned. By 1831, Mexico was placing troops in Texas to enforce its new laws. It feared that Andrew Jackson would try to claim Texas as a United States territory.[241] Austin's "indentured servant" loophole lasted until April of 1832, when the state legislature closed it. Austin stated at that time: "Nothing is wanted but money, and negros are necessary to make it." As historian Burrough opines, Austin was a "frontier intellectual" who "understood slavery was morally repugnant but who nevertheless owned slaves because it was the best way to make

[238] Levy, p. 19; Burrough, p. 44.

[239] McNeese, pp. 39, 41; Burrough, p. 32.

[240] Burrough, p. 32; Tinkle, p. 88; Levy, p. 18; McNeese, p. 42.

[241] Ibid., p. 33; McNeese, pp. 42, 44; Tinkle, p. 15; Levy, p. 18.

money. In other words, Stephen F. Austin was a sellout . . ." Austin wrote the legal code for Texas, including the punishments for runaway slaves.[242]

To make matters worse, cotton prices began to soar in 1831, reaching a 15-year high by 1835. Worldwide demand for finished cotton was growing. Thanks to the invention of the cotton gin three decades earlier, cotton production increased 600 percent in the four-year period ending in 1835. Meanwhile, illegal immigrants from America were pouring into Texas, doubling its population during those four years.[243] Trouble was indeed brewing.

By 1834, Santa Anna had decided that Mexico was not ready for democracy. He declared himself dictator. He also nullified the Mexican constitution. As Burrough puts it, Santa Anna's real allegiance was to himself.[244] Meanwhile, President Andrew Jackson sought to buy Texas from Mexico for $5 million.[245]

Stephen F. Austin

A perfect storm had formed in Texas involving cheap land, increased cotton production, a booming textile industry, and growing worldwide demand for cotton. The slave population in America would quadruple between 1800 and 1860, going from 900,000 to nearly 4 million. All

---

[242] Ibid., pp. 15, 18–23, 41.

[243] Ibid., p. 34.

[244] Levy, pp. 7, 19; McNeese, p. 70; Burrough, p. 44.

[245] Burrough, p. 74.

of the prime land in Alabama, Mississippi, and Louisiana had been taken, so those seeking to grow cotton looked to Texas. Some say that the Texas Revolution was not about freedom, but about the freedom to own slaves.[246]

William Travis

In 1831, William "Buck" Travis, a 22-year-old, "chest-thumping" Alabama lawyer who had killed a man for "trifling" with his wife, fled to Texas never to return. He lived in a boarding house, liked to gamble, and wore flamboyant clothing, including a white hat with "the broadest brim imaginable" and red pants. Travis was complicated. He had a reputation as a ladies' man, though most of his conquests were with prostitutes and slaves. As historian Tim McNeese puts it: "Despite his taste for partying and constant women, he was known as a gentleman. Perhaps surprisingly, he was also known as a highly religious man."[247]

Travis moved to Galveston in 1832. He was convinced that Texas and Mexico were on a collision course and he joined the War Party, a group of Texans determined to pursue independence. In short order, Travis was at the center of trouble as the "loudest and most persistent member" of the War Party.[248]

As a lawyer in Texas, Travis represented a Louisiana slave owner who had come to Texas to reclaim two runaway slaves. However, the Mexican commander at the Anahuac fort in east Texas declared the fugitives to be citizens of Mexico and refused to return them. That commander was Juan Bradburn (formerly John Bradburn of Kentucky), who was disliked by many for his arrogance and his high-handed manner. Travis delivered a letter to Bradburn, claiming that 100 soldiers were coming to the fort to retrieve the two slaves. In response, Bradburn declared martial law and arrested Travis, but would not disclose the charges against him. Bradburn then declared that Travis would be executed. Soon a boat carrying 100 Texans headed downriver toward the Anahuac fort. After nearly nine

---

[246] Ibid., pp. 4–6.

[247] Tinkle, pp. 44, 61,64; Hoyt, pp. 18, 95-IX; McNeese, pp. 45, 93; Burrough, p. 37.

[248] McNeese, p. 47; Burrough, p. 55.

hours of fighting and two-thirds of Bradburn's men dead or wounded, the Anahuac fort surrendered in June of 1832.[249] Martial law was soon rescinded and Travis was released. Bradburn resigned and fled to the United States.[250]

William Travis was "ambitious, well read, self-focused, moody, touchy, and easily offended. But he was also a man of action and principle." He was high strung, and his temper was "nearly ungovernable." During one court appearance he pulled a knife on the opposing lawyer. Travis was "hugely ambitious, yet haughty, humorless, and quick to take offense" and had a "big chip on his shoulder."[251] His success at Anahuac led to Santa Anna's decision to send troops into Texas. As Burrough says, "If ever a man could be said to have single-handedly started the Texas Revolt, it was the histrionic, melodramatic, oversexed, underprincipled 'Buck' Travis." He was the "loudest, angriest voice in Texas."[252]

Stephen Austin had tried to calm things down. He met with newly elected President Santa Anna in the summer of 1833 to try to convince him to recognize Texas as a Mexican state. Santa Anna denied the request and imprisoned Austin for a year and a half. Austin was then released but had to remain in Mexico until July of 1835—two years after his trip had begun. By then, Santa Anna had already declared himself dictator.[253] And while Austin was imprisoned, a fellow named Sam Houston had gotten involved.

249 Hoyt, pp. 18–19.
250 Ibid., pp. 18–19.
251 McNeese, p. 45; Tinkle, p. 44; Burrough, pp. 56–57.
252 Levy, p. 31; Burrough, p. 56–57; Tinkle, p. 59.
253 Levy, p. 19; Hoyt, pp. 32, 33; McNeese, pp. 47–49; Tinkle, p. 15.

William Travis

Sam Houston

In 1832, at the age of 38, Sam Houston decided to turn his life around and go to Texas. He had run away from home at age 16 after his father died, and lived among the Cherokee Indians in Tennessee. He served under General Andrew Jackson in the War of 1812, whatever the hell that was all about, before studying law, becoming the attorney general of Tennessee, and serving in the U.S. House of Representatives at the age of 30. By the age of 34, in 1827, Houston was governor of Tennessee.

Houston was flamboyant. He married a woman 15 years younger, but the marriage lasted only three months, with some blaming its failure on Houston's drinking. Others suspected that his bride was still in love with someone else. Humiliated, Houston resigned his governorship and went to live in Oklahoma with the Cherokee, who Andrew Jackson had by then ordered to move west of the Mississippi River.[254]

Houston stayed with the Cherokee for three years. They called him the "Big Drunk," as he spent much of his time drinking. He straightened himself out a bit, married a Cherokee woman, and appeared in Washington in 1830 as a member of the Cherokee delegation to the United States government. Houston appeared in buckskin pants,

[254] McNeese, pp. 50–51; Kilmeade, pp. 5–7.

a turban, and a brightly colored blanket over his shoulders. Andrew Jackson welcomed him warmly.[255]

Sam Houston also visited Jackson at the Hermitage in Tennessee before he left for Texas, and Jackson lent him $500 (almost $12,000 today) to help him get started. He arrived in Texas on December 10, 1832 and soon concluded that Texas should be independent from Mexico. Houston settled in Nacogdoches to practice law. Already well known as the former governor of Tennessee, he soon became a leader in the community. He spent $375 of the money from Jackson ($9,000 today) to buy 4,428 acres of land.[256]As Santa Anna became more tyrannical, Austin's influence diminished. Houston's grew. He stood at six feet two inches and continued to wear Indian clothing from time to time.[257]

The Conflict Grows

By June of 1835 William Travis was at it again. Santa Anna had reopened the customs house in Anahuac and was serious about collecting import taxes. Several of Travis's law clients had had their imported goods impounded, and to Travis this was "tyranny." Travis and twenty men loaded cannon onto a ship and crossed Galveston Bay. As historian Edwin Hoyt puts it, Travis "rounded up a bunch of his well-liquored friends and set out for Anahuac." When the Mexican commander there inquired about their purpose, Travis demanded his surrender. The Mexicans indeed surrendered.[258]

---

[255] McNeese, p. 51; Burrough, p. 64; Kilmeade, pp. 12–13; Hoyt, p. 144.

[256] Kilmeade, pp. 17–18, 22; McNeese, pp. 49–52; Levy, p. 25.

[257] McNeese, p. 52; Kilmeade, p. 1; Tinkle, p. 18.

[258] Hoyt, pp. 34, 37; Levy, p. 31; Burrough, pp. 58–59; Tinkle, p. 173.

Sam Houston

Texans were stunned. Travis had gone too far. He was harshly criticized by many, but when an arrest order for Travis was issued one month later, the Texans became outraged at Mexico instead. They called for a "consultation" to be held on October 15, 1835, in the tiny town of Washington-on-the-Brazos to discuss how to respond to Santa Anna's replacement of a republic with a dictatorship.[259] They were affronted both by the order to arrest Travis and by the threat to local government power under which slavery had continued to exist. As one settler put it, Texans would be in a situation "worse than that of the most degraded slaves."[260]

The Texas leaders consistently framed the fight as one to preserve "natural rights" and "property"—an economic issue rather than a moral one. They claimed to be in a "glorious revolution about liberty and freedom," likening the struggle to the second coming of the American Revolution. Northern abolitionists, however, viewed it as a pro-slavery rebellion. Mexico saw it as a secret plot by the United States to take Texas. After unsuccessful U.S. efforts to buy Texas from Mexico in 1825 and 1828, many wondered why Andrew Jackson's protege, Sam Houston, had come to Texas in the first place.[261]

[259] Burrough, pp. 59–60; Hoyt, p. 37; McNeese, p. 57; Tinkle, p. 173.

[260] Burrough, p. 71.

[261] Ibid., pp. 64, 72–76.

One month later, in September of 1835, Stephen Austin returned to Texas following his imprisonment in Mexico. He no longer promoted loyalty to the Mexican government. Instead, he said, "War is our only recourse." It must be "war in full," he added, and "there must now be no half way measures."[262]

Santa Anna soon sent General Cos, his "elegant and dandified" brother-in-law, to Texas with 500 men to bring the Texans back into line.[263] Cos was a veteran soldier, but he was a political general with little military vision or strategy. His men wore blue uniforms with white sashes and tall hats.[264]

On October 1, General Cos sent a hundred Mexican cavalrymen to the town of Gonzales to retrieve an old cannon. Mexico had given the cannon to the town of two dozen settlers four years earlier to ward off Comanche Indian attacks. But, as punishment for Texan resistance to Santa Anna's government and in an effort to disarm the Texans, the Mexican army now demanded it back. The Texans refused. Though the cannon had long before been removed from its carriage and had no ammunition, the Texans refurbished it and mounted it on a wagon. They began making ammunition out of slugs of iron bar, along with cut-up horseshoes and pieces of chain.[265]

When the Mexican troops appeared on the far bank of the river, 300 Texans appeared on the opposite bank with the cannon. They had draped a white sheet on it bearing an image of the cannon along with the words "Come and take it!" A lot of yelling back and forth across the river took place. The next morning, the Texans forded the river with the cannon and fired it, following up with a charge against the Mexican army. The Mexican troops retreated to San Antonio. Though the volunteers believed that they had defeated an invading army, the Mexican officer

---

[262] Tinkle, pp. 89, 173; Burrough, p. 6; Stephen F. Austin to Columbia Committee, September 19, 1835, cited in Cantrell, p. 312; McNeese, p. 58; Kilmeade, p. 30.

[263] Tinkle, pp. 10, 173; McNeese, p. 57; Kilmeade, p. 28. Note: Whether Cos and Santa Anna were in fact related is not certain. Some say that this familial connection was fabricated as part of the traditionalist narrative in order to portray Santa Anna as being vengeful at the Alamo due to his relative having been shamed there.

[264] Kilmeade, pp. 43–44; Hoyt, p. 35.

[265] Tinkle, p. 173; Kilmeade, pp. 30–36; Hoyt, p. 39.

on the scene had in fact been ordered not to fight. Many hailed this first battle of the Texas Revolution as the "Lexington of Texas." News of the victory at Gonzales quickly spread and 200 men soon left from New Orleans to head for the fight in Texas.[266]

Two days later, Santa Anna dissolved the state governments of Mexico. Six days after that, Texans captured the Mexican fort in Goliad, which was only 93 miles from Gonzales and full of arms, supplies, and money. Fewer than 50 Mexicans were at the fort when the Texans chopped their way into the place. The surprised officer in charge surrendered immediately.[267]

Stephen Austin showed up in Gonzales on October 11. The Texans unanimously chose him as their leader. Though he had no military experience, Austin and 300 men set out the next day on a 75-mile march to San Antonio with their "Come and Take It" flag leading the way. Most of his men were on foot.[268]

Austin was not a natural military leader, but he accepted the position in the hope of unifying his "motley mix" of volunteers. They wore buckskin britches and sombreros and they carried hunting knives, shotguns, and Kentucky rifles. The volunteers were untrained and hot-blooded. William Travis joined them along the way. So did Jim Bowie.[269]

Jim Bowie

Born in Kentucky and raised in Georgia, Bowie had come to Texas from Louisiana in 1828 in search of silver. At six foot one with red hair, he was already famous for killing two armed men with his big knife on a sandbar in the Mississippi River. He had also killed three more men with his knife in Texas when they ambushed him.[270] Historian Janey Levy describes him as a "reckless, violent man." His famous knife had a blade

---

[266] Hoyt, pp. 42–47; Levy, p. 21; Kilmeade, p. 38; Burrough, p. 62.

[267] Tinkle, pp. 173–174; Kilmeade, p. 41.

[268] Hoyt, p. 47; Kilmeade, pp. 43–44; Burrough, p. 63.

[269] Kilmeade, pp. 44, 46, 68; Burrough, p. 63; Hoyt, p. 46.

[270] Tinkle, pp. 46–47; Kilmeade, p. 21; McNeese, p. 54.

between 9 and 15 inches long. Bowie was handsome and likable, but he had a hair-trigger temper.[271]

He also had a gift for making and losing money. Bowie gambled, smuggled slaves, dealt in stolen goods, operated a Louisiana steam mill for grinding sugar cane, and sold Arkansas and Louisiana land under fraudulent deeds before heading to Texas. After he found no silver, Bowie was introduced by Stephen Austin to the powerful Veramendi family of San Antonio. He married the beautiful Veramendi daughter and joined the Catholic Church.[272]

With the help of the Veramendis, Bowie soon became a Mexican citizen, qualifying him to buy nearly 50,000 acres of Texas land at five cents per acre. He persuaded friends of the Veramendi family to do the same and then sell their land to him. In short order, Bowie owned 750,000 acres. He was appointed as a land commissioner and proceeded to sell thousands of acres of public land for personal profit. As historian Burrough puts it, if Bowie had stayed in the United States, "there's a decent chance he'd have ended up swinging from a rope."[273]

Bowie was colorful and he was crooked. According to Burrough: "Bowie was a seasoned swindler, always on the make, a man who fled to Texas rather than face the consequences of a series of land frauds he had attempted back in Arkansas and Louisiana. In Coahuila, Bowie managed to bribe his way to a massive land grant, only to have Santa Anna annul all such sales. It was at this point that he started badgering folks to try to take Santa Anna down." Bowie's wife and kids and in-laws all died of cholera in 1833. After that, he tried to drink the pain away. Jim Bowie was brave, aggressive, and cool under fire. In San Antonio, he was also known as "the braggart."[274]

By mid-October of 1835, Mexican General Cos had 650 men in San Antonio and was aware of Austin's approach. Austin in turn sent Bowie ahead to scout out the Mexican troops in San Antonio. Bowie

---

[271] Levy, p. 28; McNeese, p. 54; Kilmeade, p. 21.

[272] Tinkle, pp. 48–49; Levy, p. 30; Hoyt, p. 120; Burrough, p. 84; Kilmeade, p. 22.

[273] Tinkle, p. 49; Hoyt, pp. 120–121; Burrough, p. 83.

[274] Burrough, pp. 53, 86; Tinkle, pp. 50–51; Kilmeade, p. 47.

reported back that the Mexican troops in San Antonio were short on food and could be starved out in five days.[275]

While Austin was making his way toward San Antonio, Sam Houston showed up at his camp. Houston had been in east Texas trying to raise an army. Now he was on his way to the October 15, 1835, Consultation of Texas to sketch a plan for the governance of Texas in the wake of Santa Anna's recent dissolution of the state governments. In order for the Consultation to meet, a quorum was needed, so Houston was seeking delegates from among Austin's men. As historian Brian Kilmeade puts it: "Instead of arriving to help in the fight, Houston would rob the army of fighters."[276]

Austin's soldiers gathered and the issue was raised whether to "stay and fight" or "depart and debate." Houston declared flatly that they needed more training and were ill-equipped to succeed in an assault on San Antonio. According to him, they would fare better to return to Gonzales for the winter and create a real army, rather than to attempt a suicidal assault on San Antonio. Austin strongly disagreed. Everyone voted on the issue and the vast majority favored an assault.[277]

On October 25, Houston headed on to the Consultation with twenty delegates from Austin's army. At the Consultation, they debated whether to fight for complete independence from Mexico (the War Party) or for Mexican statehood and rights under the Mexican Constitution (the Peace Party). Surprisingly, they decided to defend the Mexican Constitution.[278] At the Consultation, Sam Houston was named commander of a "regular army" to be formed, and a fellow named Henry Smith was chosen as governor. A legislature known as the Council was formed and everyone agreed to reconvene on March 1, 1836.

Houston was charismatic and the natural choice for commander, seasoned from his days under Jackson in the War of 1812 against the British. During that war, at the age of 21, Houston had taken a nearly fatal arrow to the thigh and a bullet to the shoulder in Mississippi

---

[275] McNeese, pp. 58–59; Kilmeade, pp. 43, 48, 49.

[276] Kilmeade, pp. 45, 49–50.

[277] Ibid., pp. 50–51; Burrough, p. 65.

[278] Kilmeade, p. 52; Tinkle, pp. 16, 174; Burrough, p. 65.

while routing the Red Stick Indians, a potential ally for the British. As Kilmeade states, Houston "was eager to be a hero at any cost, but instead had become a casualty and had learned that courage must be calculated or else will get you killed."[279]

Austin, who was in charge of the volunteer militia, continued to move his men toward San Antonio. They were unpaid, did not wear uniforms, and provided their own guns and ammunition. Austin soon received 100 reinforcements and now had 400 men. On October 27, he sent Jim Bowie ahead once again, this time with 92 men, to find the best position for staging the attack. Austin wanted to move his troops to that place by nightfall.[280]

Bowie found the perfect place only three miles from San Antonio. But he ignored Austin's command and stayed the night at the newly found location without telling Austin. As Kilmeade puts it, Bowie was "a man possessed of an independent streak wider than the Mississippi." Mexican General Cos soon learned from his spies that Bowie and his small group were nearby, so he sent 300 or more hundred soldiers toward Bowie during the night. They surrounded the Texans.[281]

In the morning, a Mexican cannon fired at Bowie's men, but hit the trees overhead, showering ripe pecans down on them. Bowie and his men then shot the artillerymen and charged toward the cannon. When they reached it, they pivoted it and shot into the Mexican troops, who ran in full retreat with 14 dead and 39 wounded. One Texan was killed. Bowie had won the Battle of Concepcion. Austin's troops soon joined him.[282]

Three days later, Austin began the siege of San Antonio, saying, "What we want to do now is starve them out." Cos was indeed running low on food and ammunition, and 200 of his men had deserted. Austin, who now had 600 men, invited Cos to surrender. Cos refused, stating that his orders required him to fight to the death. He figured that if

---

[279] Kilmeade, pp. 1–3, 49, 69; Tinkle, p. 174; Hoyt, p. 151.

[280] Kilmeade, pp. 51–52; McNeese, p. 59; Hoyt, p. 50.

[281] Kilmeade, pp. 54–58; Burrough at p. 67 says 400 soldiers.

[282] Kilmeade, pp. 58–60; Burrough, p. 67.

things got bad in San Antonio, his men would retreat to the Alamo four hundred yards out of town.[283]

During the siege, Austin's men grew frustrated after weeks of inaction. Some left, including Jim Bowie, who departed in a huff and made his way over to the Consultation, where he got drunk with Sam Houston night after night. Those who stayed raised so much hell that Austin sent a request to the nearby town of San Felipe "in the name of Almighty God" not to send over any more alcohol.[284]

Though Sam Houston was the chosen commander of the Texas army, he was not in charge of the volunteers at San Antonio—and Stephen Austin was determined to capture the town before his leadership of the volunteers ended. Austin ordered an attack, but many of his officers refused, basing their unwillingness on what Houston had said. Austin called off the attack. Shortly afterward he resigned as their leader in order to fill a new position as envoy to the United States to request a loan for the new Texas government. By then, more than 250 of his 600 volunteers had gone home, feeling that their time had been wasted.[285]

Jim Bowie

[283] Hoyt, p. 51; McNeese, pp. 63, 66; Kilmeade, p. 64; Burrough, p. 68.

[284] Kilmeade, pp. 66–67; Hoyt, pp. 51, 144; McNeese, p. 62; Burrough, p. 68.

[285] Kilmeade, pp 69–75; Tinkle, p. 174; Burrough, p. 69; Hoyt, p. 51.

A fellow named Burleson replaced Austin. Burleson had fought in the war of 1812. He was also the leader of the officers who had refused to obey Austin's order to attack. Burleson was ready to retreat into winter camp, as suggested by Sam Houston. Then a volunteer named Ben Milam, who had been jailed by Santa Anna and recently released, got the volunteers all riled up. On December 5, Milam and more than 300 men attacked San Antonio, breaking into houses in the town to find cover from the Mexican cannon fire. The streets of San Antonio were filled with grapeshot and the Texans were pinned down. To advance through the town, the Texans used battering rams made out of logs to "mouse hole" through the adjoining adobe walls of houses.[286]

The fighting in San Antonio went on for four days as the Texans slowly advanced on the town plaza, where the Mexican army had placed their cannon in fortified positions. While looking through a field glass to plan his next step, Ben Milam was shot in the head by a sniper and died on the spot. As the Texans advanced from house to house toward the town plaza, General Cos moved his headquarters to the Alamo.[287]

Another 600 Mexican troops then arrived (without bringing any food). The Mexican army now outnumbered the volunteers by a factor of two or three to one.[288] But, eventually, the Texans reached the house of a priest in town. From that location, their rifles could sweep the town plaza. The Mexican troops had to withdraw to the Alamo as well. As they did, 200 of them deserted. As Kilmeade says, "Cos was in deep trouble and he knew it."[289]

Cos surrendered his 1,100 men at the Alamo on December 9, 1835. The seven-week siege of San Antonio was over. The terms of surrender took 12 hours to negotiate. Under the surrender, Cos was released after swearing not to fight the Texans again. His men were sent toward Mexico City. They were allowed to keep their personal weapons, along with one cannon for protection against Indian attacks, but Cos left behind 21

[286] Kilmeade, pp. 39, 71, 77, 82; Hoyt, pp. 45, 52, 56–57; https://en.m.wikipedia.org/wiki/Mexican-American_War, p. 72, accessed March 27, 2022.

[287] Hoyt, pp. 45, 57, 60, 62; Kilmeade, p. 81.

[288] Kilmeade, pp. 63, 82; Tinkle, p. 174; McNeese, pp. 62, 65; Levy, p. 21; Hoyt, p. 58.

[289] Kilmeade, p. 83.

cannon and 500 muskets. The 60-day enlistments of the Texas volunteers had expired, so they disbanded. Many went home for Christmas with no plan of returning.[290]

At that point, most Texans thought the war was over and that Mexico would recognize Texas as an independent territory. William Travis, never moderate, felt certain that Mexico would never again invade Texas. In contrast, Houston issued a call for volunteers to reinforce San Antonio, which he knew the Mexican army would try to retake. While many rejoiced, Sam Houston suspected that the battle in San Antonio should never have occurred and that the Alamo was a fort that could not be held.[291]

On Christmas Day of 1835, Santa Anna and his army set off toward Texas with little planning or forethought. He was furious about the outcome in San Antonio and he ordered Cos to turn around and head back toward the Alamo. When the news of Santa Anna's approach reached the hard-drinking Sam Houston in January of 1836, he was, as he stated, "most miserably cool and sober." In mid-February, Santa Anna's troops ran into a blizzard. They had no tents and some of the men froze to death. Many deserted along the way.[292]

Meanwhile, in early January of 1836, the Council decided to move the fighting closer to the border in an effort to get the fighting out of Texas. So 200 of the volunteers in San Antonio, including Jim Bowie, headed for Matamoros, nearly 300 miles due south and just across the Rio Grande in Mexico. Having no money in its treasury to pay the soldiers, the Council had instead promised them that they could ransack the town and keep the spoils. For that mission, the Matamoros volunteers took most of the horses, provisions, and medicine from the Alamo, leaving behind 104 men. When Sam Houston learned of the Matamoros plan, he called it an "absurdity." The Matamoros force was disorganized and the whole plan was soon scrapped when more Mexican troops appeared

---

[290] Hoyt, p. 65; McNeese, p. 66; Tinkle, pp. 20, 23, 174; Kilmeade, pp. 84–85; Levy, p. 21.

[291] Tinkle, pp. 20, 24–25; McNeese, p. 66; Levy, p. 25; Kilmeade, p. 85,

[292] Tinkle, pp. 10, 175; McNeese, pp. 67, 70, 72; Kilmeade, p. 86; Hoyt, p. 70.

there. The Texans in the Matamoros expedition withdrew 25 miles north of Matamoros to the fort in Goliad.[293]

Santa Anna

Antonio Lopez de Santa Anna was born into a well-to-do family in Veracruz and joined the military at age 16. He had fought well against the Spanish in 1821 and again when Spain tried to retake Mexico in 1829, driving them out with a much smaller force and becoming the nation's savior. He often referred to himself as the "Napoleon of the West," as did others. In fact, he was a Napoleon fanatic, an avid collector of Napoleon artifacts who kept portraits of Napoleon on the walls of his estates. (The formal term for information and artifacts relating to Napoleon is *Napoleoniana*.)[294]

Santa Anna was a wealthy landowner and a tall, handsome ladies man who adored elaborate military garb. One of his uniforms was said to have been so heavily laden with silver that, when the metal was later melted down, it yielded a set of spoons. He was also a lifelong gambler.[295]

[293] Kilmeade, pp. 87–90; Tinkle, pp. 175–176; Hoyt at p. 66 says that only 80 men were left at the Alamo; https://en.wikipedia.org/wiki/James_Fannin, p. 2, accessed February 17, 2022.

[294] Kilmeade, pp. 23–24; McNeese, p. 70; https://military-history-fandom.com/wiki/Antonio_Lopez_de_Santa_Anna, p. 6; Tinkle, p. 87–88; https://www.history.com/news/6-things-you-may-not-know-about-santa-anna, p. 2, accessed February 18, 2022.

[295] McNeese, p. 70; https://military-history-fandom.com/wiki/Antonio_Lopez_de_Santa_Anna, p. 3, accessed February 20, 2022.

Santa Anna

As Kilmeade puts it, Santa Anna "seemed to believe that cruelty was usually the best strategy." His minister of war soon issued a decree stating that any foreigners entering Mexico to join the rebellion would be treated as "pirates" and executed if captured.[296]

Though Santa Anna enjoyed holding power, he did not want the work that came with it. He lived in Veracruz and let his subordinates do the work. Santa Anna was married twice, but did not personally appear at either ceremony, sending a proxy instead. Both women were wealthy; historian Will Fowler suggests that, since the marriages were arranged, Santa Anna's failure to appear resulted from the purely financial nature of the transactions.

Santa Anna was opportunistic and "constantly changed with the political winds." He is said to have been capricious, opinionated, stubborn, and often foolish. A handsome, aristocratic womanizer, Santa Anna was also a scheming, conniving, disloyal, ambitious, self-serving, manipulative, back-stabbing "autocrat who ruled with an iron fist."[297]

---

[296] Kilmeade, pp. 23–24; Tinkle, p. 89; McNeese, p. 70; Hoyt, p. 33; https://en.wikipedia.org/wiki/Battle_of_San_Jacinto, p. 2, accessed February 17, 2022; Calore, p. 56; Todish, pp. 137–138.

[297] Krauze, p. 137; Fowler, p. 35; "All the President's Women: The Wives of General Antonio Lopez de Santa Anna in 19th century Mexico." Will Fowler, *Feminist Review*, 2005, No. 79, Latin America: History, War, and Independence; Hoyt, pp. 28, 153; Kilmeade, p. 31.

On January 19, 1836, Jim Bowie and 30 men returned to the Alamo from Goliad, *perhaps* with instructions from Sam Houston to blow up the place and move its cannon to Goliad and Gonzales. Houston knew that holing up in the Alamo against a much larger army would spell disaster. Soon after arriving, however, Bowie decided not to destroy it, believing that it was too important in some way—either symbolically or as the last stronghold from which to stop Santa Anna on his way to east Texas. What's more, removal of the cannon was impossible, since most of the horses and wagons at the Alamo had been taken for the ill-fated Matamoros expedition. Bowie said, ". . . we will rather die in these ditches than give it up to the enemy." So the Alamo took on a symbolic value that was at least as important as its military value. Bowie was also determined to defend his massive landholdings. He was immensely popular at the Alamo and he now drank steadily.[298]

Many of the men in the Alamo were what Kilmeade calls "second-chance" men, running from something, whether it be failure, arrest, or debt. Texas was "the place everyone went to start their second act." But no one expected Santa Anna to appear so soon. Within a month, he would be only 50 miles away.[299]

The Alamo stood half a mile outside of San Antonio and was surrounded by cottonwood trees. It had been built by the Spanish as a Roman Catholic mission nearly 120 years before. *Alamo* is Spanish for cottonwood. The place was now a mess, with little in the way of food, gunpowder, or supplies. Those who were there were unpaid and angry about it. Two out of three were recent arrivals to Texas. Water ditches ran along two sides of the Alamo, as well as under its walls and into its courtyard. The area inside the Alamo was 80 yards by 150 yards. The outer walls were up to 12 feet high and 3 feet wide. A large chapel, with thicker, taller walls, and the Long Barrack were contained within the Alamo, but the roof of the Long Barrack had fallen in long before due to years of neglect.[300]

---

[298] Burrough, p. 36; Tinkle, pp. 52, 54; Kilmeade, p. 97.

[299] Tinkle, pp. 28, 175; McNeese, pp. 73–75; Kilmeade, p. 92; Levy, p. 30.

[300] McNeese, pp. 7, 75–77; Tinkle, p. 27; Levy, p. 5; Burrough, p. 80.

On February 3, William Travis arrived at the Alamo with 25 men under instructions from Texas governor Smith, who referred to the ragtag Texian volunteers as "a mob nicknamed an army." Travis soon came to agree with Bowie that the Alamo should be held as a key defense. They had one cannon that would fire an 18-pound cannonball about half a mile, along with 20 other smaller pieces of artillery. Cannonballs were in short supply, so nails, door hinges, and other metal scraps were fashioned into ammunition. With the arrival of Travis, the Alamo had 150 men. But Travis and most of his men stayed in town rather than in the old Alamo mission.[301]

Unlike Bowie, hot-headed Travis wanted to march straight into Mexico to seize its gold and silver for the Texas republic. He could not stand playing second fiddle to Bowie, who was a natural leader eager for command. As historian Hoyt puts it, Travis was "a brave, sometimes precipitate man with a yearning for glory . . ."[302]

Davy Crockett

Davy Crockett, age 49, responded to Sam Houston's call for volunteers by walking for three months to get to Texas. He was already famous, so banquets were held in his honor at stops along the way. Crockett was muscular and he was tall for his time, standing at five feet eight inches and weighing around 190 pounds. He arrived at the Alamo five days after Travis and brought with him 12 men and his own fiddle. He referred to the Mexican leader as "Santy Anny."[303]

Crockett's father had first put him in school at the age of 12, but he ran away after only four days. He returned home three years later and received another six months of schooling. From that point on, he was self-educated. He served as a scout for Andrew Jackson in Florida against the Creek Indians in 1812, but grew disgusted with American treatment

[301] Tinkle, p. 176; McNeese, p. 77; Kilmeade, p. 94; Hoyt, pp. 3, 7–8.

[302] Tinkle, pp. 54–55; Hoyt, p. 95-I.

[303] Kilmeade, pp. 97–99; Tinkle, pp. 17, 29, 176; McNeese, p. 81; https://sharetngov.tnsosfiles.com, Davy Crockett-TLSA: "Tennessee Myths and Legends," accessed July 19, 2022.

of the Indians and hired a substitute to finish his enlistment. Crockett's "picturesque and canny speech spellbound his listeners," according to historian Lon Tinkle. He once claimed to have shot 47 bears in a single month. He had even published his autobiography in 1834, *A Narrative of the Life of David Crockett of the State of Tennessee Written by Himself.* Crockett described his own eyes as being "as keen as a lizard's." Others claimed he could "climb a thorn tree with a panther under each arm."[304]

Crockett had served Tennessee for three terms in the U.S. House of Representatives, wearing his frontier garb in Washington. He was folksy, but also shrewd and forthright, and he fought for the rights of poor settlers. Crockett strongly opposed the policies of Andrew Jackson and had, over time, come to loathe Jackson and his spoils system. He voted against Jackson's Indian Removal Act—the only delegate from Tennessee to do so. Crockett also proposed abolishing West Point on the grounds that public money was being used to benefit the sons of the wealthy. However, he was unable to pass a single bill during his six years in Congress.[305]

Davy Crockett

The Whig party considered Crockett as a presidential candidate to run against Jackson in 1836. Whig politicians began ghostwriting his speeches, as well as an 1833 biography of Crockett that was filled

[304] Tinkle, pp. 84–85; Hoyt, p. 71; McNeese, p. 77; Kilmeade, p. 98; Crockett, p. 80; Williams, p. 164.

[305] Tinkle, p. 85; https://en.wikipedia.org/wiki/Davy_Crockett, pp. 5–6, citing Boylston & Wiener, pp. 16 and Groneman, pp. 96–97; https//:history.com/ 10 Things You May Not Know About Davy Crockett, Evan Andrews, August 12, 2016, accessed March 22, 2022.

with wild exaggerations in an effort to raise his national profile. Called *Sketches and Eccentricities of Colonel David Crockett of West Tennessee*, one portion read: "I'm that same David Crockett, fresh from the backwoods, half-horse, half-alligator, a little touched with the snapping turtle, can wade the Mississippi, leap the Ohio, ride upon a streak of lightning, and slip without a scratch down a honey locust; can whip my weight in wild cats—and if any gentleman pleases, for a ten dollar bill, he may throw in a panther."[306]

Andrew Jackson helped to ensure that Crockett did not get reelected for a fourth term as a Tennessee representative in 1835. After his constituents elected a rival, Crockett said, "Y'all can go to hell and I'm going to Texas." So, on November 1, 1835, Crockett indeed headed to Texas, leaving behind his wife and children, whom he intended to send for later. In Jackson, Tennessee, people swarmed into town to get a look at him. In Little Rock, they put on a dinner in his honor at the Jeffries' Hotel, where he spoke of Washington politics and Texan independence. According to historian Burrough, "after Andrew Jackson, Crockett may have been the most famous man in America in 1836," known as much for his tall tales and autobiography as for anything he had actually done.[307]

When he reached Nacogdoches, Texas, in early January of 1836, Crockett enlisted for six months as a volunteer private and was promised 4,600 acres of land as payment for his service. He described Texas in one of his letters as "the garden spot of the world." Crockett arrived at the Alamo on February 7, 1836, with his 12 men. Along with them came a Scot named McGregor, whom they had met along the way. He carried a set of bagpipes. Historian Burrough says that Crockett was looking to reenter politics in Texas and "had no intention of actually fighting anyone...But if it took a six-month stint to get into the game, he was up for it." His appearance in Texas--a place to which he had no connection-

306 Levy, p. 28; Kilmeade, p. 98; Burrough, p. 91; *Sketches and Eccentricities of Colonel David Crockett of West Tennessee*. New York: J. & J. Harper (1833); Wentworth Press (2016). ISBN 1374258121.

307 Kilmeade, p. 98; Tinkle, pp. 80–87; Levy, p. 28; https://en.wikipedia.org/wiki/Davy_Crockett, p. 7, citing Cobia, pp. 40–44; Burrough, p. 89.

-is said to be as strange as if Teddy Roosevelt had "darted onto the *Titanic* at the last minute."[308]

Stephen Austin, who was on his way to Washington to ask for soldiers and money, had made it only as far as Nashville. Sam Houston was in east Texas negotiating with the Indians, whom Santa Anna had attempted to incite into attacking the settlers. Having no soldiers in his regular army yet, Houston went on leave until the meeting of the Texas Constitutional Convention set for March 1. Meanwhile, a fellow named James Fannin in Goliad was in charge of the army.[309]

On February 2, 1836, Santa Anna reached the Rio Grande and stayed there four days to rest before fording the river. He decreed that all leaders and volunteers in the Texas revolution would be executed. For entertainment, he brought along his fighting cocks in a cart. Santa Anna had planned to deal with the Texas revolt in the spring, but when San Antonio fell he decided to handle it immediately. The Mexican inhabitants of San Antonio who were helping the volunteers panicked at the prospect of retaliation from Santa Anna if the rebellion failed and Texas did not become part of the United States. They abandoned the town in droves.[310]

On February 11, the Alamo commander, a man named James Neill, departed due to family illness. He appointed Travis as commander of the Alamo. The volunteers, however, insisted on a vote. They elected Bowie instead. But Bowie was of little help, being drunk a large part of the time, then falling ill and unable to get out of bed. So Bowie and Travis shared command, but they jockeyed for control. Travis, age 26, disapproved of 40-year-old Bowie, who laughed wildly and owned nearly a million acres of land in Texas. Though Travis and Bowie shared joint command of the Alamo, the loyalty of the men went to Bowie. But Bowie was ailing as well. He had tuberculosis, or pneumonia, cholera, or typhoid fever. He would soon go down as "the Alamo's tragic hero, a swashbuckling American archetype of romance and adventure brought low by bad luck and the bottle."[311]

---

[308] McNeese, p. 78; https://en.wikipedia.org/wiki/Davy_Crockett, p. 7; Levy, p. 28; Hoyt, p. 72; Burrough, pp. 92-93.

[309] Tinkle, pp. 12, 33–34.

[310] Ibid., pp. 18, 34, 88; Hardin (2004), p. 25; Burrough, p. 82.

[311] McNeese, pp. 78, 96; Kilmeade, pp. 100–101, 108; Tinkle, pp. 11–12, 23–25, 56, 58, 176; Hoyt, p. 73; Burrough, pp. 83, 93, 98.

After traveling 850 miles, Santa Anna appeared eight miles south of the Alamo. Everyone had been certain that he would wait until spring to appear. He had lost 400 men and supplies along the way, including 50 yoke of frozen oxen. To cross the swollen San Antonio River on the outskirts of town, Santa Anna ordered that several homes on the river banks be destroyed for lumber to create bridges. A beautiful young woman was found in one of those homes. Though Santa Anna had a wife in Mexico City, he married the young woman in a fake marriage three days later. As Kilmeade says, after fighting for Spain and then for Mexican independence from Spain, he fought now for himself.[312]

The Mexican troops wore red coats, blue trousers, and tall black helmets. Their commanders had broad sombreros, blue coats, and gold epaulets. Santa Anna was taller than most of his countrymen. He flaunted a snuffbox made of gold and wore epaulets fringed with silver. One 12-year-old boy who saw him in San Antonio later described Santa Anna as having a broad face with high cheekbones and a hard, cruel look.[313]

As Burrough observes: "Just a glance at the two armies makes you wonder what on earth the Texians were thinking when they rose in revolt . . . There was no reasonable scenario in which this was not a complete mismatch . . . on the face of it, this was shaping up to be a slaughter." The five-acre Alamo was simply too large for Travis and his 150 men to defend over an extended period.[314]

The Siege of the Alamo

Day 1

When the Mexican army came into view on February 23, the San Antonio bell tower sounded the alarm and all of the volunteers, including Travis, withdrew into the Alamo. Bowie and others gathered up bushels of corn and 30 head of cattle in town and headed into the Alamo. The Texans conceded the town and by late afternoon the Mexican army occupied San

---

[312] Tinkle, pp. 10, 39, 68, 176; Kilmeade, pp. 101,105; Burrough, p. 95.

[313] Tinkle, pp. 25, 38; Kilmeade, pp. 104, 107.

[314] Burrough, p. 83; Kilmeade, p. 114.

Antonio. Travis and Bowie wrote a joint letter that day requesting help from James Fannin, who had 400 men under his command at Goliad 100 miles away. The siege of the Alamo had begun. Travis and Bowie had decided to stay in an indefensible position. As Burrough states, they had "simply lingered too long and now they were trapped." The siege would last thirteen days.[315]

Fess Parker as Davy Crockett

The Alamo

[315] Kilmeade, pp. 106–107; Tinkle, pp. 26, 176; Burrough, pp. 98–99.

Though water flowed through the courtyard of the Alamo, the Texans dug a well inside it in case Santa Anna blocked the flow of the stream. Bowie oversaw military preparations, while Travis sent messages to nearby towns notifying them of the situation. The towns did not respond.[316]

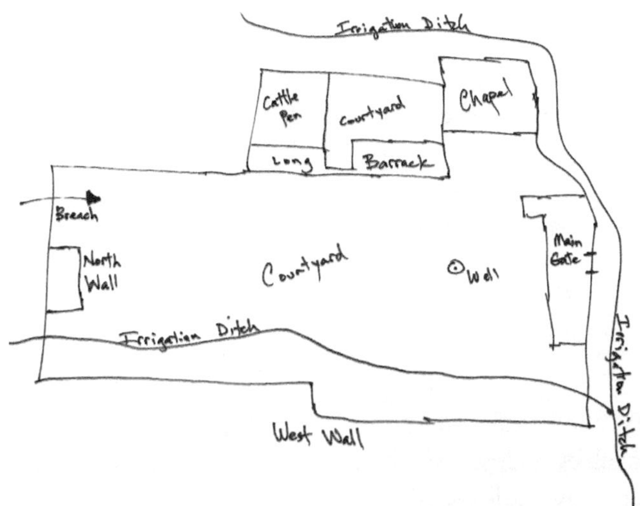

In addition to the Chapel and the Long Barrack, the Alamo consisted of a large anterior courtyard. The Alamo was built as a mission, not as a fort.

Santa Anna soon raised a red flag, indicating that no quarter would be given to the enemy. In response, Travis fired the 18-pound cannon at him. Before the cannon was fired, however, Bowie had heard a bugle call from the Mexican army, signaling an invitation to discuss matters. So Bowie sent out a rider with a white flag to find out if Santa Anna would allow the volunteers to surrender and leave, just as the Texans had allowed General Cos to do at the Alamo two months earlier. Santa Anna was angry by that time and responded that he would accept only a surrender with no conditions attached. However, he did offer amnesty to all Tejanos (native inhabitants) inside the Alamo. After Bowie advised

[316] Tinkle, pp. 30–31.

them to take the offer, most of them left. Bowie took to his bed with a high fever that night and turned over all command to Travis.[317]

The land was flat and dense with mesquite thicket and Santa Anna knew that he would lose a great number of men in a direct assault. He also did not have heavy siege artillery, having travelled 850 miles to get there. So he waited, surrounding the Alamo to starve the inhabitants and prevent reinforcements. The men in the Alamo were vastly outnumbered. They had enough food, including beefsteak (but no coffee) to last a month, and enough gunpowder to last two weeks. Travis then administered a "never surrender" oath to his men. Meanwhile, Santa Anna's numbers continued to grow, though many of his soldiers were conscripted from jails in Northern Mexico and deserted along the way.[318]

Day 2

By February 24, Santa Anna's men were digging trenches so that they could approach ever closer to the Alamo. Travis sent a letter to the town of Gonzales, but it was addressed "To the People of Texas and all Americans in the World." Soon it appeared in two newspapers. His letters were dramatic, and intentionally so, in an effort to urge the general populace to come to his aid. Travis wrote:

> "I am besieged by a thousand or more of the Mexicans under Santa Anna—I have sustained a continual Bombardment & cannonade for 24 hours & have not lost a man—The enemy has demanded a surrender at discretion, otherwise, the garrison are to be put to the sword, if the fort is taken—I have answered the demand with a cannon shot, & our flag still waves proudly from the walls—*I shall never surrender or retreat. Then*, I call on you in the name of Liberty,

[317] Ibid., p. 39; Burrough, p. 98; McNeese, pp. 8, 81; Poyo, pp. 53, 58; Lindley, pp. 94, 134; Hoyt, p. 78.

[318] Tinkle, pp. 11, 40, 44, 57, 67, 69, 70.

> of patriotism & . . . everything dear to the American character, to come to our aid, with all dispatch—The enemy is receiving reinforcements daily & will no doubt increase to three or four thousand in four or five days. If this call is neglected, I am determined to sustain myself as long as possible & die like a soldier who never forgets what is due to his own honor & that of his country—*Victory or Death.*"[319]

Though people reacted to the Travis letters, no new volunteers reached the Alamo before it fell. Burrough observes: "It is one of the Texas Revolt's dark little secrets that . . . the great mass of Texians and Tejanos wanted nothing to do with Travis or the Alamo or fighting Mexican soldiers. Most had never wanted to revolt in the first place. Others, it's clear, were downright skeptical of Travis's pleas. He was, after all, a known troublemaker . . . Foremost among Travis's skeptics was none other than Sam Houston . . ."[320]

Day 3

The weather turned intensely cold on February 25. Two hundred of the Mexican troops tried a frontal assault that day, but were easily repelled by the Alamo Kentucky long rifles that could fire accurately at more than 200 yards. In contrast, the Mexican smoothbore "Brown Bess" muskets could fire 100 yards and were wildly inaccurate. Santa Anna's men then took up positions behind a group of adobe huts near the walls of the Alamo as a staging point for a later assault. That night, however, the Alamo volunteers torched the huts, taking away cover for the Mexican troops. Up to this point, couriers and civilians came in and out of the Alamo with ease. But none of the messengers that Travis had sent out

319 McNeese, p. 84; Burrough, pp. 103–104; Tinkle, p. 75.
320 Levy, p. 32; Burrough, pp. 104–105; Kilmeade, p. 112.

had returned to the Alamo. Doubt was setting in about help being on the way.[321]

There were no holes in the mission walls for the Texans to shoot through. Instead, they had to stand above the walls to fire, with their heads and shoulders exposed. The Mexican army continued to receive reinforcements. Some Mexican soldiers indeed tried to cut off the water supply to the Alamo by damming the tributary that flowed through its courtyard with logs, but they were cut down by gunfire from the mission.[322]

Day 4

On February 26 at Goliad, James Fannin received a second message from the Alamo asking for help. He had ignored the first request. Fannin, age 32, was from Georgia. He had attended West Point for 18 months before returning home, purportedly to attend to sick family members, though his departure was under clouded circumstances. Fannin had arrived in Texas one year before and was engaged in slave smuggling. He was now rich.[323]

Fannin had been commissioned by Sam Houston as a colonel in the regular army, and while Houston was away meeting with the Cherokee to keep them at peace, Houston put Fannin in charge of the regular army. But Fannin was an ineffective commander. He was aloof and his men refused to accept his discipline. He had even written to the acting governor of Texas a few weeks earlier saying, "I do not desire any command, and particularly that of chief. I feel, I know, if you and the council do not, that I am incompetent." Fannin was crippled by indecision. He had also been the leader of the failed Matamoros expedition in January.[324]

---

[321] Hoyt, p. 84; Kilmeade, p. 111; McNeese, p. 85; Burrough, pp. 103, 105; Tinkle, p. 92.

[322] Tinkle, pp. 92–93.

[323] McNeese, p. 86; Chariton, pp 133, 136; https://en.wikipedia.org/wiki/James_Fannin, p. 2, accessed February 17, 2022; Tinkle, pp. 99–100.

[324] Chariton, pp. 138, 142; Burrough, p. 107; https://en.wikipedia.org/wiki/James_Fannin, p. 2, accessed February 17, 2022.

With 400 of his men, Fannin eventually left the fort in Goliad to head to the Alamo 93 miles away. But they were poorly prepared, with little ammunition or food, and they had no horses, so their wagons were drawn by oxen. In fact, three of their wagons broke down on the first day and they spent the night still within sight of Goliad. Their oxen, turned loose to fodder on that first evening, wandered off, leaving no way to haul their supplies. So they spent the entire next day rounding up the oxen. They then learned that another portion of Santa Anna's army was only 50 miles away, so they turned around and went back to Goliad to protect it. Fannin never sent a messenger to the Alamo to say that he was not coming. Historian McNeese characterizes Fannin's effort as "ill-fated" and "halfhearted."[325]

James Fannin

Day 5

In desperation, Travis sent out two more messengers. In New Orleans, posters appeared encouraging volunteers to go to the Alamo. One poster falsely claimed that the Texans had fought off Santa Anna, killing or wounding 500 Mexican soldiers without any Texan casualties, and that an army was on the way to relieve the siege.[326]

[325] McNeese, p. 86; Tinkle, pp. 104, 110; Hoyt, pp. 84–85.
[326] Tinkle, p. 96; Ward (1996), p. 75.

Day 6

On February 28, a messenger who had left Goliad two days earlier arrived at the Alamo saying that Fannin was on his way. By now, however, Fannin had turned back. So Travis believed that Fannin was en route, while Santa Anna already knew from his own spies that he was not. The volunteers inside the Alamo waited in hope of reinforcements, drinking and playing cards while Crockett and McGregor distracted them with the fiddle and the bagpipes.[327]

Day 7

A cold front came in on February 29 with hail, high winds, and a temperature near freezing.[328] Nothing else happened that day.

Day 8

From Gonzales, 32 men arrived at three in the morning on March 1 and sneaked into the Alamo. Though Travis thought that more men were on the way with Fannin, these men were the last to arrive. Santa Anna had encircled the Alamo. Some of the men inside believed that he had let the new arrivals enter so that the total number of dead would be increased. The Mexican army at the Alamo was now somewhere between 1,500 and 6,000 strong.[329]

Meanwhile, the Texas Convention began meeting at Washington-on-the-Brazos, 150 miles from the Alamo. One delegate from each of the 59 Texas settlements attended. They met in a crude frame building that had cloth stretched across the windows to block the cold wind.[330]

Day 9

[327] McNeese, p. 88; Tinkle, p. 112; Kilmeade, p. 116.

[328] Burrough, p. 106.

[329] Tinkle, pp. 105–108, 111, 117; Kilmeade, p. 117; Hoyt, p. 85.

[330] Ward (1996), p. 73.

The Texas Convention adopted the Texas Declaration of Independence on March 2, saying: "We do hereby declare that our political connection with the Mexican nation has forever ended, and that the people of Texas do now constitute a free, sovereign, and independent republic." The accompanying Constitution guaranteed slavery and prohibited emancipation. The men inside the Alamo never learned of this. On that same day, 1,000 more reinforcements arrived for Santa Anna.[331]

Day 10

Sam Houston decided he would soon begin making his way toward the Alamo. Meanwhile, Travis learned from a messenger that Fannin was not coming. Travis wrote what would be his last letter to the government.[332]

According to historian McNeese, the volunteers at the Alamo continued to fly the Mexican flag in support of the Mexican Constitution, not knowing that the Convention nearby had already declared independence the day before. In contrast, Chariton states that, "given the disposition of the men inside the Alamo, which was overwhelmingly in favor of independence, it seems highly unlikely that a Mexican flag of any kind would have been allowed to fly over the mission." By then, the Mexican army had fired more than 200 shells into the Alamo, but there were still no fatalities among the volunteers.[333]

Day 11

Travis had by now sent a dozen or more couriers through enemy lines to ask for help. In the distance he saw the Mexican troops building ladders to scale the Alamo walls. Davy Crockett offered, "I think we ought to march out and die in the open air. I don't like to be hemmed up."[334]

---

[331] Kilmeade, p. 118; Burrough, p. 111; https://en.m.wikipedia.org/wiki/Constitution_of_the_Republic_of_Texas, p. 2, accessed March 10, 2022; Tinkle, pp. 115, 122; Hoyt, p. 89.

[332] Kilmeade, p. 118; McNeese, p. 92; Hoyt, pp. 87, 91.

[333] Chariton, p. 230; McNeese, pp. 92, 95; Kilmeade, p. 119.

[334] McNeese, pp. 8, 84; Tinkle, p. 91; Kilmeade, p. 120; Hoyt, p. 98; Burrough, p. 112.

Day 12

There were 182 men in the Alamo on March 5. Travis assembled them in the courtyard and Jim Bowie was brought out on his cot. Travis informed the men that help was not coming. He said that he had deceived them in this regard and that he had in turn been deceived by others. This is all according to a fellow named Louis Rose, who supposedly later jumped over a wall of the Alamo and escaped along the river. According to Rose, Travis drew a line in the dirt with his sword and said, "I now want every man who is determined to stay here and die with me to come across this line." All but two men stepped across the line. One was Jim Bowie, who then asked that his cot be moved across the line. The sole remainder was Rose, who later claimed that Davy Crockett told him, "You may as well conclude to die with us, old man, for escape is impossible." Rose gathered up his bundle of unwashed clothes and jumped over the wall as the others watched.[335]

Rose's story first came to light, however, in 1873—roughly 37 years after the fall of the Alamo—and his "line in the sand" story is considered by many to be nothing more than popular legend. As Burrough comments, the story "refused to die" because it was "just too good." To this day, there is no evidence that Rose was ever at the Alamo. However, in 1988, the Daughters of the Republic of Texas installed a five-foot brass line at the Alamo as a tribute to the legend of the line in the sand.[336]

The Alamo defenders wore all sorts of clothing, including hunting shirts and blankets. Travis, however, may have worn a uniform consisting of a gray coat with stripes, pantaloons, and a cap, along with his sword. Some insist that he wore plain clothes, because the formal uniform that he had ordered had not yet arrived. Walt Disney depicted him in full uniform, sword and all.[337]

Though some of Santa Anna's officers advised waiting for two more days until two larger cannon would arrive, Santa Anna insisted that the

[335] Ward (1996), p. 73; McNeese, p. 99; Tinkle, pp. 117–120; McNeese, p. 98.
[336] Tinkle, p. 120; Hoyt, p. 104; Chariton, pp. 175–193; Burrough, pp. 157–163.
[337] Tinkle, p. 134; Chariton, p. 238–239; Kilmeade, p. 94.

troops be ready to attack the next morning. He had grown impatient and was eager to attack. The temperature that night neared freezing.[338]

Day 13

The attack began on March 6 with a bugle blast at five o'clock in the morning. Columns of Mexican soldiers approached from all four directions, with five hundred or more men in each column. They had lain flat on the ground overnight in position and they now carried 28 ladders to scale the walls. Santa Anna had provided them with alcohol in liberal amounts shortly before the attack. Behind them was the Mexican cavalry to prevent their desertion. The attack caught the Texans by surprise. Though Travis had posted three sentries outside the Alamo, they were either asleep or dead and gave no warning of the coming attack.[339]

The Mexican army band began playing the *Deguello*, an ominous Moorish battle march that meant "throat cutting" and indicated that no quarter would be given. General Cos, who had sworn at the Alamo less than 90 days before not to fight again in Texas, led his men in the attack. Santa Anna employed Napoleonic tactics, throwing an overwhelming force at the enemy with little regard for casualties. He observed the battle on horseback near a small house 500 yards away.[340]

The Texans each had three or four loaded rifles, so they could fire rapidly in succession. The first assault brought staggering Mexican losses, as Santa Anna had expected. Travis was shot in the forehead early on in the fighting and was among the first defenders to die.[341]

A second assault was needed quickly, before the Mexican troops lost their resolve. It began at 5:30 in the morning and, in the confusion, the Mexican columns shifted, resulting in more concentrated approaches from the north and west. As a result, the Texan cannons on the south and east walls of the Alamo were of no use. The second assault was repelled as well, with the ladders being pushed away from the walls. Mexican soldiers

---

[338] Kilmeade, pp. 120–121.

[339] McNeese, p. 101; Tinkle, pp. 126–128; Burrough, p. 117.

[340] McNeese, p. 103; Hoyt, pp. 105–106; Tinkle, pp. 129, 142; Kilmeade, pp. 124–127.

[341] Burrough, p. 117; McNeese, p. 104; Levy, p. 39.

climbed over their dead and wounded while trying to reach and scale the walls. The Alamo cannon were loaded with nails, chain links, and pieces of horseshoes, but could not be pointed downward and became useless once the attackers reached the base of the Alamo walls. According to one Mexican captain, the man in the peculiar cap (Crockett) stayed calm.[342]

The third attack was successful. With three of the four Mexican columns converged on the north wall, they breached it and entered the courtyard. From there, combat with rifle, bayonet, and knife took over. The Texans were now shooting in every direction to defend attacks from every direction. They now had one loaded gun each and, with no time for reloading after each shot, they began using their rifles as clubs. Mexican soldiers fired in every direction as well, killing many of their own men along with the volunteers.[343]

The Texans soon had to take refuge in the Long Barrack, but in short order its doors were blown open by their own 18-pound cannon, which the Mexican soldiers had spun around and fired. Eventually, the fighting made its way into the chapel, where Jim Bowie was killed on his cot. As for Crockett, no one knows for certain how he died. Some say he was captured along with seven other men and that they were all executed.[344]

The entire Battle of the Alamo lasted only 90 minutes. It was all over by 6:30 in the morning. Late that afternoon, the bodies of all 182 Alamo dead were burned, with the exception of one whose brother was in the Mexican army. The Mexican soldiers were buried in the nearby cemetery. When it became full, the mayor of San Antonio ordered the rest to be thrown into the river.[345]

Most historians have concluded that the Mexican forces ranged from 2,300 to 2,500 and that their casualties (dead and wounded) ranged from 500 to 600. Given that only about 1,800 of those men were involved in the assault, that means that Santa Anna lost one-third of his attacking troops. That is an extremely high percentage.[346]

---

[342] Burrough, p. 120; Kilmeade, p. 125; Tinkle, pp. 130–133; McNeese, p. 104.

[343] Tinkle, pp. 134–135; Kilmeade, p. 130; Hoyt, p. 108; Burrough, p. 121.

[344] Tinkle, p. 135; McNeese, pp. 106, 109; Kilmeade, p. 130–135; Hoyt, p. 109.

[345] McNeese, pp. 112–113; Hoyt, pp. 112, 124–126; Tinkle, p. 153; Kilmeade, p. 139.

[346] Chariton, pp. 223–224.

Contrary to longstanding assumptions, however, the men in the Alamo likely believed that they were fighting against General Sesma, rather than against Santa Anna. Four days before the final attack, Sam Houston wrote, "The Alamo is besieged by two thousand of the enemy, under General Sesma." Travis wrote two letters before the attack, each mentioning Sesma. The evidence also strongly suggests that the men in the Alamo considered themselves to be fighting for independence and not for restoration of the Mexican constitution.[347]

Some say that all of the men at the Alamo died fighting. Others say that fifty or sixty men jumped over the mission walls and made a run for it, taking cover in a drainage ditch and heading toward the road to Gonzales before being slaughtered by the Mexican cavalry. This is based on an interview with a Mexican sergeant 42 years after the Alamo fell, but it is consistent with the account given five days after the Alamo by General Sesma, who indeed commanded the cavalry during the battle. Nobody is saying that these men were not brave or were unwilling to fight. They were "forced out" of the mission by "overwhelming numbers." As historian Chariton points out, these men were brave no matter what and "it is a miracle that they stayed as long as they did." He also suggests that we get the facts straight.[348]

The final appeal for help that Travis had written to the Council arrived after all of the men at the Alamo were dead. Not knowing this, some members of the Council wanted to adjourn and march to the Alamo. Sam Houston disagreed, arguing that if Texas went to war before setting up its structure, disaster would result and they would be "nothing but outlaws." He convinced the Council to remain in session and finish its business. Houston is said, at least by historian Tinkle, to have "made the choice that history has judged best."[349] I do wonder, however, whether Bowie's refusal to blow up the Alamo as Houston had ordered played a part in this decision.

---

[347] Ibid., pp. 226, 229.

[348] Kilmeade, p. 133; Hoyt, p. 110; Burrough, pp. 123–126, quoting historian William Davis as to being forced out by overwhelming numbers; Chariton 33, 35.

[349] Kilmeade, pp. 140–141; Tinkle, p. 123.

There were 15 Alamo survivors—women, children, and the two noncombatant slaves of Bowie and Travis who had been inside the mission. Santa Anna spared them, giving them each two pesos and a blanket. One of the women was Susannah Dickinson, whose husband had just died in the fighting. According to her, Santa Anna tried unsuccessfully to adopt her infant daughter that day shortly after the battle ended. She refused and was sent off. Many of her statements about the Alamo, however, have proven to be untrue. Most oddly, no journalist or historian interviewed her until 1874—nearly four decades after the fall of the Alamo. Her statements were "likely the product of editorial prompting," as Chariton puts it, since Dickinson was probably not in a position during the attack to see the events she described. She was not a reliable witness and "told her story many times and with many variations." As for Rose's line in the sand story, Susanna Dickinson sometimes confirmed it and at other times denied it.[350]

Santa Anna referred to the Alamo as "a small affair." When he reported the outcome of the battle to his secretary of war and navy in Mexico, he overstated the number of Texans by a factor of three or more and understated his own losses.[351]

The Runaway Scrape

Three days after the Alamo fell, the town of Gonzales was the first to learn of the outcome. Houston first heard the news when he arrived in Gonzales two days later on March 11. He wrote to James Fannin that day, ordering him to blow up the fort in Goliad and to retreat to avoid the large Mexican forces. He also sent out letters to politicians blaming Travis and Fannin for the fall of the Alamo.[352]

Houston allowed the Texas settlers to use his army wagons to flee toward Louisiana in what became known as the Runaway Scrape. Anything that could not be carried was burned, including the town

[350] Tinkle, pp. 143, 150, 152; Levy, p. 39; McNeese, p. 80; Chariton, pp. 208–209, 214; Hoyt, pp. 118, 121, 126; Burrough, p. 159.

[351] McNeese, p. 112; Kilmeade, p. 134–136.

[352] Tinkle, p. 148; Kilmeade, p. 142; Hoyt, p. 128; Burrough, pp. 130–131.

of Gonzales. The army's only two cannon were thrown into the river. Houston declared, "Our forces must not be shut up in forts, where they can neither be provided with men nor provisions. Long aware of this fact, I directed on the 16th of January last that the artillery should be removed and the Alamo blown up . . ." He also wasted no time in casting the blame on Bowie, though Houston's letter to governor Smith of January 16 had merely said: ". . . *if you should think well of it, I will* remove all the cannon and other munitions of war to Gonzales and Copano, *blow up the Alamo*, and abandon the place . . . *the sooner I can be authorized the better* . . ." Many, say, however, that the order was in fact given and that Bowie changed his mind after he reached the Alamo.[353]

As historian Kilmeade observes: "Santa Anna had succeeded in striking fear in the hearts of those who opposed him. But he had also provoked rage." He had "overplayed his hand," providing a cause that would unite the Texas volunteers. In all, "He hadn't put out a fire: He had lit one."[354]

A large number of Mexican soldiers deserted after the Alamo, leaving Santa Anna with a greatly reduced force. But Santa Anna was overconfident and nevertheless split his army in two in order to accelerate his victory over the Texas volunteers. He also sent a separate army of 1,400 men under General Urrea to Goliad. Meanwhile, Sam Houston was on the move, retreating from the Mexican troops, and his army was increasing daily. Houston had heard no word from Fannin, whom he had ordered to leave Goliad four days before. The news of the Alamo was spreading and thousands of Texans waited in panic for ferries at river crossings.[355]

On March 19, thirteen days after the Alamo fell and seven days after receiving Houston's order to retreat, Fannin was still at Goliad, though Houston had ordered him to move 30 miles eastward to avoid the approaching Mexican army. Fannin simply could not decide what

---

[353] Tinkle, p. 148; Burrough, p. 132; Moore, pp. 55–59; Hoyt, pp. 1, 7, 130–132; Chariton, p. 6, with italics added to the language of the January 16 letter from Houston to Smith.

[354] Kilmeade, pp. 143–144; McNeese, p. 115.

[355] McNeese, p. 116; Hoyt, p. 130–131.

to do. First he ordered all of the artillery buried. Then he changed his mind and had it all dug up. When he and his men finally began moving, they went less than ten miles from Goliad before getting trapped on the open prairie by Mexican troops under General Urrea. Fannin's men were outnumbered nearly three to one.[356]

Over his officers' objections, Fannin had ordered his men to camp on the open prairie, rather than in the thick woods one mile ahead that would have provided protection. When the Mexican army appeared, Fannin's troops pulled their wagons in a circle and piled up their supplies to create a breastwork for defense. They even shot some of their oxen and piled them up as well. In short order, the men were surrounded. They had no access to water and had accidentally burned their food supply while torching the fort at Goliad before departing. By daylight, even more Mexican soldiers had arrived, bringing their total to more than a thousand.[357]

Fannin and his men surrendered that day to General Urrea, who said that he did not have the authority to negotiate the terms of surrender. They were marched back to Goliad, where they were held for a week. Then they began marching again in what they believed to be a march to the Gulf of Mexico to board a ship and be paroled to New Orleans. Shortly after the marching began on March 27, however, 371 of Fannin's men were gunned down from behind in accordance with orders from Santa Anna, despite Urrea's attempt to persuade him otherwise. Santa Anna later tried to blame Urrea for the slaughter.[358]

Fannin was killed at Goliad separately, by firing squad. His body was burned. Roughly two dozen of his men were spared, being doctors and carpenters needed by the Mexican troops. Some others escaped and survived to tell the story of the massacre. As historian Wallace Chariton puts it, "It would appear that Fannin was correct when he said he was no commander." Historian Hoyt adds that "Fannin was an ambitious man whose abilities did not match his aspirations. He would not follow

---

[356] Hoyt, p. 133; Levy, p. 42; Tinkle, p. 149; Kilmeade, pp. 147–150.

[357] Kilmeade, pp. 151,154–155; Hoyt, p. 134.

[358] Kilmeade, pp. 157–158; Hoyt, pp. 68, 135–137; McNeese, pp. 116–117; Tinkle, p. 149; Burrough at p. 134 says 390 men.

orders, and this failing led to the destruction of his command and his own death." After the Alamo and Goliad, Santa Anna expected nothing short of total capitulation by the Texans.[359]

The first published account of the Alamo soon ran in the *Telegraph & Texas Register*. As historian Levy states: "Already the Alamo's defenders were being elevated to legendary status—hailed as godlike . . ." In harsher terms, Burrough says that the newspaper account served to "distract people from the uncomfortable truth of what a bone-headed loss the Alamo actually was." He adds: "The *Telegraph*'s big lie was that the Alamo fighters were serving a strategic purpose as a rear guard, that their deaths had purchased precious time for Houston's army . . . The fact is, as painful as it may be to hear, the Alamo's trapped defenders died for pretty much nothing."[360]

As Houston and his men retreated from Santa Anna, they destroyed everything along the way that might be of use to the Mexican army. Houston's army was now 600 strong, but most had no fighting experience. Houston retreated in an erratic, zig-zagging pattern in order to stay just out of range of the Mexican army. Then he put a river between his men and Santa Anna and burned the ferry after completing the crossing. That bought him some time to get his men organized. And they needed it. Some were hot-blooded and eager to avenge the Alamo. Houston wanted to win the war. Not wanting his men "shut in forts," Houston relied on mobility and surprise. All told, Sam Houston used Fabian strategy, since a head-on confrontation against a much larger force would surely fail.[361]

While Houston and his men retreated, the settlers of Texas ran for their lives by any means possible in the Runaway Scrape. As Hoyt describes it: "In the houses doors stood open, beds were unmade, uneaten breakfasts were still on the tables, unwashed dishes still in the sinks, pans of milk moldering in the dairies . . . In the fields, cattle were grazing in the luxuriant stands of grass and hogs wallowed comfortably in the mud puddles. All

[359] Chariton, p. 145; Kilmeade, p. 159; Hoyt, pp. 54, 137,174.

[360] Levy, pp. 39–40; Burrough, p. 135.

[361] Ward (1996), p. 75; Kilmeade, pp. 161–164.

this had been abandoned. But as they fled, the Texians were burning with resentment and determination. The Mexicans would pay."[362]

Houston's army continued to grow as fear spread across Texas. By April 5, he had 1,200 men. Houston soon learned of Fannin's surrender, but did not yet know of the massacre that had followed. As to the surrender, Houston said: "I deplore it and can only attribute the ill luck to his attempting to retreat in daylight in the face of a superior force. He is an ill-fated man."[363]

Sam Houston's men hated retreating; 200 of them deserted, with some seeing his unwillingness to fight as cowardice. Settlers jeered Houston as he passed through. Houston continued retreating after leaving 500 men behind to slow down the Mexican advance. This appeased those who were eager to fight, especially since the officers that he left behind had refused to retreat further.[364]

Houston was determined to fight Santa Anna on favorable terms, rather than let a desire for revenge lead to disaster. He drilled his remaining 500 men for a week, shaping them into a fighting force as Santa Anna approached. Others criticized Houston, such as Texas president Burnet who wrote: "Sir: The Enemy are laughing you to scorn. You must fight them. You must retreat no further." In fact, the complaints among Houston's men grew so strong that he posted notices in the camp stating that anyone attempting to take over his leadership would be court-martialed and shot.[365]

Santa Anna assumed that the rebellion was over when Fannin surrendered. But when he told his officers that he intended to return to Mexico City, they objected, stating that the fighting was not done. With General Urrea doing so well in battle, Santa Anna grew concerned about being outperformed. He stayed. As Hoyt states, Urrea was "a thoroughly competent professional soldier. If Santa Anna had taken his military advice, Texas might still be part of Mexico." But by now Santa Anna was

---

[362] Kilmeade, p. 216; Hoyt, p. 139.

[363] Burrough, p. 134 says Houston instead had 1,400 men; Kilmeade, pp. 165, 167; Hoyt, p. 139.

[364] Hardin (1994), pp. 183–184; Ward (1996), p. 75; Kilmeade, pp. 171–177; Moore, pp. 134–137; Hoyt, p. 140.

[365] Hoyt, p. 139; Kilmeade, pp. 173–176; Moore, p. 185.

driven by an "incautious determination" to capture the Texas leaders. He had already divided his army and was advancing ahead of its other divisions.[366]

Santa Anna left some of his men behind to fight against the 500 soldiers that Houston had left behind. He crossed the Brazos River on April 12 with 700 men. Houston and his men had crossed the river only shortly before. Santa Anna continued to violate basic military strategy by separating his army in the presence of the enemy. He was hell-bent on ending the rebellion sooner rather than later, and he was convinced that Houston would not fight. Santa Anna then unwittingly marched past Houston's zig-zagging troops, who were suddenly behind him.[367]

Some of Houston's men wondered whether he intended to retreat all the way to Louisiana to get Andrew Jackson and the United States involved. When his army reached a fork in the road on April 16, the left fork led to safety in Nacogdoches and the right fork led to Santa Anna. Without waiting for instructions from Houston, 300 soldiers headed toward Santa Anna. Another 200 deserted toward Nacogdoches. It is not known what Houston had been planning to do. He now had fewer than 800 soldiers, including the 500 he had left behind to slow down the Mexican army.[368]

Three days later, Houston sent out a scouting party to determine Santa Anna's whereabouts. It returned with a captured soldier who told them that the Mexican army had no idea where Houston's army was and that Santa Anna was marching toward the San Jacinto River. He also said that more men were on the way under General Cos. Houston decided that it was time to fight. He could launch a surprise attack on Santa Anna's diminished forces at the San Jacinto River, but he needed to do so quickly before Santa Anna's full army reassembled.[369]

---

[366] Hoyt, pp. 69, 142; The Oxford Companion, p. 635.

[367] Hoyt, p. 142–143; Kilmeade, p. 179–180; Burrough, p. 138; Ward (1996), p. 75.

[368] Kilmeade, pp. 181–182; Hoyt, p. 146.

[369] Kilmeade, pp. 188–189.

Showdown at San Jacinto

Santa Anna's scouts soon learned that Houston was less than a one-day march away. Believing that Houston was still retreating, Santa Anna planned to attack him on the near side of the San Jacinto River before Houston could cross. So with each planning to surprise the other, both armies raced toward the river, with Houston arriving three hours ahead on April 20. He selected a grove of live oak trees on high ground for cover. The open prairie lay in front of his army. His back, however, was against the water, leaving no way to retreat. It is not clear why he put his army in that trapped position. His army was roughly 25 miles east of present-day Houston, Texas. By now, it had retreated more than 200 miles in its zig-zag pattern.[370]

Santa Anna soon appeared and chose to make camp in a vulnerable location over the protests of his officers. As one officer later wrote, "The camping ground of His Excellency's selection was in all respects against military rules. Any youngster would have done better." Then Santa Anna ordered some of his troops to advance toward the live oak grove, seeking unsuccessfully to lure the Texans into an open field battle. Later, over Houston's objection, some of his more hot-headed men went out to fight the enemy. Furious, Houston ordered them to countermarch back to safety. One soldier yelled "Countermarch yourself!" as he passed Houston on the way to the fight. Those men soon raced back. Both armies then spent the night in position approximately 500 yards apart.[371]

On the morning of April 21, General Cos indeed arrived with 400 or more men at Santa Anna's encampment. They had marched all night without food or rest and they were exhausted. Santa Anna's men had likewise been up most of the night building fortifications out of saddles, sacks of beans, and brush. Meanwhile, Houston had the bridge behind Santa Anna destroyed, preventing escape.[372]

---

[370] Ibid., pp. 191–196; Hardin (1994), pp. 200–201; Moore, p. 258; Hoyt, p. 149.

[371] Moore, p. 287; Hoyt, pp. 150, 153; Ward (1996), p. 78; Hardin (1994), pp. 204, 208; Davis (2004), p. 267; Kilmeade, pp. 197–199; Burrough at p. 139 says 1,000 yards.

[372] Kilmeade, p. 200; Hoyt, pp. 154–155; General Sam Houston, Texian Officials, HQ of the Army, April 25, 1836, reproduced in the *Daily National Intelligencer*, June 11,

The 500 men who had been left behind to slow down the Mexican army rejoined Houston, who now had between 800 and 900 soldiers. Santa Anna had between 1,300 and 1,500. Houston then held a rare council of war with his officers to determine whether to attack or be attacked. They voted by a two to one margin to wait to be attacked. The day lingered on. By mid-afternoon, with no action from the Texans, Santa Anna allowed his tired men to stand down and to stack their guns. Some slept while others ate or bathed. Santa Anna did not post any pickets to warn of an attack. That is when Houston's army attacked.[373]

Creating a distraction on Santa Anna's left by sending in 61 men on horseback, Houston's infantry attacked on the right. Houston rode his horse along the battle line, which stretched for half a mile. Chaos ruled among the Mexican troops when they realized that the attack was on. Houston had two horses shot out from under him during the battle. As he mounted his third horse, he was was shot in the ankle with a musket ball.[374]

The battle lasted only 18 minutes before the Mexican army abandoned its campsite and fled, but the killing afterwards lasted for hours, despite Houston's attempt to stop it. During the fighting, the Texans hollered "Remember the Alamo!" One Texan later described it as "the most awful slaughter I ever saw." Those who fled ran into the water and were all bunched together as the Texans began firing from the bank. As Hoyt notes, "It was like shooting fish in a barrel."[375]

During the Battle of San Jacinto, 630 Mexican soldiers were killed. Another 650 surrendered, of which 200 were wounded. Others fled, including Santa Anna, who took off on one of his officer's horses. Among

---

1836, Volume XXIV, Issue 7280, p. 2, Washington, D.C.

[373] https://en.wikipedia.org/wiki/Battle_of_San_Jacinto, p. 1, accessed February 17, 2022; Kilmeade, p. 202–203; Moore, pp. 292, 328; McNeese, p. 118; Hoyt, p. 154; Burrough, p. 140.

[374] Kilmeade, pp. 204–207; Hoyt, p. 158.

[375] Davis (2004), p. 271; Hardin (1994), pp. 211, 213; Tinkle, p. 149; McNeese, p. 118; Hoyt, p. 163.

the Texans, there were 11 killed and 30 wounded. At the end of the fighting, Houston tried to dismount but collapsed from loss of blood.[376]

Less than a month after Fannin's men were gunned down, Santa Anna had walked into the trap set by Sam Houston, who would soon become president of the independent Republic of Texas. Burrough says, "what gives the Alamo its resonant symbolism is the power its story had on the men who won at San Jacinto. It was there the words 'Remember the Alamo' entered history . . ." Historian Heather Cox Richardson opines: "'Remember the Alamo!' became a cry that justified the annexation of Texas, particularly by leaders . . . that had formed around Andrew Jackson. They developed the concept of 'Manifest Destiny': that it was the inevitable, God-ordained future of America to take over the entire continent."[377]

Santa Anna was captured the following day, as was General Cos. Santa Anna was found in a ravine, lying motionless under a blanket. He was wearing a private's jacket as a disguise, but his identity was soon revealed when the other prisoners shouted out his name as he appeared. Many of the Texans wanted to execute Santa Anna on the spot. Santa Anna declared that, if his life would be spared, he would call off the rest of the nearby Mexican army and its 3,500 men.[378]

Santa Anna was taken to Sam Houston and had the gall to declare through an interpreter, "I put myself at the disposal of the brave General Houston. I wish to be treated as a general should be when a prisoner of war." He went on to say "that man may consider himself born to no

---

376 Kilmeade, p. 208; Burrough at p. 141 says 600 Mexican soldiers dead, and also says 9 Texans died and 6 more would die of their wounds; Kilmeade, p. 210; Hoyt, pp. 159, 162–164 says 630 Mexicans killed, 730 Mexican prisoners of which 200 were wounded, and 9 Texans killed; https://en.wikipedia.org/wiki/Battle_of_San_Jacinto, p. 1, accessed February 17, 2022; McNeese at p. 119 says 650 Mexicans killed, 650 Mexican prisoners. He also says 2 Texans killed and 23 wounded. Ward (1996) at p. 78 says there were only 6 Texans killed.

377 Tinkle, p. 149; McNeese, p. 120; Burrough, p. 142; Richardson, pp. 57–58.

378 McNeese, p. 118; Levy, p. 119; Kilmeade, p. 211; Hardin (1994), pp. 215–216; Hoyt, pp. 167–168; Davis (2004), p. 272; Tinkle, p. 149; https://en.wikipedia.org/wiki/Battle_of_San_Jacinto, p. 4, accessed May 9, 2022.

common destiny who has conquered the Napoleon of the West. And now it remains for him to be generous with the vanquished."

Houston replied, "You should have remembered that at the Alamo."

Santa Anna went on, "What happened at the Alamo—I was only obeying the orders of my government."

Houston lost his temper. "You are the government of Mexico, sir. A dictator has no superior. What about the murders at Goliad?"

Santa Anna lied. "Those were the responsibility of General Urrea. And when I have the opportunity I shall have him executed."[379]

Houston stated that he did not have the authority to negotiate and that he could merely spare Santa Anna's life if he would order his army to move across the Rio Grande River. Santa Anna agreed and thereafter negotiated with the government of Texas for several weeks regarding the terms of surrender.[380]

Three weeks later, in May of 1836, Santa Anna signed a peace agreement known as the Treaty of Velasco, recognizing the independence of Texas and pledging not to attack it. He later repudiated the treaty after returning to Mexico, claiming that it was made under duress. He also signed a "secret" treaty that freed him to return to Mexico in exchange for his promise to try to persuade Mexico to recognize Texas as an independent state of Mexico and to accept the Rio Grande River as the border between Mexico and Texas. In fact, Santa Anna boarded a ship to Mexico on May 14, but was pulled off by Texan soldiers who placed him under military arrest. He remained a prisoner in Texas, and the government of Mexico refused to recognize any agreements signed by a prisoner.[381]

Many Texans wanted to execute Santa Anna, but Houston was opposed to it, seeing it as a violation of the rules of civilized warfare. He also wanted to use Santa Anna to sell the idea of an independent Texas to Mexico. Houston wrote to Andrew Jackson, who saw it the same way. At Jackson's invitation, Santa Anna set out to Washington, D.C., on

---

[379] Hoyt, pp. 167–168.

[380] Ibid., p. 169; Davis (2004), p. 282.

[381] McNeese, p. 119; Lack, p. 104; Hoyt, pp. 170, 173; Kilmeade, pp. 217–220; Davis (2004), p. 288.

November 20 with a military escort to protect him from assassination. While Santa Anna made his way to Washington in December of 1836, Stephen F. Austin died of pneumonia. Historian Hoyt attributes his death to the decline in health that occurred during his imprisonment in Mexico.[382]

Santa Anna Makes Acquaintances

Santa Anna arrived in Washington to meet with Jackson in January of 1837, nine months after he had been captured. Though Jackson had been informed by the Mexican ambassador that, as a prisoner, Santa Anna did not speak for Mexico, Jackson nevertheless treated Santa Anna as a head of state during his six-day visit. He honored Santa Anna as such at a dinner attended by representatives from other countries.

During his visit with Jackson, Santa Anna suggested that the United States pay $3.5 million to Mexico for Texas. Jackson had previously offered $5 million before the fighting had begun. Jackson also knew that Texas, soon to be recognized by the United States as an independent republic, would not agree.[383]

When Santa Anna departed Washington on a ship to Veracruz, Jackson hoped he would indeed persuade Mexico to accept the Treaty of Velasco and the independence of Texas. However, Mexico had a new government in place by then, declaring that Santa Anna was no longer president and that the treaty was invalid. Meanwhile, Texas was eager to join the union and both Jackson and Houston were in favor of that. But slavery was a contentious issue. As a slaveholding state, the admission of Texas was not politically feasible. When Santa Anna arrived in Mexico, he went to his estate, where he wrote an explanation of the Battle of San Jacinto that blamed another general for the defeat.[384]

Though most Texans assumed that the Mexican army would re-enter Texas quickly, only occasional skirmishes occurred over the years

---

382 Hoyt, pp. 15, 176; Kilmeade, p. 221.

383 Tinkle, p. 150; Kilmeade, pp. 222, 227.

384 https://en.wikipedia.org/wiki/Antonio_Lopez_de_Santa Anna, p. 10; Kilmeade, p. 223; Hoyt, pp. 177–178.

until Texas and Mexico declared an armistice in June of 1843—seven years after the Alamo.[385]

Meanwhile, Santa Anna redeemed himself in Mexico one year later by fighting off the French, who sent troops into Mexico in 1838. During the battle, he was hit by a cannonball in the leg, which had to be amputated. It was buried at his home in Veracruz, but four years later, when he once again became president in 1842, Santa Anna ordered that the leg be buried with full military honors in Mexico City. It arrived in an ornate coach and the ceremony involved cannon fire, poetry readings, and speeches. Santa Anna lost power and fled two years later, when several Mexican states challenged taxes that he had imposed. An angry mob dug up his buried leg and dragged it through the streets shouting "Death to the cripple!" Santa Anna was soon captured and imprisoned in exile in Cuba.[386]

War with Mexico

The Republic of Texas was in effect an independent country, but most Texans wanted to join the United States. Mexico did not recognize Texas independence, but England, France, and the United States did.[387]

Texas became the twenty-eighth American state in December of 1845, nine years after the Alamo and six months after James K. Polk was elected president. Polk had been narrowly elected on a platform of expanding U.S. territory in Oregon and Texas. He advocated expansion, whether peacefully or by armed force. Polk then signed a treaty with England as to Oregon so that he could focus on Mexico.[388]

The southern boundary of Texas was in dispute. Mexico continued to refuse recognition of the treaty signed by Santa Anna nine years

385 Lack, p. 201; Henderson, p. 125; https://en.wikipedia.org/wiki/Battle_of_San_Jacinto, p. 5, accessed February 17, 2022.

386 https://en.wikipedia.org/wiki/Antonio_Lopez_de_Santa Anna, pp. 10–11; Fowler, p. 239; Camnitzer, p. 199; https://www.history.com/news/6-things-you-may-not-know-about-santa-anna, p. 1; accessed February 18, 2022.

387 https://en.m.wikipedia.org/wiki/Mexican-American_War, p. 20, accessed March 27, 2022.

388 Ibid., p. 33.

earlier while a prisoner during the Texas Revolution. It asserted that the southern border of Texas was the Nueces River, farther north than the Rio Grande. So the land between these two rivers was contested territory. To complicate matters, in 1846 alone, the presidency of Mexico changed hands four times.[389]

Polk was determined to acquire Texas by force if not by purchase. He sent representatives to meet secretly with Santa Anna, who was exiled in Cuba. Polk obtained a promise from Santa Anna that, if the United States would help him pass through the U.S. naval blockade of Mexico, then Santa Anna would broker a deal between the United States and Mexico for Texas. But at the same time that Polk's diplomats were negotiating with Santa Anna, Polk sent troops to the contested territory in the hope of luring Mexico into starting a war. Mexican forces indeed attacked American soldiers in the contested territory, killing 11 and capturing 52. The United States declared war. Polk told Congress: "Mexico has passed the boundary of the United States, has invaded our territory and shed American blood upon American soil."[390]

After Santa Anna was allowed to pass through the blockade in August of 1846, he denied any familiarity with an offer to sell the Texas territory. Mexico's defeats early in the war with America soon set the stage for Santa Anna to become head of the Mexican army. Congressman Abraham Lincoln called Polk's claim that American blood had been shed on American soil "a bold falsification of history." Ulysses S. Grant likewise opposed the war and stated years later that the main goal of the American army advance to the Rio Grande was to provoke the war without attacking first, so as to reduce political opposition. Others opposed the war, including Frederick Douglass, Ralph Waldo Emerson,

[389] Ibid., pp. 1, 23; Stevens, p. 11.

[390] https://en.wikipedia.org/wiki/Antonio_Lopez_de_Santa Anna, pp. 11–12; Guardino, p.71; https://en.m.wikipedia.org/wiki/Mexican-American_War, pp. 39, 43; Message of President Polk, May 11, 1846, https://web.archive.org/web/20080725155106/http://www.yale.edu/lawweb/avalon/president/messages/polk01.htm.

and Henry David Thoreau. Walt Whitman, in contrast, endorsed it enthusiastically.[391]

Southern Democrats favored the war with Mexico as an element of "Manifest Destiny" that would add slave-owning territory to the United States. That phrase was coined in 1845 by the editor of the *Democratic Review*, who said it is "our manifest destiny to overspread the continent allotted by Providence for the free development of our yearly multiplying millions." In contrast, the Northern Whigs wanted to strengthen the country through industrialization, rather than through land expansion.[392]

The Mexican-American war lasted one year and nine months. The largest battle of the war was at Buena Vista, where American troops were almost routed. They somehow managed to hold their position with the aid of a volunteer regiment commanded by Jefferson Davis, and rather than attack the following day to finish off the Americans, Santa Anna retreated. Many historians agree that he could have won the Battle of Buena Vista if he had fought to its conclusion. Jefferson Davis was eager to take Cuba as well under the Manifest Destiny doctrine; he considered the Gulf of Mexico a "basin of water belonging to the United States."[393]

The Americans then invaded Mexico by sea with 12,000 men at Veracruz under General Winfield Scott. Fighting side by side under Scott were Robert E. Lee, George Meade, Ulysses S. Grant, James Longstreet, and Stonewall Jackson. Other American military officers who would reappear in the Civil War as adversaries 12 years later fought in the Mexican-American War, including George McClellan, Jefferson Davis, George Pickett, Joseph Johnston, and Braxton Bragg. Veracruz fell after a 12-day siege, during which many Americans contracted yellow fever.

---

391 https://en.m.wikipedia.org/wiki/Mexican-American_War, pp. 44–47, 56, accessed March 27, 2022; Guardino, p. 206; Bauer, p. 370.

392 https://en.m.wikipedia.org/wiki/Mexican-American_War, p. 50, accessed March 27, 2022; John O'Sullivan, "Annexation." *United States Magazine and Democratic Review* 17, no.1, July-August 1845: pp. 5–10.

393 https://en.m.wikipedia.org/wiki/Mexican-American_War, pp. 74, 78, accessed March 27, 2022; Foote, volume 1, p. 15; Christensen, p. 161; Loveman, p. 70.

Santa Anna counted on tropical disease to take its toll on the Americans as they marched their way inland.[394]

Chapultepec Castle

With 8,500 men, Winfield Scott then marched toward Mexico City. But Santa Anna had 9,000 men entrenched along the main road. Robert E. Lee found terrain that Santa Anna had not defended because it seemed impassable, so the Americans changed course, passing through the rough terrain, outflanking Santa Anna and obtaining the high ground. The Mexican army was routed. Fifteen years later, Winfield Scott would advise Lincoln to name Lee as head of the Union army. Lee would decline, stating that though he was opposed to secession he could "take no part in the invasion of the southern states."[395]

---

[394] https://en.m.wikipedia.org/wiki/Mexican-American_War, pp. 79–81, accessed March 27, 2022.

[395] Ibid., p. 82, accessed March 27, 2022; Sneiderman, p.118.

In Mexico City, the Battle of Chapultepec took place in September of 1847. Built in 1785, the castle of Chapultepec stood on a hill. Its named was derived from the Nahuatl language meaning "on the hill of the grasshopper." It was considered sacred by the Aztecs. A large number of American marines died during the storming of the castle. To this day, the red stripe on the trousers of marine officers is known as the "blood stripe" commemorating those at Chapultepec. The Marine Corps hymn also refers to the corridors of the castle at Chapultepec as the "Halls of Montezuma," though the castle was built more than two centuries after Montezuma was overthrown.

The Battle of Chapultepec is a point of pride for Mexico as well, even though it lost that battle. At the time of the battle, the castle served as a military academy and six young cadets died during the fighting, with one wrapping himself in the Mexican flag and leaping from the castle to his death rather than surrender. These Niños Héroes (Boy Heroes) are memorialized by a huge monument in Mexico City.

During the war, Santa Anna's prosthetic leg was captured by infantry from Illinois. While resting during lunch, he had removed the leg, and he fled without it during a surprise attack. It remains in the Illinois State Military Museum as a war trophy despite repeated requests by Mexico for its return.[396] Under Santa Anna's command, Mexico City fell.

The Mexican-American War was the second costliest war in American history in terms of the percentage of soldiers who died: nearly 17 percent, with most dying from illness, disease, or accident, rather than from combat. The only more costly war in this regard was the Civil War, at 21 percent. In contrast, World War I and World War II were 2.5 percent and Korea and Vietnam were 0.1 percent.[397]

The war ended in early 1848 with the signing of the Treaty of Guadalupe Hidalgo. That treaty acknowledged the independence of Texas and established the border at the Rio Grande. It also ceded

---

[396] https://en.m.wikipedia.org/wiki/Chapultepec_Castle, p. 1, accessed March 28, 2022; https://en.wikipedia.org/wiki/Antonio_Lopez_de_Santa Anna, p. 12, accessed February 17, 2022; https://www.history.com/news/6-things-you-may-not-know-about-santa-anna, p. 2; accessed February 18, 2022.

[397] White, p. 96.

California, Nevada, Utah, and most of New Mexico, Arizona, and Colorado to the United States, along with parts of Oklahoma, Kansas, and Wyoming. In exchange, the United States paid $15 million and also assumed $3.25 million of debt owed by Mexico to American citizens. All told, 338 million acres were ceded at five cents per acre. When the treaty was signed, however, no one yet knew that gold had been discovered in California only ten days earlier.[398]

This map shows Mexico before it ceded California, Nevada, Utah, Arizona, New Mexico and Texas under the Treaty of Guadalupe Hidalgo in 1848 and another 18 million acres in 1854 under the Gadsden Purchase.

[398] https://en.m.wikipedia.org/wiki/Mexican-American_War, pp. 6–7, 98, accessed March 27, 2022; Smith (1919), vol. 1, p. 241; Our Public Lands. U.S. Department of the Interior, Bureau of Land Management (1958), p. 7; Richardson, p. 58.

Soon the question of whether to annex all of Mexico surfaced. Strong objection was raised in Congress on several grounds, including race, with Senator John Calhoun of South Carolina arguing that annexation would threaten American institutions and character: "Ours, sir, is the Government of a white race," he asserted. At one point, Polk wanted to send troops into Yucatan, but Congress refused.[399]

In his memoirs, Grant characterized the war as "one of the most unjust ever waged by a stronger against a weaker nation." The Mexican-American War inflamed the opposing views on slavery in America as debate continued regarding the scope of westward expansion.[400]

The Aftermath

Santa Anna was blamed for losing the war and was again sent into exile in 1848, this time to Jamaica and Colombia, but he once again returned to Mexico five years later after the government was overthrown. He declared himself dictator for life and held the title of "Most Serene Highness." Santa Anna was driven from power in 1855, after selling another 18 million acres of southern Arizona and New Mexico to the United States in the Gadsden Purchase. He had sold the land to raise money for the Mexican army to defend against continuing U.S. encroachments. He went into exile once again, spending time in Cuba, Colombia, and Saint Thomas. While in Cuba, he was tried in absentia and all of his estates were confiscated by the Mexican government.[401]

Santa Anna returned yet again to Mexico 11 years later, in 1865, to try to take back power, but was sentenced to death. That is when his friend, Gilbert Thompson, sailed to Mexico and smuggled him out

[399] https://en.m.wikipedia.org/wiki/Mexican-American_War, pp. 96, 106, accessed March 27, 2022; Merry, pp. 414–415; Christensen, p. 220.

[400] https://en.m.wikipedia.org/wiki/Mexican-American_War, p. 109, accessed March 27, 2022; "Ulysses S Grant Quotes on the Military Academy and the Mexican War."Fadedgiant.net; Personal Memoirs of General U. S. Grant — Complete by Ulysses S. Grant. Project Gutenberg Literary Archive Foundation. June 2004; Hine, p. 211.

[401] Kilmeade, p. 227; https://en.wikipedia.org/wiki/Antonio_Lopez_de_Santa Anna, pp. 2, 14–15, accessed February 17, 2022; Warren, pp. 49–50.

of the country. Thompson was the son of the governor of New York, who had been luxuriously hosted by Santa Anna in Mexico during his reign. The son brought Santa Anna to Staten Island, where Santa Anna lived for nearly ten years and entertained many guests, including General Winfield Scott who had defeated him in the war.[402]

While on Staten Island, Santa Anna tried unsuccessfully to raise money to take over Mexico one more time. He also brought in the first shipment of chicle to the United States in 1869. Derived from the Aztec language, *chicle* means "sticky stuff" and it comes from tree sap. In his quest for money, Santa Anna planned to use chicle as a less expensive substitute for rubber in tires. That failed. But an American associate of his, Thomas Adams, who had bought one ton of chicle from Santa Anna for the rubber experiments, later used the chicle to develop one of the first chewing gums in the United States. He flavored the chicle, rolled it into balls, and began selling it at local pharmacies in 1871 as Adams New York Chewing Gum.

The Mayans had been chewing chicle long before that and Santa Anna had chewed chicle in Mexico to calm his nerves. In 1899, 23 years after Santa Anna's death, the Chiclets brand would be introduced by Thomas Adams. It was chicle, coated with hard sugar and dyed various colors. Santa Anna did not create Chiclets, but he did play some inadvertent role in bringing chewing gum to the United States.[403]

---

[402] https://www.history.com/news/6-things-you-may-not-know-about-santa-anna, p. 1; accessed February 18, 2022; https://en.wikipedia.org/wiki/Antonio_Lopez_de_Santa Anna, p. 15, accessed February 17, 2022; https://silive.com, "The World Leaders Who Walked Among Us." September 18, 2011, updated January 3, 2019, Thomas Matteo for the *Staten Island Advance*.

[403] https://historyofyesterday.com/general-santa-annas-chewing-gum-legacy-296d2878e557, accessed March 27, 2022; Anarumo, p. 75; https://en.wikipedia.org/wiki/Chiclets.

After Santa Anna imported chicle in an unsuccessful attempt to provide a less expensive substitute for rubber, Thomas Adams developed a chicle-based gum that ultimately evolved into Chiclets.

After receiving amnesty and reentering Mexico at the age of 80, Santa Anna died impoverished two years later in Mexico City in 1876, 40 years after the fall of the Alamo. He was the quintessential strongman, serving repeatedly as a military general, president, and dictator and reversing himself whenever convenient. Santa Anna had opposed Mexican independence, then fought for it, then supported the new Mexican emperor, then revolted against him. He was a master of self-promotion, somehow rebuilding his reputation after major military losses. In all, Mexico lost half of its territory due to Santa Anna's military failures in the Texas Revolution in 1836 and the Mexican-American War in 1848. As one historian puts it, "his usual habit was to ally with the wealthy and privileged, but his immediate concern was to be on the winning side in any battle." No street, monument, or statue in Mexico is named for him.[404]

Santa Anna served as president somewhere between 4 and 11 times, depending on how the counting is done. He also spent a total of 23 years in exile during his lifetime. In his autobiography, *The Eagle*, he portrayed himself as a simple man who had the best interests of his people at heart. In contrast, biographer Fowler says: "He was also notoriously corrupt and amassed a formidable fortune at the height of his career by lining his pockets with government funds. He was charismatic and charming. He was also forceful and ruthless." Yet Fowler also claims that Santa Anna was "not always a tyrant" and that he served as dictator "on only three occasions." This may be true to some extent, but his slaughter of nearly 400 captured men in Goliad, combined with his other behavior during his lifetime, leave no doubt that, at a minimum, he was a true piece of work.[405]

---

[404] https://en.wikipedia.org/wiki/Antonio_Lopez_de_Santa_Anna, pp. 1, 4, 15, accessed February 17, 2022; Fowler, p. xviii, xix.

[405] https://www.history.com/news/6-things-you-may-not-know-about-santa-anna, p. 1; accessed February 18, 2022; Burrough, p. 70; Anarumo, p. 76; Fowler, pp. xii, xxvi, xxi.

Santa Anna, age 61

Sam Houston remarried four years after the Alamo at the age of 47 and had eight children. He later served two terms in the U.S. Senate and was the governor of Texas when the Civil War approached. Houston opposed secession and was removed from office after refusing to sign an oath of allegiance to the Confederacy. His children deserted him over this issue. Ever the pragmatist, Houston stated, "The North is determined to preserve this Union. They are not a fiery, impulsive people as you are, for they live in colder climates. But when they begin to move in a given direction, they move with a steady momentum and perserverance of a mighty avalanche; and what I fear is, they will overwhelm the South." Sam Houston died in Texas at the age of 70 in 1863, three weeks after the Battle of Gettysburg.[406]

Alamo Mythology

As Burrough puts it, on March,1836, "around two hundred men were killed by Mexican troops at an old Spanish church outside San Antonio known as the Alamo. On this we can agree. But after that, pretty much everything—who died, how they died, why they died, and what they

[406] Hoyt, p. 145; Kilmeade, pp. 228–230.

represented—has been a topic of debate ever since." For nearly 25 years after the Alamo fell, those who wrote about it were fiction or travelogue writers. Over time, the Alamo became a ruin, with its walls torn down by the Mexican army after the battle and the only standing structures being the chapel and the vine-covered Long Barrack.[407]

Then, in 1860, the first work that resembled modern professional history appeared. Even in that work, the author stated that on the second day of the siege, Jim Bowie climbed up a timber scaffolding to position a cannon. While on the scaffolding, Bowie had a coughing fit and momentarily let go of the cannon, which pivoted and nearly rolled off of the scaffolding. Bowie stopped it from rolling off after struggling with it for several minutes. Then he fell off of the scaffolding and crushed his ribs on the ground. Bowie remained on a cot for the rest of the siege. That author later admitted that he had made the whole thing up. We now know that Bowie was instead laid up by typhoid fever or some other disease.[408]

By the fiftieth anniversary of the Alamo in 1886, the Long Barrack had been sold and converted into a grocery store. There was no Alamo commemoration nor any effort at historical preservation. When the state of Texas bought back the Long Barrack in 1905, a lifelong battle over the Alamo began between two members of the Daughters of the Republic of Texas. One wanted to return everything to the way it looked at the time of the battle. The other wanted to tear the Long Barrack down altogether to make way for a memorial park. By 1913, annual commemorations were underway, and in November of 1940, the Cenotaph was installed in the Alamo Plaza, with statues of Travis, Crockett, Bowie, and Travis's second cousin, James Bonham, standing at its base and the names all of the defenders chiseled into the marble and granite.[409]

In February of 1955, Walt Disney aired the episode with Fess Parker as Davy Crockett at the Alamo. That episode showed Travis drawing the line in the sand and Crockett swinging his rifle, Old Betsy, like a club in

---

[407] Burrough, pp. 1, 144–147.

[408] Burrough, pp. 151–152; Tinkle, pp. 56, 58.

[409] Burrough, pp. 165, 171, 190.

a fight to the death. And "The Ballad of Davy Crockett," sung by Fess Parker and Buddy Ebsen, was mesmerizing.

> Born on a mountain top in Tennessee,
> Greenest state in the land of the free,
> Raised in the woods so he knew every tree,
> Kilt him a b'ar when he was only three,
> Davy, Davy Crockett, king of the wild frontier!

The song went on to claim that Crockett had won the Indian war single-handedly and that he had patched up the crack in the Liberty Bell.

Americans spent $100 million on Crockett paraphernalia during the first sixty days after the airing. Disney's three-part miniseries was then converted into a full-length film known as *Davy Crockett: King of the Wild Frontier*. Then John Wayne came out with his own traditionalist Crockett movie, *The Alamo*, in 1960. The Cold War was on and Wayne, an arch conservative, sought to liken Santa Anna's oppression to the Soviet Union.[410]

Historian Burrough observes that the traditional Alamo narrative went unchallenged for 150 years and was fiercely guarded by the "cult-like Daughters of the Republic of Texas, which by the 1960s had evolved into a kind of paramilitary Junior League." The traditional Alamo narrative has been characterized as "Texas tub-thumping." As traditionalist Lon Tinkle wrote, the Alamo participants viewed themselves as "rising up against tyranny to demand their promised statehood and freedom." As Kilmeade says: "The Alamo itself assumed a place in the history and the mythology of Texas. The narrative is irresistible: Brave men fighting for freedom and democracy are crushed by a brutal autocrat and then avenged."[411]

The cover of historian Tinkle's 1958 book, *Thirteen Days to Glory: The Siege of the Alamo*, describes the narrative as a "minute-by-minute, bullet-by-bullet story of how 182 tough Texans fought off for 13

---

[410] Ibid., pp. 198–204.

[411] Ibid., p. 218; Tinkle, p. 9; https://www.kirkusreviews.com/book-reviews/bryan-burough/forget-the-alamo/accessed March 10, 2022; Kilmeade, p. 227.

desperate days an army that outnumbered them 30 to 1." Tinkle was hired as a historical advisor for John Wayne's 1960 film, *The Alamo*. In fact, the movie was so inaccurate that Tinkle demanded that his name be removed from the movie credits. As historian Timothy Todish puts it, "not a single scene" in that film corresponded to a "historically verifiable incident." Tinkle, who is said to be a "stout traditionalist," is "beloved by many Alamo enthusiasts and ridiculed by historians."[412]

All Hell Breaks Loose

In 1978, all hell broke loose when Dan Kilgore published a book citing the statements of seven Mexican soldiers who confirmed that Crockett had surrendered and was executed. In fact, that was the account that was widely accepted back in 1836 and for nearly 120 years afterward. Then Disney changed the narrative in 1956. The Texan outrage at Kilgore's new information was predictable, with the Corpus Christi *Times* saying, "Any Texan worth his lizard skin cowboy boots and Willie Nelson albums knows better than to smear the legend of Davy Crockett."[413]

Then along came Jeff Long's *Duel of Eagles* in 1990, "characterizing the Texas Revolution as a secessionist revolt intended to defend Texas' slave-based economy," according to Burrough. In his book, Long stated: "For over a century, historians simply gave the Alamo myth a free pass. It continually shocked me that my book had never been written." In reaction, the *Houston Chronicle* wrote: "If he isn't careful, Jeff Long may become the Salman Rushdie of Texas." Sure enough, Long began receiving death threats. His *Duel of Eagles* is the "big bang of Alamo revisionism," according to Burrough, who also refers to it as a "screaming banzai charge against everything John Wayne held dear."[414]

Ironically, revisionism within the context of the Alamo means reassessing the facts in order to get them uncontaminated by traditionalist myths. However, the revisionist books about the Alamo that appeared after *Duel of Eagles* were by academic presses and were mostly ignored.

---

[412] Tinkle, book cover; Todish, p. 188; Burrough, pp. 235, 312.

[413] Burrough, pp. 233–237; Kilgore and Crisp, p. 59.

[414] Burrough, pp. 239–242.

As fifth-generation Texan and self-described "Alamo junkie" Wallace Chariton states with regard to the truth about what happened in San Antonio, "permanent intrigue seems to be the destiny of the Alamo."[415]

Nagging Questions

1. Did Sam Houston really order Bowie to blow up the Alamo, or did he just make that up later to avoid blame for the slaughter that occurred?

For a long time, historians have argued over whether the order was actually ever given. Houston had written to the governor of Texas on January 17 (eight weeks before the Alamo fell) saying: ". . . *if you should think well of it, I will* remove all the cannon and other munitions of war to Gonzales . . ., *blow up the Alamo*, and abandon the place . . . *the sooner I can be authorized the better* . . ." There is no clear answer as to whether Houston actually ordered Bowie to blow up the place. He may have verbally ordered Bowie to do so and then written to the governor for confirmation. Houston of course consistently stated after the Alamo that he had given the order.[416]

Historian Hoyt says that the orders were clear, though Bowie said that they were discretionary. In his letter to governor Smith, Bowie did not even mention blowing up the Alamo nor any order to do so. Instead, he said that he did not want to allow the Mexicans to have the Alamo and that he would "rather die in these ditches than to give it up to the enemy."[417]

Interestingly, when Houston received word on March 13, 1836, of the fall of the Alamo, he wrote a letter that same day blaming Fannin for not coming to their aid. But as historian Chariton puts it: "Now, hold on Sam, what happened to 'blow up the Alamo'?" Chariton rightfully asks why Houston did not blame Bowie for not following his orders. It was not until two days later, on March 15, that Houston first wrote that he had ordered Bowie to blow the place up. Chariton takes the gloves off,

---

[415] Chariton, p. xii.

[416] Ibid., pp. 6–9, with emphasis added to quote; Hoyt, p. 1.

[417] Hoyt, p. 1; Letter from James Bowie to Governor Henry Smith, February 2, 1836.

saying: "Could it be he was covering his backside? Bowie certainly was not around to dispute his story."[418]

Lastly, Burrough offers: "There are those who believe Sam Houston never really wanted Bowie to blow up the Alamo, that he only said so later to rationalize his lethargy. But there are real-time letters that make clear he did, and that he allowed Bowie to make the decision. When Governor Smith learned this, in fact, he sent a letter to Bowie countermanding Houston's order."[419]

2. Why did Fannin not come to the aid of the Alamo?

Fannin was "the one man in Texas who might, just might, have saved the Alamo," according to Chariton. Fannin's excuse of a broken down wagon for failing to come to the aid of the Alamo is "a little hard to swallow," he adds. Sam Houston was similarly critical at the time, saying that "owing to the breaking down of a wagon," Fannin abandoned the march and left the Alamo volunteers to their fate. Of course, Houston's criticism was part of his effort to cast blame away from himself.[420]

Chariton asks two questions relating to Fannin: (1) Why did he not go to the Alamo? and (2) Would it have made any difference even if he had done so? On the first question, Chariton believes the answer lies in Fannin's self-pity and indecision. One of Fannin's soldiers wrote about him in a letter home saying, "I am sorry to say that the majority of soldiers don't like him, for what reason I don't know, unless it is because they think that he has not the interest of the country at heart, or that he wishes to become great without taking the proper steps to achieve greatness."

As for the second question, the answer seems to be no. If Fannin had gone to the Alamo, the total number of men there would have been about 600, which was probably not enough to fend off Santa Anna's army. In addition, Santa Anna received even more men and artillery soon after Fannin would have arrived. What's more, Santa Anna knew from his spies that Fannin had left Goliad headed for the Alamo. If Fannin had

[418] Chariton, pp. 15–17.
[419] Burrough, p. 88.
[420] Chariton, pp. 132–133.

proceeded on his march, the cavalry brigade that Santa Anna had dispatched upon learning of Fannin's march would likely have slaughtered Fannin's troops before they ever reached the Alamo.[421]

3. Did all of the men in the Alamo die fighting as traditionalists would have us believe?

A sizeable amount of evidence, some it more recent, indicates that seven men surrendered and were promptly executed by Santa Anna. According to Chariton, "Over the years, however, as the story of the dramatic stand in the Alamo gained prominence, the part about possible survivors somehow slipped between the historical cracks." He goes on to observe that "in many ways Texas history is like an ocean: what you see on the surface is not necessarily an indication of what lies underneath." In fact, even the number of men who died in the Alamo is not certain, ranging from 160 to 183.[422]

4. How did Davy Crockett die?

It is not known whether Crockett died fighting or was one of the men executed shortly after their surrender. As Chariton states, Crockett's "pedestal became one of the tallest" and when Walt Disney told us that Crockett died bravely fighting, the "proof seemed self-evident." After the "Disneyfication" of Crockett's legacy, however, new information appeared from different sources in 1968, 1975, and 1978 suggesting that Crockett was indeed captured and executed. As Chariton puts it, "The real truth is, we may never know how Davy died." As another historian puts it, historians have been able to back up opposing theories with "voluminous evidence."[423]

---

[421] Ibid., pp. 142–144; Hoyt, p. 132.

[422] Chariton, pp. 20–23, 165–174.

[423] Ibid., pp. 39–41, 63; *Corpus Christi Times*, July 31, 1974; "Born on a Mountaintop: On the Road with Davy Crockett and the Ghosts of the Wild Frontier by Bob Thompson, Crown Publishing," Christopher Corbett, *Washington Post Book Review*, March 22, 2013; https://en.wikipedia.org/wiki/Davy_Crockett, p. 9, citing Hilley, Kenneth, "The Mysterious Death of David Crockett," https;//stmuhistorymedia.org/the-mysterious-death-of-david-crockett, *Texas Monthly*, December 13, 2019.

Some, however, consider the suggestion that Crockett died other than while fighting to be "blasphemous." Though Susanna Dickinson said Crockett died fighting in the Alamo, most historians find her an unreliable witness who changed her story over the years. And while one Mexican officer said he recognized Crockett's dead body wearing the coonskin cap in the plaza shortly after the fighting ended, another stated that Crockett surrendered and was executed.[424]

There is a lot of mythologizing when it comes to the Alamo. For example, historian Tinkle declared in all seriousness that the Texans "were expert marksmen, accustomed to bringing down a squirrel a hundred yards away with a shot between the eyes."[425] At a hundred yards, a person can barely see a squirrel, much less shoot between eyes that are spaced an inch and a half apart. And who speaks in big game terms of "bringing down" a squirrel?

What we do know is that Davy Crockett was born not on a mountaintop in Tennessee, but in a cabin alongside the Nolichucky River in what was at that time known as the independent territory of Franklin, previously part of North Carolina. He did not kill a bear when he was only three and he preferred to be called David. But "The Ballad of Davy Crockett" sung by Fess Parker and Buddy Ebsen in the Walt Disney show said so, and that ballad was the number one song on the U.S. charts for four weeks in 1955. It was number one in France for five weeks. Senator Estes Kefauver of Tennessee even wore a coonskin cap during his 1956 run for vice president. In all, the Davy Crockett character has appeared in more than 20 films and has been played by Fess Parker, John Wayne, Brian Keith, Johnny Cash, and Billy Bob Thornton, among others.[426]

Fess Parker, a Texan, was only 30 years old when he played the role of 49-year-old Davy Crockett for Disney. This led to a "merchandising frenzy for coonskin caps and all things Crockett." Parker stood at six feet

---

[424] https://en.wikipedia.org/wiki/Davy_Crockett, p. 9, citing Paulsen, Barbara, "Say It Ain't So, Davy." https://www.texasmonthly.com/article/say-aint-davy, *Texas Monthly*, February 9, 2017; Burrough, p. 133; Hoyt, pp. 122–123.

[425] Tinkle, p. 77.

[426] en.wikipedia.org/wiki/The_Ballad_of_Davy_Crockett, pp. 3–4, accessed April 9, 2022; https://en.wikipedia.org/wiki/Davy_Crockett, p. 1, 12, accessed February 17, 2022.

six inches and seemed like the real thing.[427] By the time he reached age 49, Parker had retired from acting altogether and had started a vineyard and a hotel in California. His fancy, 360-room Santa Barbara beachfront hotel opened as Fess Parker's Red Lion Inn in 1985. It had that widely recognized bell-shaped mission hump on its front just like the Alamo. When the Alamo battle was fought, however, the bell-shaped hump did not yet exist. It was installed by the United States army in 1858, 22 years later, while converting the Alamo into a supply depot. Parker's hotel name was later changed to Fess Parker's Doubletree Hotel. I stayed at it with my wife and kids in 2011. It was fabulous. It is now the Hilton Santa Barbara Beachfront Resort.[428]

Parker's vineyard opened in 1988. It appeared under another name in the movie *Sideways* in 2004. Parker died in 2010 in California at the age of 85. To this day, the Fess Parker wine bottle labels bear the logo of a coonskin cap.[429]

So What Was the Alamo About?

According to Burrough, "For the first 150 years after the battle, few disagreed—at least publicly—with the 'traditional' notion that its defenders were fighting for their 'freedom' against the 'oppression' of a crazed Mexican tyrant . . ." As late as 1986, the history of the Alamo was considered to be "an academic backwater best abandoned to amateur writers."[430]

One sixth-generation Texan traditionalist, Michael Lind, has even written a 281-page, 6,006-line cringeworthy poem in iambic pentameter

---

[427] https://en.m.wikipedia.org/wiki/Fess_Parker, p. 6, accessed February 18, 2022, "Fess Parker, Who as Davy Crockett Set Off Coonskin Cap Craze, Dies at 85." Richard Severo, *New York Times*, March 19, 2010.

[428] Burrough, p. 151; Hoyt, p. 180.

[429] https://en.m.wikipedia.org/wiki/Fess_Parker, p. 10, accessed February 18, 2022; https://www.fessparker.com/our-wines, accessed February 19, 2022.

[430] Burrough, pp. 1, 3.

about the Alamo. It took him 12 years to write it. He describes the return of General Cos to the Alamo after having surrendered there:

> Back in December, he had held this fort
> against the rebel ranks, only to lose
> his honor with the cannon in that court
> when he surrendered. Months had made the hues
> grow pale, but still he felt the purple bruise
> upon his soul, still felt disgrace's twinge.
> This morning Cos would relish his revenge.

And of the charismatic and ruthless Santa Anna seeing the dead body of Travis during the aftermath of The Alamo, he writes:

> The conqueror removed his plumed crescent,
> a gesture imitated all around
> by men who watched their master, grown quiescent,
> study his foe awhile without a sound.
> Then General Santa Anna faintly frowned.
> "At last, Guillermo Travis. Why, you are
> so young, to have begun so great a war.[431]

The cover of the book containing the poem describes the Alamo as one of the "great mythic moments" in U.S. history. To me, *mythic* means fictional or imagined or embellished, as contrasted to factual. Perhaps the intended word was *legendary*, meaning well known, with some parts of the Alamo legend appearing to be without factual basis and perpetuated for the glory of Texas.

At the Alamo, I saw only the chapel. I do not remember seeing the Long Barrack and I had no idea that the Alamo, with its courtyard and outer walls, was a much larger compound at the time of the battle. I mentioned this recently to my sister-in-law and she said that when she saw the Alamo it indeed looked "dinky." Apparently that is what a lot of

---

[431] Lind, pp. 197, 280.

visitors experience: "This is it?"[432] I was also left with a sense of awe and sadness, along with some confusion about why the whole thing occurred and what it was about.

The Daughters of the Republic of Texas ran the Alamo for more than a hundred years. One critic referred to them as "a tea club running a historical site." They budgeted a whopping $350 a year for site preservation and requested that Alamo visitors be silent because the place was "like a church." Finally, in 2011 they were placed under the supervision of the General Land Office of the State of Texas, also known as the GLO. Three years later, in 2014, George P. Bush (Jeb's oldest son) became head of the GLO. That same year, Phil Collins (the drummer for Genesis) offered his 206-piece collection to the Alamo. It is said to include Jim Bowie's knife and Davy Crockett's shot bag. But Collins had two conditions for the donation: everything must be displayed in a single place and, if a new museum would be built to house the artifacts, then ground had to be broken within seven years. Fortunately, Bush sent the Daughters of the Republic of Texas packing in 2015.[433]

Current Confusion

Phil Collins holds the world's largest collection of Alamo artifacts. As a kid, he too saw Fess Parker and John Wayne portray Davy Crockett and he caught the Alamo fever. Some think he has gone overboard on the Alamo paraphernalia, with the London *Daily Mail* saying he is "one drumstick shy of a pair." Historian Burrough calls him "the ultimate true believer." He is a "traditionalist," absorbing all Alamo myth as gospel.[434]

In contrast to Phil Collins, Ozzy Osbourne wandered into the Alamo plaza in 1982 in a mid-afternoon stupor and urinated on the Cenotaph, unaware of or indifferent to its sanctity in Texas. He was

---

[432] Burrough, p. 247.

[433] Ibid., pp. 218, 248, 261, 264–267, 286–288, 293.

[434] Ibid., pp. xx, 321; "I Remember the Alamo: How a Psychic Cook Called Carolyn Convinced Phil Collins He's a Reincarnated American Hero." Alison Boshoff and Annette Witheridge, *Daily Mail*, November 26, 2010, https://www.dailymail.co.uk/femail/article-1333165/How-psychic-cook-called-Carolyn-convinced-Phil-Collins-hes-reincarnated-American-hero.html.

holding a bottle of Courvoisier and wearing his girlfriend's evening gown. His band was set to play at the convention center that night and his girlfriend had gotten so tired of his drinking that she had hidden his clothes. Osbourne was banned from playing San Antonio for years after that, until he apologized and paid a $10,000 donation to charity.[435]

The Alamo stands 900 feet from the Bonham Exchange, a gay bar opened in 1980 and named after James Bonham, whose statue appears at the base of the Cenotaph. Bonham served as the messenger who carried through enemy lines the letters from Travis pleading for help. The three-story Bonham Exchange features ten bars, drag shows, and 25,000 square feet of dance floor.

As Burrough, a fifth-generation Texan, opines: "The Alamo has always loomed at the center of the Texas mythos . . . the idea, deeply held among generations of Texans, that the state is special, somehow a cut above the Delawares and Rhode Islands of the world." The Alamo was invoked by LBJ to create support for the Vietnam War. Over the years, it has been cited by "patriots" in opposition to communism, immigration, and other things.[436]

The state of Texas protects the traditionalist view fiercely, with governor Greg Abbott in full support of the requirement that students be taught a "heroic" version of Alamo history. Burrough asserts: "Given the fact that its defenders were fighting to form what became the single most militant slave nation in history, that men like Bowie and Travis traded slaves, and that the 'Father of Texas,' Stephen F. Austin, spent years fighting to preserve slavery from the attacks of Mexican abolitionists, one would think the post–George Floyd era might have brought to Texas a long-overdue reevaluation of its history. By and large, that hasn't happened."[437]

In preparation for the construction of a new $450 million museum to house the Phil Collins collection, the Texas state planners began considering changes that might be made, including relocation of the

[435] Burrough, p. xxii.

[436] Ibid., p. xxiii.

[437] Ibid., p. xxiv-xxv, p. 282.

Cenotaph 500 feet south in 2019. In response, angry traditionalists wearing camouflage and carrying assault rifles protested in Alamo Plaza.[438]

The Alamo project was called Reimagine the Alamo. It included fixing up the downtrodden Alamo Plaza and, according to Bush, having the Alamo serve as a "centerpiece for taking on the controversial issues of the past," including slavery, which he mentioned. It would also include recognition of the role played by Tejanos in helping the volunteers battle against Santa Anna. But as traditionalist pressure on Bush increased, he stepped back from revisionism. Soon his team backpedaled, explaining that "reimagining" the Alamo did not mean changing the traditional narrative. Instead, it meant "reimagining the experience people have when they come to the Alamo." The Alamo is now promised to be a "world-class destination."[439]

As it turns out, many items in the Collins collection are of questionable authenticity. Phil Collins began collecting every Alamo artifact that he could find in 2004. Working with the owner of the History Shop around the corner from the Alamo, Collins visited the Alamo three or four times a year to walk through the place and look at new artifacts that the shop owner had found for him. Collins spent $750,000 at one auction in Dallas. The Collins collection includes what is claimed to be Jim Bowie's knife, for which Collins paid $1.5 million. It also holds what is claimed to be Bowie's sword and Crockett's rifle.[440]

According to Burrough, "Serious Alamo collectors watched Collins build his collection from a distance with bemusement, wondering if he had more money than sense." But it did not really matter until he donated his collection to the state of Texas in 2014 for display in a museum. By then, Collins had also published a 2012 illustrated book detailing his collection. About the book, one expert on Alamo artifacts says, "Just about everything they said was used at the Alamo, these are not Alamo-related items. This book, it embarrasses collectors. It embarrasses me . . . A lot of people believe the Collins stuff is the real thing. It's not." And of the seven knives shown in the book, only one may be authentic according

[438] Ibid., pp. xxvi, 285, 295.

[439] Ibid., pp. 294, 297–300, 302, 307.

[440] Ibid., pp. xxvii, 308, 313, 316–319.

to Mark Zalesky, the editor of *Knife Magazine.* As for the Jim Bowie knife, Zalesky says that the knife was likely made in England in 1971 or 1972. It is not made from the steel used in the early 1800s. As Zalesky summarizes, "It's fake." In all, fifteen of the most noteworthy pieces in the Collins collection are of "highly questionable authenticity," according to professor Stephen Hardin. To add further to the drama, an artifacts dealer and a historian who were involved with the Collins collection sued Burrough in June of 2022 for defamation, claiming that his assertion that the artifacts may be fraudulent has destroyed their reputations.[441]

The problems with the Collins collection were an "open secret" in the world of collecting, according to Burrough. But nobody communicated their concerns to the GLO when it began talking with Collins back in 2014. One staff member at the GLO does not recall any due diligence having taken place regarding the collection. "Our job was to get the most [press coverage] out of that as we could. It wasn't to make sure that that knife that he is holding was actually Jim Bowie's knife." As a result, the former official historian of the Alamo says, "I don't think the GLO or the Alamo are prepared for or have any idea the ruckus the collecting world is going to raise once the collection is made public."[442]

In May of 2020, young people marching in response to the George Floyd murder likened the Alamo to a Confederate war statue. They spray painted the Cenotaph with arrows facing downward beside the words "white supremacy," "profit over people," and "the Alamo." The GLO soon installed a barrier across the front of the Alamo to protect if from damage.[443]

From the conservative side, pressure continued against Bush's "reimagining" plan. As one fundraiser for the Alamo Foundation sees it: "All of a sudden, after years of agreement on telling the story of all the layers of history of the site, everyone now seems to want this to be John Wayne's Alamo." As Burrough puts it, the men at the Alamo "fought for

[441] Ibid., pp. 320–326; "Su-suit-io: Alamo Experts Sue Authors of a Book Suggesting They Sold Phony Artifacts from the Battle to British Pop Star Phil Collins." Daniel Cassidy, *The Art Newspaper*, June 23, 2022, http://theartnewspaper.com, accessed July 16, 2022.

[442] Burrough, pp. 327–328, 332.

[443] Ibid., pp. 335–336.

freedom, just not everybody's freedom . . . Maybe it's time to forget the Alamo, or at least the whitewashed story, and start telling the history that includes everyone."[444]

As of April 2022, the Alamo struggle continues. The budget for the reworking of the site, including the new museum, has been cut from $450 million to $388 million—and $174 million of that money must still be raised. The whole project is expected to be completed in 2025. The Cenotaph will not be moved. Even with all of this delay, Phil Collins still appears to be all in.[445]

Country singer Billie Joe Shaver remembered the Alamo in "The Heart of Texas":

> The heart of Texas is where I was born
> By twist of fate the Lone Star State's where I'm coming from
> God almighty's been good to me.
> Where I grow'd up learning about the Alamo
> With a swelling pride down deep inside me saying, "Go, man, go"
> You can be all you want to be.
> Yeah, it's right there where the best is
> Smack dab in the heart of Texas, thank you ma'am.

Later in the song, he adds:

> I made my music from coast to coast
> Been over the water, couldn't get no hotter
> Then I dang near froze
> Remember the Alamo!
> The road was long but the heart is strong

---

[444] Ibid., pp. 337–342.

[445] "Alamo plan takes shape under new vision, and it's $60 million cheaper." Iris Dimmick, August 10, 2021, https://www.sanantonioreport.org/new-alamo-plan-details-coming; https://www.thealamoorg./support/alamo-plan, accessed March 11, 2022.

I was Texas born and raised and Texas is still my home
Texas is home sweet home.
Yeah it's right there where the best is
Smack dab in the heart of Texas, thank you ma'am.
Where my songs are always playing
And them good ol' Texas girls say, "Honey, where ya been?"
Yeah it's right back where where the best is
Smack dab in the heart of Texas, thank you ma'am.

A few weeks after we saw the Alamo in the summer of 1965, we were at the Mormon Tabernacle in Salt Lake City. There I saw the actor with the big long beard who played Cincinnatus, the innkeeper, alongside Fess Parker on the *Daniel Boone* show. I had my coonskin cap on and he talked to me. I was on cloud nine all day, oblivious to anything that the Tabernacle had to offer. I am eager to see the new Alamo museum, if and when it opens. I will probably leave the place with the same combination of awe, sadness, and confusion that I had nearly 60 years ago.

Chapter 4

The Civil War

The Civil War involved two war zones or "theaters." The Eastern Theater encompassed Virginia, Maryland, and Pennsylvania. The Western Theater ran west from North Carolina and south from Kentucky. Most soldiers remained in a single theater during the war, but a few—including Grant, Hood, and Johnston—fought in both. And battles sometimes occurred in both theaters at or near the same time. I approach the war according to theater, in an effort to keep things straight. Naturally, there is some overlap from time to time. The timeline appearing at page 188 serves as an overview and may be helpful.

1862
The Eastern Theater: McClellan Talks the Talk

George McClellan arrived in Washington to a cheering crowd in late July of 1861. Five days earlier, the Union army under Irvin McDowell had lost at the first battle of Bull Run in Virginia. On arrival, McClellan was appointed by Lincoln as the new commander responsible for protecting Washington. He was 34 years old. McClellan wrote to his wife, Ellen, that same day saying: ". . . I seem to have become the power of the land . . . I almost think that were I to win some small success now I could become Dictator or anything else that might please me—but nothing of that kind would please me—therefore I won't be Dictator. Admirable self-denial!"[446]

McClellan had won two small victories in West Virginia that earned him national recognition. The *New York Herald* called him the "Napoleon of the Present War" and others referred to him as "Young Napoleon." McClellan had a tendency toward self-aggrandizement and unmerited self-congratulation, posing for photographs with one hand tucked inside his coat like Napoleon.[447]

The son of a prominent Philadelphia surgeon, George McClellan stood at five feet eight inches. His soldiers admiringly referred to him as "Little Mac." He graduated 2nd in his class out of 59 cadets at West Point at the age of 19. His closest friends at school included Stonewall Jackson, George Pickett, and several other Southerners who later fought against the Union. Pickett graduated 59th in that class.[448]

As was customary at West Point, those at the top of the class became engineers and those in the middle were assigned to cavalry or artillery. The bottom went into the infantry.[449] On occasion, a cadet with good grades would intentionally accrue demerits in order to be relegated to a cavalry position that they desired, rather than becoming an engineer.

McClellan served as an engineering officer during the Mexican-American War. Resigning after 11 years in the army, he then became a chief engineer and a president in the railroad business. When the Civil War broke out four years later, his former Southern classmates approached him about joining the Confederacy. McClellan was opposed to interference with slavery, but he was also opposed to secession. He favored a war policy that involved a "polite war" with no emancipation,

---

[446] Sears (1988), p. 72, 93–95; Beagle, p. 1274; Beatie, p. 480; Eicher, pp. 372, 856.

[447] Sears (1988), p. 93; Goodwin, pp. 378–379; https://www.history.com/this-day-in-history/lincoln-removes-mcclellan, p. 1, accessed May 2, 2021; Beagle, p. 1274.

[448] Eicher and Eicher, p. 371;"Facts, Information and Articles about George McClellan." Ed Bonekemper, *History.Net.* Tysons, VA: Historynet LLC, December 2010; Foote, vol. 2, p. 531.

[449] "Robert E. Lee, the King of Spades," Bob Duncan, February 16, 2014, https://www.columbiadailyherald.com/article/20140216/OPINION/302169932, accessed May 10, 2021.

since he viewed slavery as being recognized in the Constitution. Lincoln held the same view until August 1862.[450]

George McClellan was a great organizer, and he whipped the army into shape for the defense of Washington. He fortified Washington like no tomorrow and his army nearly quadrupled in six months, from 50,000 to 192,000 men. His soldiers loved him and he returned their worship with a jaunty salute. However, McClellan argued frequently with the government about strategy, favoring one big Napoleonic-style battle to end it all. He proposed adding 100,000 more men and more guns.[451]

Within a month after his arrival in Washington, McClellan declared a state of emergency, believing that the Confederacy had 100,000 troops facing him when in fact they only had 35,000. Two weeks later, he raised his estimate to 150,000 Confederates. McClellan refused to share his strategy with the U.S. War Department. And though he was a capable army builder in the early stages of the war, he was a "sluggish and paranoid field commander who seemed unable to muster the courage to aggressively engage" the Confederate army. Lincoln and others grew impatient with McClellan's slowness to attack as the Confederates massed near Washington. But McClellan wanted to have "everything ready in case of defeat and keep our lines of retreat open."[452]

---

[450] Rafuse, pp. 47–49; Rowland, pp. 260–261; Sears (1988), pp. 16–17, 66–69; https://bobcivilwarhistory.wordpress.com, p. 3.

[451] Sears (1988), pp. 98–99, 101–104, 110; Foote, vol. 1, p. 241.

[452] Sears (1988), pp. 101–104, 110, 136–137; Beatie, pp. 471–72; https://www.history.com/this-day-in-history/lincoln-removes-mcclellan, p. 1, May 2, 2021; Foote, vol. 1, p. 242.

George McClellan

Privately, McClellan called Lincoln a "well-meaning baboon." After McClellan had been in Washington for five months, Lincoln visited his home, waiting for 30 minutes before being told that McClellan had gone to bed. After waiting seven months with no action by McClellan, Lincoln met with other top military officers in Washington.

"If General McClellan does not want to use the army," he declared in exasperation, "I would like to borrow it for a time."

Lincoln issued an order requiring all armies to begin offensive operations by the middle of month eight. McClellan replied to the order with a 22-page letter objecting to Lincoln's plan and proposing another, the success of which McClellan said he was certain. Lincoln approved the plan. McClellan stayed in Washington and continued training his army.[453]

The Confederates under Joseph Johnston were indeed just outside Washington. For months, McClellan planned to attack them. Ultimately, he concluded that Johnston's fortifications were overwhelming, so he tried to go around them instead. But by the time he did so, he discovered that Johnston had secretly withdrawn. McClellan caught hell from the press

[453] Foote, vol. 1, p. 240, 249; McPherson (1988), p. 364; Sears (1988), pp. 132–133, 140–141, 149, 160; McPherson (2008), p. 66; Hyatt, Michael, https://michaelhyatt.com/5-characteristics-of-weak-leaders/ p. 2, accessed May 2, 2021.

and from Congress, particularly when it was learned that as Johnston withdrew he had fooled McClellan by replacing his cannons with logs that were painted black. Moreover, Johnston's troops had been only half the size that McClellan had estimated.[454]

George McClellan devised a new scheme involving a Union advance up the Virginia Peninsula to Richmond. But before heading south to face the enemy, he addressed his troops: "I am to watch over you as a parent over his children; and you know that your general loves you from the depths of his heart. It shall be my care, as it ever has been, to gain success with the least possible loss; but I know that, if necessary, you will willingly follow me to our graves for our righteous cause."[455]

In month nine (March of 1862), McClellan's army finally sailed to the southern tip of the Virginia Peninsula. His "armada" had 121,500 men, 1,150 wagons, 15,000 horses, and a lot of equipment and supplies. They traveled by 113 steamers, 188 schooners, and 88 barges. Lincoln thought that McClellan had left too few soldiers to protect Washington and that he had been deceptive in reporting the strength of his force there, counting troops as being ready to defend Washington when in fact they were elsewhere. McClellan assured Lincoln that he would "carry this thing through handsomely."[456]

Little Mac intended to work his way up the Virginia Peninsula and take Richmond. But he stood still on the Peninsula for a month, preparing. By then the Confederates under Johnston had built fortifications 14 miles wide across the Peninsula at Yorktown. These were far too wide for the number of Confederates available to hold them, but McClellan believed that the rebels had two or three times more soldiers than they actually had. His belief was further fueled by one Confederate officer who created the illusion that many troops were present and that more troops were arriving by having small groups of his soldiers march in a circle, passing the same opening in the woods over and over, coupled with a lot of noise. In actuality, McClellan had the superior number of forces.[457]

---

[454] Foote, vol. 1, p. 264; Sears (1988), pp. 168–169.

[455] Symonds, pp. 140–146; Sears (1992), pp. 15, 25; Foote, vol. 1, p. 167.

[456] https://www.history.com/this-day-in-history/lincoln-removes-mcclellan, p. 1, accessed May 2, 2021; Sears (1988), pp. 167–169; Foote, vol. 1, p. 269.

[457] Foote, vol. 1, p. 399; Bailey (1983), p. 99; Sears (1992), pp. 42–43.

Joseph Johnston

Joseph Johnston was a 55-year-old Virginian who resigned from the United States army when the South seceded. His brother was a U.S. congressman and his nephew a senator. Johnston graduated 13th out of 46 from West Point in the same class with Robert E. Lee. Jefferson Davis was also at the academy when he was there. After school, Johnston fought in the Mexican-American War with Lee, in the Wyoming Territory against the Sioux, and in Kansas during the violence over slavery. Along the way, he served as a mentor and close friend to junior officer George McClellan.[458]

Johnston had played a critical role in defeating the Union army at the first battle of Bull Run (also known as the first battle of Manassas), where the U.S. army had marched toward Richmond at the outset of the war thinking that it would easily overcome the ragtag Confederate army. Any expectation that the war would end quickly and easily had ended at Bull Run.[459]

Joseph Johnston

[458] Symonds, pp. 10–11, 28, 72–80, 373; "A Much-Respected, and Conflicted, General of the Confederacy." Frederick N. Rasmussen, *The Baltimore Sun*, July 29, 2011.

[459] Symonds, pp. 112–124; McMurry, p, 193; Coski, p. 9.

Joe Johnston considered his Peninsula fortifications at Yorktown to be indefensible with his 54,000 soldiers. He had half the number of soldiers that McClellan had and McClellan had artillery support from the navy on the nearby James and York rivers. So Johnston withdrew from Yorktown, leaving some Confederate forces at Williamsburg to slow down any chase that McClellan might give. McClellan did not give chase. In fact, he did not even know that Johnston had left.

When McClellan was finally ready to attack the Yorktown fortifications, he learned that Johnston had split for Richmond. He made this discovery when one of his officers went up in a hot air balloon and saw that the Confederate fortifications were empty. McClellan was skewered publicly when it was shown that he had vastly overestimated the strength of Johnston's fortifications and had once again been given the slip. McClellan had now been in command for 11 months.[460]

After withdrawing, Johnston planned to fortify Richmond. But Jefferson Davis labelled his withdrawal a "precipitate retreat," concluding with Lee that the Peninsula had to be held. So Johnston returned to Yorktown, waiting to defend against McClellan's imminent attack. But McClellan did not attack, though he had told Lincoln, "I shall push the enemy to the wall." As Johnston put it, "No one but McClellan could have hesitated to attack." McClellan's "own ripe imagination" had convinced him that he could not prevail. He claimed to have only 85,000 men, though he had reported 108,000 to Lincoln.[461]

McClellan then decided to lay siege to Yorktown, rather than attack it. Meanwhile, Johnston withdrew to Williamsburg. Politicians in Washington were livid, labelling McClellan a Confederate sympathizer who had designed a plan to move the main Union army to the Peninsula in order to create a clear path for a Confederate attack on Washington. McClellan had also told Lincoln that 77,456 soldiers remained in Washington to protect it, whereas there were only 29,000 after adjusting for McClellan's double counting of some men and his counting of others who had not yet arrived.

---

[460] Symonds, pp. 140–146, 153–159; Sears, (1992) pp. 15, 25, 40–110; Rafuse, p. 211; Esposito, map 41; Burton, p. 24; Salmon, p. 79.

[461] Foote, vol. 1, pp. 402–413; Sears (1992), pp. 40–110; Symonds, pp. 153–159.

"You must act," Lincoln wired to McClellan.

"We shall soon be at them," McClellan replied, "and I am sure of the result."[462]

McClellan advanced to Williamsburg, attacking Johnston on May 5. In a fierce defensive battle, the Confederates somehow held their line until dark and then retreated up the Peninsula toward the Chickahominy River. By late May, McClellan was within six miles of Richmond. The Union army with its superior numbers had indeed prevailed at Williamsburg, but McClellan mischaracterized it as a "brilliant victory" over superior forces. As one historian suggests, McClellan simply could not bring himself to engage in what Lincoln called "the awful arithmetic" of battle. As a result, Lincoln was "forced to turn his considerable intellect toward the study of war." Lincoln even came to the Peninsula by boat to observe the situation, and he went ashore to inspect things personally.[463]

Johnston eventually abandoned his position at the Chickahominy River as well and McClellan came within four miles of Richmond—close enough to hear the downtown clocks ringing. In Richmond, the Confederates packed gold reserves onto a train that stood ready to go in case the Union army broke through. McClellan had more than 128,000 men, but he was convinced that Johnston's army of 54,000 really had 180,000 soldiers.

"If I am not reinforced," he said, "it is probable that I will be obliged to fight nearly double my numbers."[464]

McClellan also convinced himself that the only way to succeed would be to put Richmond under siege, rather than to attack. While he planned his siege of Richmond on the last day of June 1862, McClellan was surprise attacked by Johnston. McClellan had divided his army, leaving its components vulnerable.

Johnston had taken his time in getting ready for the attack, driving Jefferson Davis nuts in the process. Johnston had announced on Monday

---

462 Foote, vol. 1, pp. 408–409.

463 Ibid., p. 411; Sears, (1992), pp. 40–110; Symonds, pp. 153–159; https://bobcivilwarhistory.wordpress.com/2012/01/28/command-profile-george-b-mcclellan/ pp. 1, 4, accessed May 2, 2021; Sears (1992), pp. 89–92.

464 Sears (1992), pp. 103–104; Foote, vol. 1, pp. 418, 422.

that he would attack that Thursday. But by Thursday, McClellan had moved backwards, so the attack was cancelled. It seems that Johnston was every bit as cautious as McClellan. Then Johnston received reinforcements, bringing his total to 75,000 men.[465]

Johnston attacked near Richmond at Seven Pines, conducting what historian Shelby Foote calls "unquestionably the worst-conducted large-scale conflict in a war that afforded many rivals for that distinction." Through confusion, lack of communication, and bungled marches, the Confederates ended up with 6,134 dead or wounded. The Union had 5,031. Johnston's attack plan was aggressive, but it was too complex for his soldiers to execute. Yet it did stop McClellan, who never advanced farther on Richmond. Johnston was wounded in the battle and replaced by Robert E. Lee.[466]

George Armstrong Custer

Custer fought under McClellan on the Peninsula, capturing 50 Confederates in an attack that McClellan called a "very gallant affair." He was 23 years old. As Foote puts it, Custer's "love of combat was only exceeded by his ache for glory . . ." Born in Ohio, he grew up with the nickname "Autie." Custer was a life-long practical joker who flaunted rules and tested boundaries, having one of the worst conduct records in West Point history with 726 demerits. He graduated 34th out of 34 cadets in 1861. But the Civil War was breaking out and trained officers were needed. Some historians suspect that Custer deliberately kept his class rank low so that he would be assigned to the infantry or cavalry. He soon became brigadier general of the Michigan volunteers.

George Custer was a publicity hound. He was 5 feet 11 inches tall and weighed 160 pounds, and as an officer he had wide latitude in his uniform, which was often seen as gaudy.[467] One soldier recalled, "A showy

[465] Foote, vol. 1, pp. 407, 440–444.

[466] Ibid., pp. 445, 449; Sears (1992), pp. 111–145; Eicher, p. 323; Symonds, pp. 160–174.

[467] Foote, vol. 2, p. 571; "West Point's Worst Cadet: George Armstrong Custer." Duane Schultz, *History.Net*. July 6, 2017, accessed June 2, 2020; Carhart, p. 39; Wert (1996) p. 21; Tagg, p. 184; Frost, p. 187.

uniform for Custer was one of command presence on the battlefield: he wanted to be readily distinguishable at first glance from all other soldiers. He intended to lead from the front, and to him it was a crucial issue of unit morale that his men be able to look up in the middle of a charge, or at any other time on the battlefield, and instantly see him leading the way into danger." Custer was flamboyant, wearing into battle black velvet trimmed with gold lace, a crimson necktie, and a large, tilted hat, with his "long, blond ringlets flowing down to his shoulders."[468]

Robert E. Lee

Robert E. Lee was 55 years old and had not taken part in a battle since the Mexican-American War 15 years earlier. "I prefer Lee to Johnston," McClellan exclaimed, describing Lee as "too cautious and weak under grave responsibility" and "likely to be timid and irresolute in action." McClellan then sat for three weeks, awaiting 9,500 more reinforcements and waiting for the roads to dry. "After tomorrow we shall fight the rebel army as soon as Providence will permit," he indicated.[469]

Three years earlier, in October of 1859, at Harper's Ferry, Lee had been given command to suppress the uprising. John Brown had raided a federal arsenal in an effort to start an armed revolt against slavery. After capturing Brown, Lee described the event as "the attempt of a fanatic or madman." Lee was said by a colleague to be "dignified without hauteur, grand without pride . . . he evinced an imperturbable self-possession, and a complete control of his passions." While many Southerners expected a glorious war, Lee predicted that it would be long and destructive. He denounced secession as unconstitutional and "nothing but betrayal." He also stated that he would sacrifice everything "but honor" to preserve the Union. Ultimately, his sense of honor outweighed his objection to secession and that sorry son of a bitch joined the Confederacy, though

[468] Tagg, p. 184; Carhart, p. 119; https://en.wikipedia.org/wiki/George_Armstrong_Custer, p. 5, accessed May 17, 2021; www.spartacus-educational.com, George Custer, accessed May 21, 2021; Philbrick (2010), p. xvi.

[469] Foote, vol. 1, pp. 450–451, 465–467; Sears (1992), pp. 111–145; Eicher and Eicher, p. 323; Symonds, pp. 160–174.

a colleague told Lee that he was making "the greatest mistake of your life."[470]

While McClellan sat, Lee fortified Richmond by digging trenches, extending his defensive line 30 miles south to Petersburg. In Richmond, his men derisively called him the "King of Spades" for his extensive digging of trenches around the city. As one author puts it, as the war wore on, those men "stopped laughing—and started digging." During the Napoleonic wars 50 years earlier, battles had been fought in straight lines in open fields at close range. However, the smoothbore muskets used back then were "wildly inaccurate" and battles were ultimately decided by bayonet. Lee knew that better muskets were now in use and that the stand-in-the-open battles of the past no longer worked. So he began digging trenches. As a result, the war was fought in part by shovel. Lee's digging presaged the trench warfare seen fifty years later in World War I.[471]

Robert E. Lee was foremost an engineer. He received no demerits at West Point and was called "The Marble Model" of a soldier by his classmates.[472] His 32 years of military service prior to the Civil War consisted mostly of engineering projects in Georgia, Virginia, Michigan, Missouri, and Iowa.

Born in Virginia, Lee graduated 2nd out of 45 cadets from West Point. He was 5 feet 11 inches tall, weighing 165 pounds. During the Mexican-American War, he had distinguished himself by finding an attack route that was not defended because Santa Anna had thought the

---

470 Freeman (1934), pp. 394–395; "Col. Robert E. Lee's Report Concerning the Attack at Harper's Ferry." University of Missouri – Kansas City School of Law. October 18, 1959. Archived from the original on July 22, 2010; Ford (1963), pp. 305–306; "The General in His Study." Elizabeth Brown Pryor, *New York Times*, April 19, 2011; "Robert E. Lee's 'Severest Struggle.'" Elizabeth Brown Pryor, *American Heritage*, Winter 2008, vol. 58, issue 1.

471 *Foot Soldier: The Rebels.* Prod. A&E Television Network. Karn, Richard, The History Channel, 1998; "Robert E. Lee, the King of Spades," Bob Duncan, February 16, 2014, https://www.columbiadailyherald.com/article/20140216/OPINION/302169932, accessed May 10, 2021.

472 "Robert E. Lee, the King of Spades," Bob Duncan, February 16, 2014, https://www.columbiadailyherald.com/article/20140216/OPINION/302169932, accessed May 10, 2021.

terrain impassable. There Lee met Ulysses S. Grant and they worked together. His commander, Winfield Scott, called him "the best officer in the army." Lee later served as superintendent of West Point for three years, from 1852 to 1855.[473]

When his father-in-law died, Lee took a two-year leave of absence to run the plantation, including its hundreds of slaves. He was a strict disciplinarian who gave harsh punishments. When three runaway slaves were captured, Lee had them whipped and then ordered that their backs be washed with brine. He recaptured runaway slaves and he separated slave families.[474]

On the Peninsula, Lee sent out cavalryman Jeb Stuart to determine McClellan's positions and plans. Stuart disappeared for three days, rattling McClellan by riding full circle around his army, gathering intelligence and interrupting his supply line. Along the way, Stuart captured 165 Union soldiers, 260 horses and mules, and supplies, with little or no resistance from the Union Cavalry, which was commanded by Stuart's father-in-law.[475]

Stuart had been a cadet at West Point when Lee was superintendent there. He wore "thigh-high boots, yellow sash, elbow-length gauntlets, red-lined cape, soft hat with the brim pinned up on one side by a gold star supporting a foot-long ostrich plume." As far as being outnumbered by the Union army, Stuart said, "We must substitute esprit for numbers. Therefore I strive to inculcate in my men the spirit of the chase."[476]

---

[473] Davis (1999), pp. 21, 111; Foote, vol. 1, p. 586; "Robert E. Lee, the King of Spades," Bob Duncan, February 16, 2014, https://www.columbiadailyherald.com/article/20140216/OPINION/302169932, accessed May 10, 2021.

[474] "Will of George Washington Parke Custis (March 2, 1855)." *Encyclopedia Virginia*, https://encyclopediavirginia.org, accessed June 13, 2022; Wesley Norris, interview in *National Anti-Slavery Standard* (April 14, 1866) 4, reprinted in Blassingame, pp. 467–468; "The Myth of the Kindly General Lee." Adam Serwer, *Atlantic*, accessed August 29, 2017; "Robert E. Lee Was Not the George Washington of His Time. But a Lot Ties Them Together." Ann M. Simmons, *Los Angeles Times*, August 18, 2017, accessed June 13, 2022. ISSN 0458-3035.

[475] Eicher, 2001, pp. 280–281; Foote, vol. 1, p. 471; Wert (1996), pp. 93–101; Davis (1957), pp. 111–130; https://en.wikipedia.org/J._E._B._Stuart, p. 1.

[476] Foote, vol. 1, p. 471.

Lee soon attacked McClellan on the Peninsula in a series of battles known as the Seven Days Battles. McClellan was unnerved, reporting that he faced 200,000 Confederates. In fact there were roughly half that many. After several days of fighting, McClellan wrote to Washington: "I am obliged to fall back . . . Attacked by greatly superior numbers in all directions . . ." McClellan had been tricked a second time by a small group of Confederate soldiers marching and countermarching to give the appearance of a much larger force. He withdrew to a safer strategic position and then inflicted a large number of casualties on the Confederate army. But by withdrawing, he also let go of Richmond. McClellan blamed Lincoln for this change in circumstances.[477]

On several occasions, McClellan was absent when the fighting took place on the Peninsula. He was five miles away with no telegraph communication during one battle and on a boat ten miles away during another. He took pride, however, in the organized manner in which his army retreated with its 25,000 tons of food, 3,600 wagons, and 2,500 head of cattle. McClellan referred to it as a "change of base," rather than a retreat.[478]

Summing it all up, McClellan told Washington: "I have lost this battle because my force was too small . . . I again repeat that I am not responsible for this . . . If, at this instant, I could dispose of 10,000 fresh men, I could gain a victory tomorrow . . . the Government has not sustained this army . . . You have done your best to sacrifice this army." McClellan's officers saw it as "a big skedaddle."[479]

Lee was determined to pursue McClellan on the Peninsula. However, he was unable to catch up with McClellan's men and position them in a way to destroy "those people," as he always referred to the Union. At Malvern Hill, Lee made one last attempt to destroy McClellan's army, to no avail. He suffered three times more dead and wounded than McClellan, who was on high ground with many more soldiers than Lee. Yet McClellan ultimately ordered a retreat, though his officers protested,

[477] Ibid., pp. 477, 491; Rafuse, p. 231; Beagle, p. 1275.

[478] Sears (1999), p. 16; Foote, vol. 1, p. 492. This is reminiscent of Washington's "alteration of our position" when abandoning New York.

[479] Foote, vol. 1, pp. 493, 500.

with one saying, "such an order can only be prompted by cowardice or treason." As Foote puts it, McClellan's view was that he "had not lost: he had 'failed to win.' Nor had he been out-fought: he had been 'overpowered.' So he said." During the Seven Days Battle, McClellan had 26,463 of his men killed, wounded, or captured.[480]

Lee's army simply could not catch up to McClellan's retreating forces, so Lee sent Jeb Stuart and his cavalry ahead in pursuit. Stuart found them camped beside the James River. McClellan had failed to protect his army from attack from the heights overlooking the encampment. Though Stuart knew that Lee's army was making its way to him, Stuart could not resist. He fired his one cannon down at the Union army, alerting it of its vulnerability without doing any real damage. As Foote says, ". . . it was a case of too little too soon."[481]

The secretary of war came to the Peninsula to urge McClellan to attack. McClellan claimed that he had 88,665 men while Lee had 200,000. In reality, Lee had 56,000. McClellan requested 30,000 additional soldiers and when the secretary indicated that no more than 20,000 were available, McClellan said he was "willing to try it." Yet the next day, he wired the secretary asking for more on the empty belief that Confederates were "pouring into Richmond from the South." Based on this misinformation, the secretary agreed that McClellan should withdraw from the Peninsula. But then McClellan protested: "Here, directly in front of this army, is the heart of the rebellion. It is here that all of our resources should be collected to strike the blow which will determine the fate of the nation . . ."[482]

Though he was a West Point student of war, McClellan had apparently not recognized the peril of proceeding up the Peninsula. Only 81 years earlier, Cornwallis had managed to trap himself there at Yorktown and had surrendered, essentially ending the Revolutionary War. McClellan lacked the gall to capture Richmond. Lee lacked the speed and manpower to capture McClellan.

---

480 Ibid., pp. 484–498, 505, 515–516, 523.

481 Ibid., p. 518.

482 Ibid., pp. 590, 594–595.

Witnessing McClellan's failed southern approach on the Peninsula, Lincoln ordered General John Pope to advance toward Richmond from the northeast. Pope had 44,000 soldiers with which to fight the 30,000 Confederates who were in his way. McClellan lingered on the Peninsula, delaying the return of his army to Washington long enough that Pope was already gone by the time McClellan's army could have provided him with reinforcements. McClellan referred to Pope as a "villain" who "ought to bring defeat upon any cause that employs him." While this was going on, Lee took a gamble, removing a large number of his soldiers from the Peninsula though McClellan was still there, in order to fight Pope up north. In order to keep McClellan stuck in place, Lee put on a "demonstration" in front of McClellan, attacking just enough to keep him busy.[483]

The Peninsula Campaign was over. The Southern press skewered Lee for the "blundering manner" in which McClellan had been allowed to escape and the "desultory manner" in which a fraction of Lee's army had pursued him. Lee agreed: "Under ordinary circumstances, the Federal army should have been destroyed."[484]

When Lee learned from a Union deserter that McClellan was at last loading his men onto boats, Lee moved the rest of his men north of Richmond to throw everything he had at Pope. It essentially became a race, with Lee trying to reach Pope before McClellan could. Lee had 55,000 men. Pope had 70,000, and a lot more on the way from McClellan. Meanwhile, the secretary of war urged McClellan to hurry up with his troops. McClellan wrote to his wife: ". . . he is not a gentleman . . . I fear that I am very mad." He finally delivered the Union soldiers to Pope as ordered, again writing to his wife: "They are committing a fatal error in withdrawing me from here, and the future will show it. I think . . . Pope will be badly thrashed within ten days, and that they will be very glad to turn over the redemption of their affairs to me."[485]

Violating the maxim that an army should not be divided in the presence of a superior enemy, Lee sent Stonewall Jackson's 23,000 troops

[483] McPherson (1988), p. 525; Foote, vol. 1, pp. 589–591.

[484] Foote, vol. 1, p. 586.

[485] Ibid., pp. 596, 605–613.

around Pope to attack his supply line while Lee's 32,000 men staged a demonstration in front of Pope to keep him occupied. Jeb Stuart had accompanied Lee in Maryland to provide intelligence on the enemy's whereabouts. However, Stuart took a five-day break along the way to attend a civilian gala ball in Maryland, leaving Lee in the dark.[486]

Stonewall Jackson

On the Peninsula, Stonewall Jackson had performed poorly, often arriving late. He was lethargic, going into bivouac in the afternoon while the rest of the army was fighting. He barely fought at all during the Seven Days, saying that he did not want his men to do all of the fighting. At one point, he remarked: "If General Lee had wanted me, he could have sent for me." Stonewall Jackson was likewise nowhere to be found as Lee chased McClellan down the Peninsula.[487]

But Jackson had performed exceptionally well in the Shenandoah Valley the year before, with three victories due to his swift maneuvers. He had combined audacity with a shrewd use of the available terrain. In the Shenandoah Valley, he used surprise and maneuver to win victories with his 17,000 men against 60,000. But now some of the Confederates began to doubt his glorious nickname, which was based on his performance at First Bull Run. There, another Confederate general had admired Jackson's closing of a gap against a heavy Union attack by saying, "Look, men, there is Jackson standing like a stone wall." Yet rumors abounded that, instead, Jackson had refused to come to the aid of his fellow soldiers, causing the Confederate general to exclaim, "There stands Jackson—like a damned stone wall." However, the Confederate general who had made the declaration was shot and killed within seconds of making it, so the true nature of the nickname was unresolved.[488]

---

[486] Ibid., pp. 610–612; Wert (2008), p. 144.

[487] Foote, vol. 1, pp. 483, 506, 587; https://www.history.com/news/10-things-you-may-not-know-about-ulysses-s-grant, p. 4, accessed June 14, 2021.

[488] Foote, vol. 1, p. 498; Freeman (1946), pp. 733–734; https://en.m.wikipedia.org/Stonewall_Jackson, p. 21, accessed July 14, 2022; See generally Goldfield, David et al. (1999). *The American Journey of History of the United States.* Prentice Hall. ISBN 0–13–088243–7.

With his 23,000 men, Jackson indeed went around Pope to attack his supply line, reaching Manassas in August of 1862. There he redeemed himself by destroying the Union depot. His men devoured bread, pickled oysters, canned lobster, cigars, coffee, molasses, and whiskey. As historian Foote says, it was "as if the mythical horn of plenty had been upended." Jackson's uniform was always badly soiled and one Northern newspaper reporter described him thus: "He was dressed in the coarsest kind of homespun, seedy and dirty at that; wore an old hat which any northern beggar would consider an insult to have offered him, and in general appearance was in no respect to be distinguished from the mongrel, bare-footed crew who follow his fortunes."[489]

When Pope learned that Lee had divided his army by sending Jackson to Manassas, he decided to crush Jackson. But when Pope's men arrived at Manassas, the supply depot was destroyed and Jackson was gone. After searching for Jackson, Pope found him.

"I see no possibility of his escape," Pope declared.

However, Jackson was neither trapped nor trying to escape. Instead, he wanted Pope to attack, though Lee had told Jackson to avoid a general engagement. Jackson noticed an approaching column of 2,800 Union soldiers on a nearby road and he attacked them with nearly twice that number from his own troops. Each side had 1,000 casualties by the time the fighting ended. But, unlike at Seven Pines, Jackson came alive. At the end of the day, he retreated and rejoined Lee's army. Pope wired Washington, stating incorrectly: "The enemy has been receiving reinforcements all day . . . I think it almost certain that we shall be attacked in the morning . . ."[490]

The Confederates were now facing Pope on the same battlefield where First Bull Run had occurred. Pope attacked. Lee counterattacked, inflicting substantial damage on the Union troops during the second battle of Bull Run. As a result, Pope was ordered to retreat to Washington and, surely enough, George B. McClellan was returned to command. Lincoln referred to Pope as "little more than . . . a first-rate clerk." But

[489] https://www.history.com/news/10-things-you-may-not-know-about-ulysses-s-grant, p. 4, accessed June 14, 2021; Foote, vol. 1, pp. 4, 35, 619, 680.

[490] Foote, vol. 1, pp. 603, 621–631.

he also did not trust McClellan, whom he thought had wanted Pope to fail. As for McClellan, Lincoln said, "If he can't fight himself, he excels in making others ready to fight." Pope was reassigned to Minnesota to fight the Sioux and remained there for the rest of the war.[491]

McClellan was now prepared to fight Lee north of Richmond, after leaving behind a junior officer with 72,500 men to protect Washington. McClellan had 88,000 soldiers; he estimated Lee to have 120,000. Lee, in fact, had 18,000.[492]

In Frederick, Maryland, some of McClellan's men found an envelope containing three cigars and Lee's written battle plans. McClellan discovered that Lee had now cut his own army into five parts. With this knowledge, McClellan became uncharacteristically bold. As Lee retreated, McClellan sent his entire left side forward. But after one hour of fighting, 12,520 of McClellan's men surrendered to the Confederates.[493]

McClellan and the remainder of his army were somehow in good spirits, however. In mid-September of 1862 they moved to Antietam Creek in Maryland, where Lee's men were on high ground overlooking a shallow valley. McClellan wanted to leave little to chance, so he decided to wait until the following day to attack. But by that time, Stonewall Jackson had arrived, bringing Lee's total to 26,000 men to fight against McClellan's 72,500. Lee attacked, sending the Union soldiers scrambling and killing or wounding 2,000 Union soldiers in 15 minutes. Confederate losses were heavy as well, though Jackson declared, "God has been very kind to us this day." Jackson was a religious fanatic who viewed the war as a religious one. After the attack, Lee asked Confederate John Bell Hood where his division was.

"Dead on the field," Hood replied.

It was the single bloodiest day in American military history.[494]

[491] Ibid., pp. 635–637, 645, 648–649.

[492] Ibid., pp. 669–672, 685.

[493] Ibid., pp. 670–675, 680.

[494] Ibid., pp. 681–685, 692, 702; McPherson (2002), pp. 129–130.

Stonewall Jackson

During the Battle of Antietam, McClellan had kept 20,000 men out of the action as a reserve against any trick that Lee might employ. McClellan defended his doing so by saying that he would not "hazard another battle with less than an absolute assurance of success." Defeat, in McClellan's mind, would have allowed a direct march on Washington by the Confederates. As Shelby Foote notes of McClellan: "It never occurred to him, apparently, to look at the reverse of the coin: to consider that Lee's army, like his own, was the only organized force that blocked the path to its capitol." By nightfall, more than one-fourth of Lee's army was dead or wounded. And though his officers objected, Lee was ready to resume fighting in the morning. However, McClellan was still convinced that he was outnumbered and decided to wait for reinforcements. The two armies therefore sat still the following day without engaging. It was a standoff.[495]

Lee then retreated from Antietam, but McClellan did not pursue him, naturally. Lincoln urged McClellan to pursue, as Lee had a smaller force with its back to the Potomac River. Instead, McClellan traded angry correspondence while Lincoln for the next five *weeks* while Lee escaped.

[495] Foote, vol. 1, pp. 700–701.

Lee had 36,418 soldiers at this point, while McClellan had 93,149. But McClellan had convinced himself that Lee had 97,445. Lincoln went to Western Maryland by train to see the situation for himself. Traveling with him was O.M. Hatch, a friend from Illinois. Overlooking McClellan's army from a ridge, Lincoln asked Hatch: "What is all this?"

"Why, Mr. Lincoln, this is the Army of the Potomac," Hatch replied.

"No, Hatch, no," Lincoln responded. "This is General McClellan's body-guard."[496]

McClellan continued calling for more and more supplies and soldiers. He soon had 133,433 men. His own quartermaster said, "no army was ever more perfectly supplied than this one has been as a general rule." Then McClellan asked for more horses, to which Lincoln replied: "To be told, after more than five weeks' total inaction of the army . . . that the cavalry horses were too much fatigued to move, presents a cheerless, almost hopeless, prospect for the future . . ."[497]

McClellan finally began to cross the Potomac River to pursue Lee, but he took nine days to cross the river and by that time Lee was long gone. That was the final straw. Lincoln removed him from command. As Lincoln told journalist and politician Francis Blair, "He has got the slows, Mr. Blair."[498]

Regarding Antietam, McClellan wrote to his wife: "Those in whose judgment I rely tell me that I fought the battle splendidly and that it was a masterpiece of art . . . I feel I have done all that can be asked in twice saving the country." The bloody fight at Antietam did, however, enable Lincoln to issue the Emancipation Proclamation, which he had been waiting to issue until there was some Union army success that would boost public support for it. The narrow Union victory at Antietam gave Lincoln the opening he needed. He issued the Emancipation Proclamation, which is said to have put the Confederacy "on the diplomatic and moral defensive."[499]

---

[496] Ibid., pp. 703–704, 749.

[497] Ibid., p. 752.

[498] https://www.history.com/this-day-in-history/lincoln-removes-mcclellan, p.2, accessed May 2, 2021; Foote, vol. 2, pp. 5, 21; Foote, vol. 1, p. 753.

[499] McPherson (1988), p. 545; Foote, vol. 1, p. 704; McPherson (2008), pp. 104–105, 129; https://en.wikipedia.org/wiki/Robert_E._Lee, p. 13, accessed April 28, 2021;

In response to criticism from newspaper man Horace Greeley for not releasing the Proclamation sooner, Lincoln wrote: "If there be those who would not save the Union unless they could at the same time save slavery, I do not agree with them. If there be those who would not save the Union unless they could at the same time destroy slavery, I do not agree with them. My paramount object in this struggle is to save the Union, and is not either to save or destroy slavery. If I could save the Union without freeing any slave, I would do it; and if I could save it by freeing all the slaves, I would do it; and if I could save it by freeing some and leaving others alone, I would also do that . . . and I intend no modification of my oft-expressed personal wish that all men everywhere could be free."[500]

The Emancipation Proclamation, issued in September of 1862, provided that any state in rebellion on the coming January 1 would have its slaves emancipated. The proclamation was expected, in part, to encourage England and France to remain with the Union. The *London Spectator*, however, noted: "The principle is not that a human being cannot justly own another, but that he cannot own him unless he is loyal to the United States." Moreover, slaves in states that were not in rebellion would remain slaves. Nevertheless, support for the Confederacy was now seen as support for slavery, so France and England would not intervene on its behalf.[501]

Jeb Stuart

Shortly after Antietam, Jeb Stuart performed another one of his rides around McClellan's massive, motionless army, covering 126 miles in 60 hours and capturing 300 soldiers and 1,200 horses. Born in Virginia, James Ewell Brown "J.E.B." Stuart graduated 13th out of 46 cadets at West Point. He was now 29 years old and commanding a cavalry. Stuart "cultivated a cavalier image . . . with a red flower in his lapel, often

https://bobcivilwarhistory.wordpress.com, p. 4.

[500] Foote, vol. 1, p. 706.

[501] Ibid., pp. 708–709.

sporting cologne." He had a "fox-hunt manner" and a "thirst for action and applause."[502]

John Bell Hood

During the Peninsula Campaign, John Bell Hood had fought under Lee, distinguishing himself by leading a brigade that broke the Union line during the Seven Days battles. But Hood wept, as more than 400 of his men, including most of the officers in his brigade, were dead or wounded.[503]

Born in Kentucky as the son of a doctor, Hood stood six foot two with a long, blond beard. He graduated 44th out of a class of 52 at West Point, where he became known as "Sam." Lee was superintendent of West Point at the time and Hood's classmates included John Schofield, whom he would later fight in Tennessee. Described by another classmate as "indomitable," Hood served for eight years in the United States army, with two years as a cavalry instructor at West Point. But he resigned immediately after shots were fired on Fort Sumter. Unhappy that Kentucky was a neutral state, Hood joined the Confederate forces of Texas as a captain. He was an avowed racist, convinced that negroes were an "inferior race."[504]

During the war, Hood was promoted for bravery, though he was often reckless if not foolhardy. He developed a reputation early in the war for hard fighting, rising from captain to colonel in five months, and six months later becoming a brigadier general. Hood was aggressive, eagerly leading his men personally into battle. He was tall and thin, with blue eyes, a massive beard, and a quiet demeanor. A "fierce light" was said to come into his eyes in the heat of battle as he became "transfigured."[505]

---

[502] Ibid., p. 750; Jermann, p. 129; Wert (2008), pp. 167–176; Thomas (1986), pp. 173–180; Davis (1957), pp. 215–237; Foote, vol. 2, pp. 306, 569, 795.

[503] McMurry, p. 51, Sears (1992), p. 243.

[504] Sword, p. 6; McMurry, p. 10; Eicher and Eicher, p. 303; Hood, p. 235.

[505] Chesnut, p. 230.

Name	Graduation Year	Class Rank	At West Point At The Same Time
Jefferson Davis	1828	23/33	Robert E. Lee Joseph Johnston
Joseph Johnston	1829	13/46	Robert E. Lee Jefferson Davis
Robert E. Lee (Superintendent 1852-1855)	1829	2/46	Joseph Johnson Jefferson Davis John Bell Hood Jeb Stuart John Schofield
Braxton Bragg	1837	5/50	William Tecumseh Sherman George Thomas
Joseph Longstreet	1838	54/56	George Thomas William Rosecrans (roommate) William Tecumseh Sherman George Pickett Ulysses S. Grant
William Tecumseh Sherman	1840	6/42	George Thomas (roommate) William Rosecrans Braxton Bragg Joseph Longstreet
George Thomas	1840	12/42	William Tecumseh Sherman (roommate) Braxton Bragg William Rosecrans John Bell Hood Joseph Longstreet
William Rosecrans	1842	5/56	Joseph Longstreet (roommate) George Thomas Ulysses S. Grant William Tecumseh Sherman
Ulysses S. Grant	1843	21/39	William Rosecrans Joseph Longstreet George Pickett Stonewall Jackson
George Pickett	1846	59/59	Stonewall Jackson George McClellan Ulysses S. Grant Joseph Longstreet
George McClellan	1846	2/59	Stonewall Jackson George Pickett Ulysses S. Grant

Stonewall Jackson	1846	17/59	George McClellan George Pickett Ulysses S. Grant
John Bell Hood	1853	44/52	John Schofield George Thomas (Artillery Instructor) Robert E. Lee (Superintendent) Jeb Stuart
John Schofield	1853	7/52	John Bell Hood Robert E. Lee (Superintendent)
Jeb Stuart	1854	13/46	Robert E. Lee (Superintendent) John Schofield John Bell Hood
George Armstrong Custer	1862	34/34	—

This table shows who knew whom at West Point.

1862
The Western Theater: Bragg Drags His Feet

Braxton Bragg and his army sat in Murfreesboro, Tennessee, thirty miles south of Nashville. It was early October of 1862, three weeks after Lee and McClellan had fought at Antietam Creek in Maryland. Bragg had recently won a tactical victory at Perryville, Kentucky, but then ordered his men to withdraw from Kentucky after midnight. One observer described his behavior as a "perplexity and vacillation which had now become simply appalling" to his officers. Bragg explained in a letter to his wife: ". . . my crime would have been unpardonable had I kept my noble little army to be ice-bound in a northern clime, without tents or shoes, and obliged to forage daily for bread, etc."

During his Kentucky invasion, Bragg had proclaimed: "Kentuckians, I have entered your State . . . and offer you an opportunity to free yourselves from the tyranny of a despotic ruler. We come . . . to restore to you the liberties of which you have been deprived by a cruel and relentless foe. We come to . . . punish with a rod of iron the despoilers of your peace, and to avenge the cowardly insults to your women . . ."[506]

[506] Foote, vol. 1, pp. 655, 739.

Bragg's soldiers were not happy with his retreat from Kentucky and many wanted him removed from command. He now sat south of Nashville, which was occupied by Union forces led by William Rosecrans. Braxton Bragg was 45 years old.[507]

A North Carolinian, Bragg had graduated 5th out of 50 at West Point 25 years earlier. He fought well under Jefferson Davis in the Mexican-American War, resigning from the U.S. army after 19 years of service in order to become a sugar plantation owner in Louisiana with his wife, a wealthy sugar heiress. During his military service, Bragg had publicly criticized his commanders to such an extent that he was found guilty in a court-martial for disobeying orders and disrespecting superior officers. He was suspended for two months. Braxton Bragg had a terrible temper and was considered the most cantankerous man in the army. Though he owned more than 100 slaves, Bragg opposed secession on the grounds that it was not constitutionally possible.[508]

Jefferson Davis visited Bragg in Murfreesboro in December to assess the situation. Then, on the day after Christmas, William Rosecrans and 44,000 Union soldiers advanced from Nashville toward Bragg, who had 37,713 men. By December 30, the two armies stood only 700 yards apart. On the last day of 1862, Bragg assaulted at dawn.[509]

Rosecrans had planned to attack after breakfast, but Bragg got the jump on him, driving the Union forces back more than two miles and capturing 3,000 men and 28 cannon. As one Confederate private recalled, he and his fellow soldiers "swooped down on those Yankees like a whirl-a-gust of woodpeckers in a hail storm." Later that day, Bragg attacked across a rocky, heavily wooded stretch of land known as Hell's Half-Acre, sending his troops straight toward heavy artillery that repulsed them. He tried three more attacks that day, all failing with devastating results. One of those attacks was led by John Breckenridge, who had served as vice

---

[507] Ibid., p. 773; http://www.battlefields.org/learn/civil-war/battles/stones-river, p. 2, accessed May 2, 2021; https://www.historynet.com/battle-of-chattanooga, p. 2.

[508] McWhiney, pp. 5–9, 24–25, 39–88, 141–143; Woodworth (1990), p. 92; de Bachelle Seebold, p. 223; Eicher and Eicher, p. 140; Foote, vol. 2, p. 170.

[509] Foote, vol. 2, pp. 82–83; http://www.battlefields.org/learn/civil-war/battles/stones-river, p. 2, accessed May 2, 2021.

president of the United States until the war broke out. After 11 hours, the fighting stopped.[510]

The Union forces managed to hold their ground, though they suffered large casualties. By nightfall, they were pinned against the Stones River. Bragg wired Jefferson Davis saying, "The enemy has yielded his strong position and is falling back. We occupy whole field and shall follow him." But both armies then sat for two days.

Bragg assumed that Rosecrans would retreat to Nashville. Rosecrans did not, though he certainly considered it. He mistakenly thought that some of the Confederates had gotten between him and Nashville, making retreat impossible. Though Bragg had driven the Union army back, he could not finish it off. As Foote puts it, "Convinced that he had won a victory, he apparently did not know what to do with it . . . What he mainly wanted, still, was for the enemy to admit defeat by retreating . . ."[511]

William Rosecrans

William Rosecrans, a 43-year-old Ohioan, had been slow in moving toward Bragg at Murfreesboro. In early December of 1862, he had received word from the head of the war department in Washington: "If you remain one more week in Nashville, I cannot prevent your removal." In his characterstic way, Rosecrans replied, "To threats of removal or the like I must be permitted to say that I am insensible." Rosecrans reportedly declared that he would not obey a direct order to move ahead until his army was ready for action "down to the final shoe nail in the final pair of shoes." He also indicated that he did not intend to move forward until he could "throw in a couple of million rations." Then Rosecrans finally began his march toward Bragg.[512]

Nicknamed "Rosy" at West Point, Rosecrans graduated 5th in a class of 56 cadets. He was therefore an engineer. One of his classmates was James Longstreet, whom he would later fight at Chickamauga. He

---

510 Foote, vol. 2, pp. 87, 89–93.

511 http://www.battlefields.org/learn/civil-war/battles/stones-river, p. 3, accessed May 2, 2021; Foote, vol. 2, pp. 18, 93–97.

512 Cozzens (1990), p. 26; Lamers, pp. 195–196; Foote, vol. 1, pp. 768–769.

then served as a professor at West Point before resigning from the army to pursue a civil engineering career, first running a successful mining business and then building an oil refinery.[513]

William Rosecrans

Rosecrans had a large, red nose and became known as "Old Rosy" to his soldiers during the war. But his "brusque, outspoken manner and willingness to quarrel openly with superiors" caused him problems. For example, he and Grant did not get along, with Rosecrans serving under him in Mississippi earlier in the war and failing to follow his orders. Grant was delighted when Rosecrans was sent off to head the troops facing Braxton Bragg in Tennessee.[514]

Ulysses S. Grant

In February of 1862, Ulysses S. Grant had captured Fort Donelson, 80 miles northwest of Nashville on the Cumberland River. The Confederates

---

[513] https://en.m.wikipedia.org/wiki/William_Rosecrans, pp. 6–9, accessed May 29, 2021.

[514] https://en.m.wikipedia.org/wiki/William_Rosecrans, pp. 4, 19–27 accessed May 29, 2021. Lamers, pp. 133–135; Woodworth, p. 229; Cozzens (1997), pp. 251–252; Foote, p. 725.

there yielded to his demand for the "unconditional and immediate surrender" of 12,000 soldiers. Thereafter, Grant was known as U. S. "Unconditional Surrender" Grant. Despite reports of Grant's drinking habits, Lincoln promoted him to major general of the volunteer troops. Lincoln may have said that, with the results that Grant was getting, if Grant was drinking whiskey then it should be ordered for every general in the army. Grant was 39 years old. He would later accept the surrender of two more Confederate armies, one at Vicksburg and another at Appomattox.[515]

Grant graduated from West Point 18 years before the war broke out. His name at birth was Hiram Ulysses Grant, but the U.S. representative who nominated him to West Point incorrectly submitted his name as Ulysses Sidney Grant and he was enrolled as Ulysses S. Grant. His classmates called him 'Sam," since to them *U.S.* stood for Uncle Sam. He was raised in Ohio and his father was a staunch abolitionist. Graduating 21st in his class of 39, Grant was quiet-natured and had few close friends, one being Confederate general James Longstreet. Grant stood at five feet, seven inches. Though he was a skilled horseman, he was assigned to the infantry in accordance with the West Point pecking order based on class standing.[516]

In the Mexican-American War, Grant served with distinction for bravery and competence. As an assistant quartermaster, he learned military logistics and supply routes, particularly with respect to a large, mobile army in enemy territory. Grant believed, however, that the Mexican-American War was unjust and that it was designed to expand

---

[515] Simpson (2014), pp. 2–3; Longacre (2006), pp. 6–7; White, pp. 9–10; Groom, pp. 138, 143–144; Brands, pp. 164–165; Smith (2001), pp. 125–134; "Blair's Bitters," *New York Times*, October 30, 1863, p. 4, column 4.

[516] Hesseltine, p. 4; Poore and Tiffany, p. 12; McFeely, p. 12; Smith (2001), pp. 24, 28–29, 83; Simon (1967), pp. 3–4; Kahan, p. 2; White, pp. 30, 43; Brands, pp. 12–13; Chernow (2017), pp. 19, 27; Longacre (2006), p. 21; Cullum (1850), pp. 256–257. There are other plausible explanations for how he became known as U.S. Grant. See Garland (1898), pp. 30–31.

slavery. He also felt that the Civil War was "divine punishment" on the United States for its aggression against Mexico.[517]

After the Mexican-American War, Grant served in the army in Michigan and New York, and thereafter in California, where he began drinking. The extent to which he drank is a subject of debate, with some saying that he was a highly functioning alcoholic. Others say that his drinking was often exaggerated by the press and by his rivals and critics. After six years of military service, he resigned from his position as an army captain at age 32, returning to St. Louis in July of 1854 to be with his wife and child. Grant was reportedly forced to resign for being caught drunk on duty. For the next seven years he struggled financially, having food but little else for his family. He farmed for four years, but gave it up after contracting malaria. He then worked, unsuccessfully, as a bill collector. In April of 1860, he moved to Galena, Illinois, to work in his father's tannery.[518]

When the Civil War broke out, Grant sought to be reinstated as an officer. George McClellan denied his request. So, instead, Grant joined the Illinois militia in April of 1861. Four months later, he was appointed brigadier general in the U.S. army, but commanded only volunteers. In a letter to his father, he wrote: "There are but two parties now, Traitors and Patriots . . ."[519]

After Fort Donelson, Grant headed south 140 miles to Corinth, Mississippi, where in April of 1862 the Confederates launched a surprise attack near Shiloh church with heavy casualties on both sides. Grant counterattacked the following morning, forcing the Confederates to retreat. Technically, Grant won the battle. But he was sharply criticized in the Northern newspapers for his heavy casualties. Grant considered resigning, but Sherman, who was there, talked him out of it. As Lincoln

---

[517] Tucker, p. 271; White, pp. 75, 80; https://en.wikipedia.org/wiki/Ulysses_S._Grant, p. 6, accessed April 28, 2021; McFeely, pp. 30–31, 37–38.

[518] McFeely, pp. 52, 55, 64–66, 77; Cullum (1891), p. 171; Chernow (2017), pp. 81–85; Farina, pp. 13, 202; "The Problem of Ulysses S. Grant's Drinking During the Civil War." Lyle W. Dorsett, *Hayes Historical Journal.* (1983) 4 (2): 37–49; Brands, pp. 77–78, 89–96; White, pp. 129–136; https://www.history.com/news/10-things-you-may-not-know-about-ulysses-s-grant, p. 3, accessed June 14, 2021; Waugh, pp. 39–40.

[519] Brands, p. 123; Bonekemper (2012), p. 21.

put it, "I can't spare this man: he fights." The Confederates abandoned Corinth in late May of 1862 and the last Confederate stronghold on the Mississippi River stood at Vicksburg, nearly 300 miles to the southwest.[520]

In November of 1862, Grant ordered his troops to incorporate former slaves into his army and to give them clothes, shelter, and wages. He had approximately 40,000 men. A month later, he issued an order expelling all Jews from his army. Why he did this is not known. Lincoln rescinded that order two weeks later. Grant was said to be hitting the bottle again. And one Chicago journalist reported hearing soldiers declare that Grant "never did amount to anything, and never would." Rosecrans, who was serving under Grant, requested a transfer out of his army.[521]

Joseph Johnston

After Joe Johnston recovered from the wound he suffered in June at Seven Pines while fighting McClellan on the Peninsula, he replaced Bragg as the Confederate commander of the entire Western Theater on November 24, 1862. And though Jefferson Davis was unhappy with Bragg's performance at Stones River, Johnston refused to assume field command there. So Bragg kept dealing with Rosecrans in Tennessee, while Johnston went to Mississippi to face Grant and Sherman.[522]

William Tecumseh Sherman

Though the Union army had gotten smeared early in the war at Bull Run, William Sherman was one of the few union officers who performed well

---

[520] Bonekemper (2012), pp. 59, 63–64; Smith (2001), p. 206; McFeely, p. 115; "Grant's Drinking or... The Beast That Will Not Die." Mike Kaplan, *Journal of Military History*, October 2015, 79 (4): pp. 1109–1119; White, pp. 223–226, 230–231; Brands, pp. 188–91.

[521] Flood, p. 133; Brands, pp. 218, 221–23; Catton (1960), p. 112; "During the Civil War, Gen. Ulysses Grant Began Expelling Southern Jews—Until Lincoln Stepped In." Erin Blakemore, *History.com*, https://www.history.com/news/ulysses-grant-expulsion- civil-war, accessed May 25, 2022; Shevitz, p. 256; Smith (2001), pp. 226–227; Miller (2019), p. 260; Foote, vol. 1, pp. 760–763.

[522] Woodworth, pp. 196–99; Symonds (1992), pp. 193–201.

there. In doing so, he impressed Lincoln, who promoted him to brigadier general in May of 1861 and sent him to protect the neutral border state of Kentucky. Sherman had graduated 6th out of 42 cadets at West Point in 1840, but he did not want such a high position. He felt tremendous stress, overestimating the size of the Confederate forces in Kentucky and requesting huge numbers of reinforcements. Ultimately, he asked to be relieved of command. His request was granted in early November and he was reassigned to a lesser position in St. Louis, where he was found to be unfit for duty. Sherman had hallucinations and contemplated suicide. The *Cincinnati Commercial* newspaper labelled him "insane." His wife picked him up in St. Louis and took him home in early December to recuperate in Lancaster, Ohio. Three weeks later, he returned to St. Louis in better condition and by February of 1862 he was back in action, serving in the Western Theater under Ulysses S. Grant. [523]

At the Battle of Shiloh, Tennessee, in April of 1862, Sherman was caught unprepared for the surprise Confederate attack, yet managed to conduct an orderly, fighting retreat that averted disaster. Three horses were shot out from under him during the battle. Sherman told Grant: "Before the battle of Shiloh, I was cast down by a mere newspaper assertion of 'crazy,' but that single battle gave me new life, and I'm now in high feather." As historian John Winters observes: "Although he was impatient, often irritable and depressed, petulant, headstrong, and unreasonably gruff, he had solid soldierly qualities. His men swore by him and most of his fellow officers admired him."[524]

---

[523] Sherman, pp. 200, 210, 216; Hirshson, pp. 90–94, 109; After Bull Run, Sherman explained to Lincoln, "my extreme desire to serve in a subordinate capacity, and in no event to be left in a superior command. He promised me this with promptness, making the jocular remark that his chief trouble was to find places for the too many generals who wanted to be at the head of affairs, to command armies, etc." in Simpson and Berlin, pp. 174, 176; *Cincinnati Commercial*, December 11, 1861; Marszalek (1992), pp. 162, 164.

[524] Eicher and Eicher, p. 485; Smith (2001), p. 212: "Ulysses in His Tent: Halleck, Grant, Sherman, and the Turning Point of the War." Carl R. Schenker, Jr., *Civil War History*, June 2010, vol. 56, no. 2, p. 175; Winters, p. 176.

Eastern Theater		Western Theatre
	April 1861	Battle of Fort Sumter Starts the War
Battle of First Bull Run in Virginia; McClellan arrives in Washington	July 1861	
	December 1861	Sherman found unfit to serve and sent home
McClellan sails to Virginia Peninsula	March 1862	
McClellan is surprise attacked by Johnston near Richmond	June 1862	
Lincoln sends Pope south toward Richmond; Jackson destroys Manassas depot behind Pope; Pope loses Second Bull Run battle and replaced by McClellan	August 1862	
Narrow Union victory at Antietam; Lee escapes across Potomac River	September 1862	
	October 1862	Bragg wins at Perryville, Kentucky but then retreats to Murfreesboro, Tennessee
	November 1862	Johnston replaces Bragg as commander of Western Theater, but Bragg still in field command in Tennessee
	December 1862	Union troops arrive in Murfreesboro
Emancipation Proclamation effective	January 1863	Battle of Stones River
Battle of Chancellorsville, Virginia	May 1863	
Battle of Gettysburg, Pennsylvania	July 1863	Confederate surrender at Vicksburg
	July 1863	Bragg reaches Chattanooga
	September 1863	Battle of Chickamauga, during which Rosecrans retreats to Chattanooga
	October 1863	Jefferson Davis in Chattanooga; Grant arrives two weeks later

Lincoln delivers Gettysburg Address	November 1863	Sherman arrives in Chattanooga; siege broken
	December 1863	Bragg resigns after Chattanooga siege is broken; Johnston replaces him
Grant becomes commander of all Union armies and of Eastern Theater field	March 1864	
Battle of The Wilderness (Virginia); Jeb Stuart and Stonewall Jackson killed	May 1864	
Battle of Cold Harbor (Virginia)	June 1864	Battle of Kennesaw Mountain (Georgia)
The Crater Explosion at Petersburg	July 1864	Hood replaces Johnston in Atlanta
	September 1864	Sherman captures Atlanta
	November 1864	Sherman begins March to the Sea
	November 1864	Battle of Franklin, Tennessee
	December 1864	Battle of Nashville
	December 1864	Sherman captures Savannah
Breakthrough at the Petersburg shad bake	April 2, 1865	
Richmond falls, Jefferson Davis flees	April 3, 1865	
Lee surrenders at Appomattox, Virginia	April 9, 1865	
Lincoln assassinated	April 14, 1865	
	April 26, 1865	Johnston surrenders in North Carolina
	May 1865	Bragg and Davis captured in Georgia
	May 1865	Hood surrenders in Mississippi

1863
The Eastern Theater: Lee Stumbles Upon Gettysburg

Gettysburg, only 85 miles from Washington, had a population of 2,400 in July of 1863. Robert E. Lee had just won the Battle of Chancellorsville in May and was brimming with confidence. This was his second march north. Though his first—nearly one year earlier—had failed at Antietam, Lee intended to march as far as Harrisburg or Philadelphia in the hope that doing so might persuade the Union to abandon the war, or encourage European recognition of the Confederacy, or entice the Union to transfer some of its troops away from Vicksburg, which was under siege by Grant. On his way to Gettysburg, Lee's army kidnapped 1,000 black civilians and sent them south into slavery.[525]

During his march northward, Lee allowed his jackass cavalry commander, Jeb Stuart, to take off around the east flank of the Union army. Stuart was notorious for riding in a circle around the opposing army. This time he disappeared for eight days. During his absence, Lee's army ran into the Union army due to lack of scouting. In fact, Lee first learned from a spy that the Union army was nearby.[526]

Some of Lee's men went into Gettysburg to look for shoes. Instead, they found Union soldiers. They reported to their officers that they saw what appeared to be part of a small Union cavalry unit. The next morning, several thousand Confederates went back to town to find those

---

[525] https://www.history.com/topics/american-civil-war/battle-of-gettysburg, p. 1, May 7, 2021; Symonds (2001), pp. 49–54; Loewen at p. 350 says: "Lee's troops seized scores of free black people in Maryland and Pennsylvania and sent them south into slavery. This was in keeping with Confederate national policy, which virtually re-enslaved free people of color into work gangs on earthworks throughout the south"; https://www.post-gazette.com/news/state/2013/06/30/Confederates-slave-hunt-in-North-a-military-disgrace/stories/201306300221; "The Soldiers' Flag?" Brooks D. Simpson, *Crossroads*, July 5, 2015, WordPress, https://wordpress.com, accessed May 22, 2022. Simpson says: "[T]he Army of Northern Virginia was under orders to capture and send south supposed escaped slaves during that army's invasion of Pennsylvania in 1863."

[526] https://www.battlefields.org/learn/civil-war/battles/gettysburg, p. 2, May 7, 2021; Foote, vol. 2, pp. 460–461.

shoes. They did not suspect that they were approaching the greatest battle of the war. It was July 1, 1863. In town, the Union cavalry formed in a line and fighting ensued. By the end of the day, the Union forces had retreated half a mile south to high ground at Cemetery Hill. When one Union commander was asked whether that high ground was the right location for a battle, he replied: "I think this the strongest position by nature upon which to fight a battle that I ever saw."[527]

Lee no doubt understood the strategic value of higher ground and he ordered one of his generals to take Cemetery Hill "if practicable." That officer determined that doing so was not practicable, so he did not attempt it. As a result, Lee's army missed an opportunity to seize the higher ground for battle before the rest of the Union army arrived.[528]

On July 2, most of the remaining solders on both sides arrived in Gettysburg, with some having marched 28 miles in 11 hours to get there. The Union army now had 94,000 soldiers. Lee had 72,000. Jeb Stuart was still riding around the countryside. Fighting took place throughout the day with more than 9,000 casualties on each side. Jeb Stuart's cavalry finally arrived around noon, but did not participate in the fighting that day.[529]

---

[527] Foote, vol. 2, pp. 461, 465; Eicher, pp. 508–509, disputes the claim that Confederate soldiers returned the next day seeking shoes, since their visit the day before would have made the lack of shoe factories or stores obvious. However, many historians accept this account, including: Sears (2003), pp. 136, 223–225; Foote, p. 465; Clark, p. 35; Tucker, pp. 97–98; Martin (1996), p. 25; Pfanz (2001), pp. 25, 294, 337–338.

[528] Pfanz (2001), p. 344; Eicher, p. 517; Sears (2003), p. 228; Trudeau (2002), p. 253. Both Sears and Trudeau say that instead the order said "if possible."

[529] Longstreet, pp. 364–368; Sears (2003), p. 257; Longacre (1896), pp. 198–199; https://www.battlefields.org/learn/civil-war/battles/gettysburg, p. 2, accessed May 7, 2021; https://www.history.com/topics/american-civil-war/battle-of-gettysburg, p. 2, accessed May 7, 2021..

Robert E. Lee

On the third and final day of the battle at Gettysburg, Lee ordered George Pickett's division to attack near the center of the Union line on the high ground. One of Lee's generals objected, but was overruled. Lee believed his men were invincible and he rejected a suggestion that he select a more favorable ground on which to fight.[530] Pickett got creamed.

The following day was July 4, 1863. In Vicksburg, Mississippi, the Confederates surrendered to Grant. In Gettysburg, Lee retreated. The Union army learned the next day of Lee's retreat, but did not aggressively pursue him, though Lincoln repeatedly urged it to do so. The Potomac River was swollen with rainwater and the pontoon bridge that Lee's army had used to cross it before the battle was destroyed. Lee's army was trapped against the river, waiting for the Union army to arrive. It did not. The Union commander, George Meade, was by nature cautious. He knew that Lee was dangerous when he appeared otherwise, particularly when in retreat.[531]

---

[530] Longstreet, pp. 386–387; Sears (2003), pp. 499–500; Glatthaar, p. 287; Fuller, p. 198, states that Lee's "overweening confidence in the superiority of his soldiers over his enemy possessed him."

[531] Foote, vol. 2, p. 587.

On July 7, Meade took a hot bath in a nearby hotel while the enemy remained trapped on the near side of the Potomac. Three days later, on July 10, Lee was still trapped against the Potomac, but the roads were drying. Meade had 85,000 soldiers with 10,000 more on the way, more than double the number of Confederates in front of him. But he stayed still. On July 14, he finally moved forward, but by the time he reached the riverbank Lee was gone. The trapped army had torn down houses and floated the timbers downstream to build pontoons for its escape. Total casualties from both sides at Gettysburg were 57,225. Gettysburg is considered by many to be the most important battle of the Civil War, often described as its turning point. Yet the war would continue for nearly two more years.[532]

Lincoln came to Gettysburg four months later for the dedication of the National Cemetery there. The principal speaker was an orator from Massachusetts who had been lined up several weeks earlier. Lincoln was asked as an afterthought to say "a few appropriate remarks," which he prepared the night before in his guest room at Gettysburg. The main orator spoke for two hours. In contrast, Lincoln's remarks were so brief that he was finished speaking before the photographer could take his photo. Puzzled, scattered applause followed Lincoln's words.[533]

> Fourscore and seven years ago our fathers brought forth upon this continent a new nation, conceived in liberty and dedicated to the proposition that all men are created equal. Now we are engaged in a great civil war, testing whether the nation, or any nation so conceived and so dedicated, can long endure. We are met on a great battlefield of that war. We are met to dedicate a portion of it as the final resting place of those who here gave their lives that that nation might live. It is altogether fitting and proper that

---

[532] Ibid., pp. 588, 590–592; Coddington, pp. 535–574; Sears (2003), pp. 496–497; Eicher, p. 596; Wittenberg (2008), pp. 345–346; Donald, p. 446; Woodworth (2003), p. 217.

[533] Foote, vol. 2, pp. 830–832.

> we should do this. But in a larger sense we cannot dedicate, we cannot consecrate, we cannot hallow this ground. The brave men, living and dead, who struggled here, have consecrated it far above our poor power to add or detract. The world will little note, nor long remember, what we say here, but it can never forget what they did here. It is for us, the living, rather, to be dedicated here to the unfinished work that they have this far so nobly carried on. It is rather for us to be here dedicated to the great task remaining before us, that from these honored dead we take increased devotion to that cause for which they here gave the last full measure of devotion; that we here highly resolve that these dead shall not have died in vain; that the nation shall, under God, have a new birth of freedom; and that government of the people, by the people, for the people, shall not perish from the earth.[534]

Jeb Stuart

Before Gettysburg, Jeb Stuart had fought well under Lee, though he had stumbled at Brandy Station. There, shortly after parading his cavalry to impress Lee, he was surprise attacked by the Union army. After ten hours of fighting, the Union troops withdrew across the Rappahannock River. Stuart claimed victory because he had held his position. But he was roasted by the other Confederate commanders and the Southern press. The *Richmond Examiner* called his cavalry "puffed up" and its leader "vain and weak-headed."[535]

---

534 https://www.history.com/topics/american-civil-war/battle-of-gettysburg, p. 4, accessed May 7, 2021.

535 Longacre (1986), pp. 40–41, 65–86; Sears (2003), pp. 62–64; Salmon, pp. 193, 199–203; Wert (2008), p. 239, 241–252; Davis (1957), pp. 305–312; www.civildiscourse-historyblog.com/blog/2015/5/20/scapegoat-or-scandal-jeb-stuart-and-the-battle-of-gettysburg, p. 1, accessed May 19, 2021.

Then, at Gettysburg, Stuart disappeared for his eight-day ride to go around the Union army yet again, perhaps in an effort to rescue his reputation after Brandy Station. Lee had ordered Stuart to guard Lee's army, to keep Lee informed of the enemy's movements, and to connect with General Ewell. Aware of Stuart's "fondness for adventure at any price," Lee had even gave him written orders to the same effect.[536] However, when Stuart set off with his cavalry, he encountered Union cavalry and veered off course so that he could accomplish his big ride. This prevented him from connecting with Ewell.

Stuart saw several warning signs during his big ride, but kept pushing on, straying farther and farther from his orders. And half of the cavalry soldiers he had left behind with Lee were so inexperienced that Lee did not trust their ability. The other half were experienced cavalrymen who were assigned by Stuart to guard Lee's supply line while he was gone; they were relegated to that meager role because one of their commanders had embarrassed Stuart in front of Lee and another had been engaged to Stuart's wife before the war.[537]

So Lee had no idea where Stuart or the enemy was. In essence, Lee was lost. The first rule about being lost is that you must admit that you are lost. The second rule is that, after you have admitted that you are lost, do not wander about pretending otherwise. Lee wandered about, making things worse. He groped his way across Pennsylvania, while sending out scouts to try to find Stuart, who was busy capturing nearly 400 enemy soldiers and 125 supply wagons. Lee assumed that the Union army was on the far side of the Potomac River, until he ran into it at Gettysburg. The enemy had in fact been on the same side of the river with him for two days.[538]

---

[536] Foote, vol. 2, p. 441; https://en.wikipedia.org/wiki/J._E._B._Stuart, p. 9; www.civildiscourse-historyblog.com/blog/2015/5/20/scapegoat-or-scandal-jeb-stuart-and-the-battle-of-gettysburg, p. 6, accessed May 19, 2021.

[537] www.civildiscourse-historyblog.com/blog/2015/5/20/scapegoat-or-scandal-jeb-stuart-and-the-battle-of-gettysburg, p. 13, accessed May 19, 2021.

[538] https://en.wikipedia.org/wiki/J._E._B._Stuart, p. 9; www.civildiscourse-historyblog.com/blog/2015/5/20/scapegoat-or-scandal-jeb-stuart-and-the-battle-of-gettysburg, p. 5, accessed May 19, 2021; Foote, vol. 2, pp. 445, 455, 461.

Of course, Stuart likewise had no idea where Lee was. Stuart even considered dashing into Washington on a surprise attack, but abandoned that idea. In fact, the Union army was *between* Stuart and Lee.[539]

The Union army at Gettysburg was under the command of General George Meade, whose stated goal was "to find and fight the enemy." However, he decided not to assume the offensive until the Confederates were positioned in a way that would assure Union success. As chance would have it, the Confederates chased the front portion of Meade's troops up Cemetery Hill. It was on this high ground that the Battle of Gettysburg was fought, with the Union army having both superior position and superior numbers. Lee's army had indeed positioned itself in a way that would assure Union success. Despite the obvious military disadvantage, Lee attacked.[540]

When Stuart finally showed up at mid-day on the second day of the battle, Lee said, "Well, General, you are here at last." Stuart's men and horses were too exhausted to fight that day after running all over the countryside.[541]

On the third and final day of the Battle of Gettysburg, Stuart's cavalry of 6,000 was repulsed by the Union cavalry of 5,000 under the command of George Armstrong Custer, who led the Michigan cavalry hollering "Come on, you Wolverines!" Custer rode four horse lengths ahead of his men, his "yellow ringlets streaming in the wind." Stuart withdrew from the battle, but claimed in his report that the enemy "vanished" before him "like grain before the scythe."

Custer's cavalry brigade would, by the time the war ended, have more of its men killed and wounded than any other cavalry brigade in the Union army. Of Gettysburg, Custer wrote, "I challenge the annals of warfare to produce a more brilliant or successful charge of cavalry." For his gallantry, Custer was promoted to major. He would ultimately reach the wartime rank of major general. Custer saw extensive action at Bull Run, Antietam, Chancellorsville, Gettysburg, Petersburg, and

---

[539] Foote, vol. 2, pp. 456, 459.

[540] Ibid., p. 466.

[541] Sears (2002), pp. 257–258; Longacre (2002), at pp. 215–216, states that a bitter confrontation, however, never took place; Foote, vol. 2, p. 461.

Appomattox. Throughout the war, he narrowly escaped death and severe wounds. Seven of his horses did not.[542]

J.E.B. Stuart

Over time, Jeb Stuart has become one of the scapegoats for Lee's loss at Gettysburg, in accordance with the Lost Cause narrative. Though there is much debate among historians about Stuart's behavior at Gettysburg, it is generally agreed that he acted "injudiciously." Lee has been criticized for issuing an order that allowed Stuart to use discretion. Lee also had 5,000 cavalry soldiers at his disposal while Stuart was out riding around, but he did not use them to find out where the enemy was.[543]

542 Longacre (1986), pp. 220–231; www.civildiscourse-historyblog.com/blog/2015/5/20/scapegoat-or-scandal-jeb-stuart-and-the-battle-of-gettysburg, p. 8, accessed May 19, 2021; Foote, vol. 2, pp. 569–572; Robbins (2006), p. 268.

543 Coddington, pp. 205–208; Longacre (2002), pp. 215–216; Longacre (1986), p. 271; Wittenberg and Petruzzi (2006), pp. 263–298; Wert (2008), pp. 299–302; www.civildiscourse-historyblog.com/blog/2015/5/20/scapegoat-or-scandal-jeb-stuart-and-the-battle-of-gettysburg, p. 9, accessed May 19, 2021.

Stonewall Jackson

Thomas Jonathan Jackson graduated 17th out of 59 students at West Point 15 years before the war broke out. A Virginian, he served in the Mexican-American War and then taught at Virginia Military Institute for ten years. Jackson was stern, eccentric, and unpopular with his students. He owned six slaves and organized Sunday School classes for blacks at the Presbyterian Church. One pastor described Jackson as being "emphatically the black man's friend." Historian James Roberston says that Jackson "neither apologized for nor spoke in favor of the practice of slavery. Yet in his mind the Creator had sanctioned slavery, and man had no moral right to challenge its existence."[544]

Jackson was also a hypochondriac, standing for long periods at a time to keep his internal organs in place. He could sleep anywhere at any time and occasionally fell asleep with food in his mouth. Largely deaf in both ears from serving as an artillery officer in the Mexican-American War, Jackson was also fanatically religious, believing the Civil War to be a religious crusade and refusing to fight on Sunday.[545]

Stonewall Jackson did not live long enough to fight at Gettysburg. Two months earlier, in May of 1863, at Chancellorsville, Virginia, he had taken his 30,000 men and launched a surprise attack against Union soldiers, driving them back two miles. They were in "The Wilderness," a 70-square-mile area covered with thick, tangled bushes and vines. That night, Jackson went in front of his lines to survey the situation for the next day. Returning through the thick, dark woods, he was mistaken for a Union soldier and shot three times by his own soldiers. His arm was

---

[544] Robertson, pp. 169, 191.

[545] "Educator Carleton H. Prothro Takes Up Stonewall Jackson for United Daughters of the Confederacy." *Minden Press-Herald*, Minden, Louisiana, September 24, 1989, p. 8; Cartmell, pp. 187–192; See "Onward Christian Soldier." *New York Times Book Review*, March 16, 1997, by Stephen W. Sears discussing Robertson's *Stonewall Jackson: The Man, The Soldier, The Legend*; http://www.nytimes.com/books/97/03/16/reviews/970316.16searst.html; See "Stonewall Jackson Biographer Says Religion Drove Civil War General." Davin White, *Charleston Gazette, October 15, 2010*; https://www.history.com/news/10-things-you-may-not-know-about-ulysses-s-grant, p. 32, accessed June 14, 2021.

amputated the next day and he died of pneumonia one week later at the age of 39, declaring "I have always desired to die on Sunday." Jackson's final words were: "Let us cross over the river and rest under the shade of the trees." His sister, Laura, wrote that she "would rather know that he was dead than to have him a leader in the rebel army." Stonewall Jackson is buried in Lexington, Virginia. His arm is buried at Locust Grove, 112 miles away, and has its own monument.[546]

George Pickett

George Pickett was a West Point graduate and the oldest of eight children from a prominent family in Richmond. At West Point, he was the "goat," graduating last in his class out of 59 cadets (as was Custer, 15 years later). One of his classmates was George McClellan.[547]

Pickett was a popular prankster, caring little about class standing and doing just enough to graduate. Normally, he would have been placed at some obscure posting, but the Mexican-American War had broken out and junior officers were needed. After the Mexican-American War, he went to what is now Washington State to oversee the construction of Fort Bellingham. When Virginia seceded, Pickett tried to resign in Bellingham, but was told that his resignation must occur in Washington, D.C., so he rode on a boat from Tacoma to the Isthmus of Panama, where he walked 40 miles overland to catch a ship to Richmond, where

546 "How in the World Did They Shoot Stonewall Jackson?" Kristopher White, https://www.historynet.comhow-in-the-world-did-they-shoot-stonewall-jackson.htm, p. 3, accessed May 9, 2021; Hattaway and Jones, p. 415; Woodworth (2003), p. xiii; Coddington, p. 573; Glatthaar, p. 288; Bearss, p. 202; https://www.history.com/news/10-things-you-may-not-know-about-ulysses-s-grant, pp. 5, 30, accessed June 14, 2021; Confederate General Thomas J. "Stonewall" Jackson dies, https://www.history.com/this-day-in-history/thomas-j-stonewall-jackson-dies, accessed May 9, 2021; McGuire, pp. 162–163; "Laura Jackson Arnold: Sister of General Thomas Jonathan Stonewall Jackson." *Civil War Women Blog*. November 29, 2010; "Stonewall Jackson's Arm." James Sorensen, *American Heritage*, April/May 2005; "The Curious Fate of Stonewall Jackson's Arm." https://www.npr.org, June 28, 2012.

547 Eicher and Eicher, p. 428; Foote, vol. 2, pp. 530–531, 571.

he joined the Confederate army. He then proceeded to Washington to resign from the United States army.[548]

Pickett had style. As historian Larry Tagg describes him: "Pickett made a colorful general. He rode a sleek black charger named 'Old Black,' and wore a small blue kepi-style cap, with buffed gloves over the sleeves of an immaculately tailored uniform that had a double row of gold buttons on the coat, and shiny gold spurs on his highly polished boots. He held an elegant riding crop whether mounted or walking. His mustache drooped gracefully beyond the corners of his mouth and then turned upward at the ends. His hair was the talk of the Army: 'long ringlets flowed loosely over his shoulders, trimmed and highly perfumed, his beard likewise was curling and giving up the scent of Araby.'"[549]

After Lee bombarded the Union line at Gettysburg with 150 cannon for two hours, Pickett's 12,500 men advanced over nearly one mile of open field to approach the Union line. The results were devastating; more than half of Pickett's soldiers did not return. Some reached the union line, where hand-to-hand combat ensued. As his retreating soldiers returned, Lee told them, "All this has been my fault." After the charge, 38-year-old George Pickett was inconsolable. When Lee told Pickett to rally his division for defense against a possible counter-attack, he replied, "General, I have no division."[550]

---

548 Eicher and Eicher, p. 428; "At West Point, 'Goats' Are an Exclusive Bunch." Ben Fox Rubin, *The Wall Street Journal*, November 26, 2012.

549 Tagg, pp. 236–237.

550 McPherson (1988), pp. 661–663; Clark, pp. 133–144; Symonds (2001), pp. 214–241; Eicher, pp. 543–549; Tagg, p. 240; Robert E. Lee, https://en.wikipedia.org/wiki/Robert_E._Lee, p. 13, accessed April 28, 2021; https://www.battlefields.org/learn/civil-war/battles/gettysburg, p. 3, accessed May 7, 2021.

George Pickett

Lee later admitted in a letter to Jefferson Davis: "I am alone to blame . . ." He offered his resignation, but Davis refused it. As historian Stephen Sears puts it, Lee was "thoroughly outgeneraled" at Gettysburg. Confederate General Longstreet, who had objected to Pickett's charge, explained in his memoirs: "I thought that it would not do . . . that thirty thousand men was the minimum of force necessary for the work . . . that the column as he proposed to organize it would have only about thirteen thousand men . . . that the column would have to march a mile under concentrating battery fire, and a thousand yards under long-range musketry . . . but he was impatient of listening; and tired of talking; and nothing was left but to proceed." Foote observes: "Gettysburg was the price the South paid for having Robert E. Lee as commander."[551]

Two of the most powerful symbols of the Confederacy are Robert E. Lee and Pickett's Charge. Lee holds a "divine mystique" as the ideal antebellum gentleman who selflessly served his home state. His military accomplishments are celebrated, while his blunder at Gettysburg is overlooked, even though he claimed full responsibility for it. Lee's

551 Longstreet, pp. 386–387; Sears (2003), pp. 499–500, 506; Glatthaar, p. 287; Fuller, p. 198; Coddington, p. 573; https://www.history.com/topics/american-civil-war/battle-of-gettysburg, p. 3, acessed May 7, 2021; *The Civil War, a film by Ken Burns.* Arlington, Virginia: WETA, 2002, https://lccn.loc.gov/2004615082.

subordinates are blamed for lost battles in an attempt to deflect criticism from the Lost Cause icon.[552]

1863
The Western Theater:
The Chattanooga Siege Is Broken

Ulysses S. Grant

After capturing the Mississippi state capitol at Jackson, Grant assaulted the entrenched Confederates at Vicksburg twice, suffering large losses. He then laid siege to Vicksburg for seven weeks. And he drank on occasion. Vicksburg fell on July 4, 1863—one day after the Confederate defeat at Gettysburg. Grant was then promoted to major general of the regular army, rather than of the volunteers. The Union now had control of the Mississippi River. Texas and Arkansas were now physically separated from the rest of the Confederacy.[553]

Braxton Bragg

By January 1, 1863, Braxton Bragg was beginning to realize that he was the one in trouble at Stones River in Murfreesboro. Rosecrans had shifted some of his men and artillery to a hill that posed a direct threat to Bragg's army. Over objections, Bragg ordered 4,500 men to take that hill one hour before sundown on January 2. The Union artillery blasted Bragg's men from two directions, sending them running back to their starting point. Only 2,800 made it. Total casualties on both sides for the two days of fighting were 24,988. Of all of the battles in the Civil War, this one had the highest percentage of casualties on both sides.[554]

---

552 Ulbrich, p. 1222.

553 White, pp. 243, 295; Miller (2019), p. xii; Chernow (2017), p. 236; Smith (2001), pp. 206–257; McFeely, pp. 122–138; Brands, p. 265; Cullum (1891), p. 172; Foote, vol. 1, p. 760.

554 Foote, vol. 2, pp. 98, 100; http://www.battlefields.org/learn/civil-war/battles/stones-river, p. 1, accessed May 2, 2021; https://en.m.wikipedia.org/wiki/William_Rosecrans, p. 31, accessed May 29, 2021.

Bragg's officers urged a retreat, but Bragg replied that the army would hold its position "at every hazard." The following morning, however, he learned that more Union reinforcements had arrived and that the force in front of him was now 70,000. Bragg retreated south to Tullahoma on January 3, giving the Union a narrow victory. As he had done in Kentucky three months earlier, Bragg again won a battle and then retreated. Though Rosecrans had been pinned against the Stones River in Murfreesboro three days earlier, Bragg had not finished him off. Bragg's men were discouraged by his fight-win-fall back pattern. Rosecrans was now cheered by his men, even though he allowed Bragg to withdraw without any pursuit whatsoever.[555]

Six months passed with Bragg and Rosecrans only forty-five miles apart, each getting ready. Bragg was in Tullahoma, Tennessee. He was worn out, his body covered with boils. His army now totaled 49,068.[556]

Braxton Bragg was a compulsive disciplinarian with well-organized troops and commanders who despised him. He had once served both as the commander and the quartermaster at a frontier post. As commander, he submitted a requisition for supplies. As quartermaster, he denied that request. Two unsuccessful assassination attempts were made on his life during his early career, one involving an artillery shell that exploded under his cot. Bragg had rheumatism, dyspepsia, and severe migraines that contributed to his bad personal style.[557]

Rosecrans was still in Murfreesboro, Tennessee, balking at the many urgings from Washington to get on with it. He had 80,124 soldiers, but somehow began to believe that he was outnumbered. As Foote puts it, "Old Rosy was . . . fighting a verbal holding action, not so much against the rebels in his front as against his own superiors in his rear." He rebuffed Lincoln and the secretary of war in their efforts to urge him forward. Rosecrans was simply convinced that he could never be too

---

[555] Foote, vol. 2, pp. 19, 101–103; McWhiney, pp. 350–371; Woodworth (1990), pp. 187–194; http://www.battlefields.org/learn/civil-war/battles/stones-river, p. 3, accessed May 2, 2021.

[556] Foote, vol. 2, pp. 171–173, 669.

[557] Johnson (1885), vol. 3, p. 604 footnote; Woodworth (1990), p. 240.

prepared or have too much of anything. His army at this point had more than 43,000 horses and mules.[558]

Like Bragg, Rosecrans had graduated 5th in his class at West Point. At age 43, he was two years younger than Bragg and was a tall, hard drinking, devout Catholic. Rosecrans cursed like no tomorrow and his moods swung rapidly. Old Rosy received a wire from Washington saying: "Is it your intention to make an immediate movement forward? A definite answer, yes or no, is required." Rosecrans replied: "If immediate means tonight or tomorrow, no. If it means as soon as all things are ready, say five days, yes."[559]

Finally, seven days later, on June 24, 1864, Rosecrans moved toward Bragg in the Tullahoma Campaign. As soon as he went into motion, it began to rain. It continued nonstop for fifteen days in what one Union soldier called "a genuine Baptist downpour." Then Rosecrans tricked Bragg by sending a small group toward the center of Bragg's line, while sending most of his army around one side. Bragg was slow to react. When he finally realized that the Union army was in his rear, he abandoned Tullahoma, hightailing it seventy-five miles farther south to Chattanooga. To his credit, Rosecrans performed brilliantly, outmaneuvering Bragg and incurring low casualties.[560]

---

[558] Foote, vol. 2, pp. 65, 177, 264; https://en.m.wikipedia.org/wiki/William_Rosecrans, p. 34, accessed May 29, 2021; Woodworth (1998), p. 17.

[559] Foote, vol. 2, p. 80; Woodworth (1998), p. 18; https://en.m.wikipedia.org/wiki/William_Rosecrans, p. 35, accessed May 29, 2021.

[560] Foote, vol. 2, p. 668; Woodworth (1998), pp. 19–46; Hallock, pp. 14–27; Lamers, p. 290; Korn, p. 30.

Braxton Bragg

Bragg reached Chattanooga on July 4, 1863, one day after the battle of Gettysburg and on the same day that Vicksburg fell. As Foote says, "After a year of marching nearly a thousand miles and fighting two great battles, both of which he claimed as victories though both were preludes to retreat, Bragg was back where he started."[561]

Rosecrans then pulled a similar trick on Bragg at Chattanooga, shooting cannon on the north side of town while most of his army crossed the river south of town. Bragg abandoned Chattanooga, a major railroad hub, heading south. By this time, Bragg's men were ticked off. In fact, when Rosecrans marched ten miles into Georgia on September of 1863, two of Bragg's officers refused to attack as ordered.

Then Bragg received reinforcements from Mississippi who, under the leadership of Joseph Longstreet (a West Point classmate of Rosecrans), opened a high-priced can of whupass at Chickamauga and sent Rosecrans scrambling back toward Chattanooga. Rosecrans got creamed at Chickamauga due to a clumsily worded order he gave to his men that opened a gap in the Union line rather than closing it. Longstreet jumped on that error, but the price was high due to the number of Confederate casualties. And the victory was not complete.[562]

---

[561] Foote, vol. 2, p. 674.

[562] Woodworth (1998), pp. 52–67; Hallock, pp. 44–53; Cozzens (1992), pp. 163–165.

At Chickamauga, Bragg had hoped to isolate Rosecrans from Chattanooga and destroy his army. But George Thomas, a Union officer, mounted a strong defense that allowed Rosecrans and his army to scamper back to Chattanooga. Thomas was said to have stood "like a rock" and became known as "the Rock of Chickamauga." He urged Rosecrans to return to the Chickamauga battlefield and lead the army, but Rosecrans stayed in Chattanooga. Total casualties on both sides were more than 34,000.[563]

The Confederate troops were incensed that Bragg had not pursued the Union army farther during its retreat into Chattanooga. As one of Bragg's aides put it, "Bragg . . . refused to believe that we had won a victory." In fact, when Bragg first learned of the Union retreat, he doubted it, asking the captain who delivered the news, "Do you know what a retreat looks like?" The man replied, "I ought to, General. I've been with you during your whole campaign." Despite the urgings of his officers, Bragg convinced himself the next morning not to pursue the Union army.

"What does he fight battles for?" one officer fumed.[564]

Then suddenly Bragg realized that by bringing his cannons as far as the high southern edge of Chattanooga, he had unknowingly created a siege. His cannon on Missionary Ridge looked down over the town from the south and his cannon on Lookout Mountain looked down on the town from the west. To the north and the east, the town was bordered by the Tennessee River and there were no bridges other than a temporary pontoon. Rosecrans was trapped in Chattanooga and his supply line was vulnerable. Bragg peered down upon him like Wile E. Coyote upon the Road Runner, stunned by his own good fortune and wondering how best to destroy him. Bragg was content to watch and wait; the siege of Chattanooga was simply a matter of starving out the Union forces and their horses.[565] It was late September of 1863.

---

563 https://en.m.wikipedia.org/wiki/George_Henry_Thomas, p. 17, accessed June 3, 2021; Hallock, pp. 47–87; Woodworth (1998), pp. 79–128.

564 Foote, vol. 2, pp. 757–760.

565 Ibid., p. 761; https://www.historynet.com/battle-of-chattanooga, p. 2, accessed May 29, 2021.

As for Bragg's officers who were incensed that he had not followed up more vigorously in pursuing Rosecrans before he could reach Chattanooga, Bragg relieved them of their commands. His best officer, Longstreet, wrote to the secretary of war, saying "nothing but the hand of God can save us or help us as long as we have our present commander." Things got so bad that Jefferson Davis came to Chattanooga to assess the situation, arriving on October 9, 1863. Davis decided to keep his old friend Bragg in command and to send Longstreet and his men off to Knoxville, reducing Bragg's troops by 25 percent.[566]

One week earlier and unbeknownst to Bragg, 20,000 additional Union soldiers had arrived in Chattanooga from Virginia. The Union now had 65,000 soldiers; Bragg had 52,500. Several days after departing Chattanooga, Jefferson Davis reminded Bragg of the "importance of doing whatever is to be done before the enemy can collect his forces, as the longer the time given him for this purpose, the greater will be the disparity in numbers."[567] Bragg sat.

Sherman, age 43, was also on his way to Chattanooga—from Vicksburg with 20,000 more Union soldiers. Rosecrans was criticized for putting himself in this predicament and accused by journalists of "temporizing" and having "no strength of will and no concentration of purpose." In Lincoln's view, Rosecrans was acting "confused and stunned, like a duck hit on the head."[568]

Bragg knew Sherman personally and considered him a close friend, as they had served together in Charleston, South Carolina. He also knew George Thomas, the Rock of Chickamauga, who had served under him in Charleston and who would remain a life-long friend.[569]

In October of 1863, Grant became head of all the Union armies for the Western Theater. He took a boat 400 miles up the Mississippi River from Vicksburg to Cairo, Illinois. Then he rode 280 miles by train to

---

[566] https://www.historynet.com/battle-of-chattanooga, pp. 2–3; Woodworth (1990), pp. 240, 244.

[567] Foote, vol. 2, pp. 765, 826; https://www.historynet.com/battle-of-chattanooga, p. 3, accessed May 29, 2021.

[568] Foote, vol. 2, pp. 767–768, 805; Cozzens (1992), pp. 520–21; Esposito, map 114; Woodworth (1998), pp. 129–131; Lamers, p. 361.

[569] McWhiney, pp. 34–38.

Bridgeport, Alabama, where he met with Rosecrans 45 miles southwest of Chattanooga. Rosecrans offered "some excellent suggestions," according to Grant, who wrote, "My only wonder was that he had not carried them out." Grant immediately replaced Rosecrans with George Thomas (the Rock), who was instructed to hold onto Chattanooga "at all hazards." Grant then made his way by horse to Chattanooga, arriving shortly after Jefferson Davis had visited Bragg there.[570]

Looking southward from Chattanooga toward Atlanta, Grant studied Missionary Ridge on his left, Lookout Mountain straight ahead, and Raccoon Mountain on the right. He could see the Confederate cannon posted high on the hills. As Foote describes it: "With the help of glasses he could even see the cannoneers lounging about in careless attitudes, as if to emphasize by their idleness the advantage they enjoyed." The Union soldiers only had enough ammunition to last one day. "It looked, indeed, as if but two courses were open, one to starve, the other to surrender or be captured," Grant later remarked.[571]

Within five days after Grant arrived, however, he had restored the Chattanooga supply line, which then brought food and additional soldiers on the way. To restore the supply line, he dislodged the Confederates at Brown's Ferry by sending 1,500 men in improvised pontoon transports floating quietly down the Tennessee River at three in the morning and 3,500 by land towards Brown's Ferry from another direction. Those Confederates who were not captured withdrew, leaving Raccoon Mountain and the supply line in Union hands. Sherman soon arrived in Chattanooga from Vicksburg in mid-November after riding on horseback for several weeks and catching the new supply line rail into town. Then he and Grant and the Rock of Chickamauga planned a way to break out of the siege.[572]

---

570 Foote, vol. 2, pp. 784–785, 803; https://en.m.wikipedia.org/wiki/William_Rosecrans, pp. 4–5, accessed May 29, 202; McFeely, pp. 145–147; Smith (2001), pp. 267–268; Brands, pp. 267–268.

571 Foote, vol. 2, pp. 804–805; https://www.historynet.com/battle-of-chattanooga, p. 3, accessed May 29, 2021.

572 https://www.historynet.com/battle-of-chattanooga, p. 3, accessed May 29, 2021; Foote, vol. 2, pp. 807–809, 836.

Grant got wind of Longstreet's troops being sent away, so he planned to fight his way out. He wanted the Rock to cause enough disturbance at the center of Missionary Ridge to allow Sherman to break through on the left and "roll up" the Confederate line by attacking it perpendicularly. In fact, Bragg was sending even more troops away when the Union army got into position to attack, but he called those troops back. At this point, Grant had 75,000 men and Bragg had 43,000.[573]

Before assaulting Missionary Ridge, however, Grant attacked at Lookout Mountain. On November 24, 1863, five days after the Gettysburg Address, Union troops set out at three in the morning under a heavy fog to attack on the right, up the back side of Lookout Mountain, which stood 1,200 feet above the river. Bragg found out about the attack, but did not send reinforcements, believing that the Union troops could not ascend the sheer backside of Lookout Mountain. The 8,700 Confederates on Lookout Mountain were no match for the 12,000-man Union force. And their cannon could not point downward enough to avoid overshooting the attackers. Fighting continued into the night, with neither side able to see more than a hundred feet through the dense fog. At 2:30 in the morning, Bragg ordered the evacuation of Lookout Mountain.[574]

---

[573] https://www.historynet.com/battle-of-chattanooga, p. 4, accessed May 29, 2021; Foote, vol. 2, p. 837.

[574] https://www.historynet.com/battle-of-chattanooga, p. 5, accessed May 29, 2021; Foote, vol. 2, pp. 846–848; https://en.m.wikipedia.org/wiki/Battle_of_Lookout_Mountain, p. 5, accessed May 23, 2021.

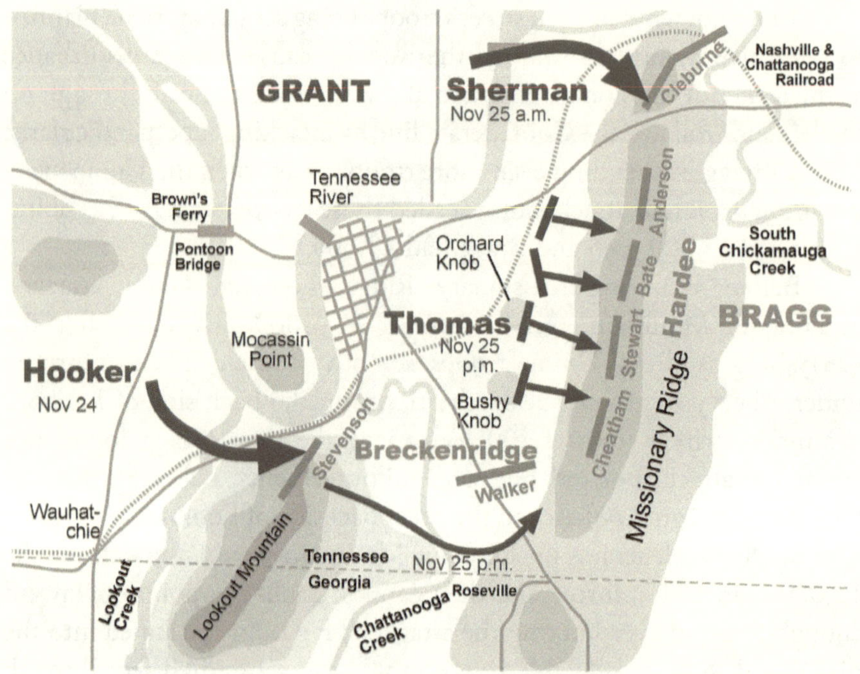

Grant then ordered the Rock to attack the Confederate center on Missionary Ridge to distract the Confederates while Sherman rolled them up from the left. However, the Rock had 25,000 men and he went wild. First he marched his troops in parade style in the valley below Missionary Ridge at the center of the Confederate line. The Confederate soldiers climbed out of their trenches on the hillside to watch. Then the parade turned into an attack and was in "mid-career" before the Confederates realized it and got back in their trenches to fight. The Union army routed them from the lower trenches and then spent the night in those trenches getting ready for the next day.[575]

As at Lookout Mountain the day before, Bragg knew what was going on below, but did not reinforce his troops, believing that he could crush the Union attackers if they were reckless enough to climb the sheer rock face of Missionary Ridge. Though the steep terrain prevented Sherman from rolling up the Confederates on the left hand side, the Union soldiers

[575] Foote, vol. 2, p. 845.

at the center broke through the line on Missionary Ridge, sending the Confederates scrambling while leaving behind a third of their cannon and 7,000 muskets. Bragg's army was routed. They retreated 30 miles south to Dalton, Georgia.[576]

After losing at Chattanooga, Bragg offered his resignation and Jefferson Davis accepted it immediately, replacing him with Joseph Johnston. As one author sums it up: "An excellent subordinate in combat, Bragg simply lacked the qualities essential for success in a field command . . . he almost invariably lacked the persistence to exploit advantages."[577]

The Union army now had control of Tennessee and had opened Georgia to invasion. Grant then devised a two-prong strategy: Sherman would attack Johnston toward Atlanta and Grant would attack Lee at Richmond. Simultaneous attacks would prevent either Confederate army from coming to the aid of the other.[578]

William Tecumseh Sherman

William Tecumseh Sherman was the red-headed son of an Ohio supreme court justice who had died unexpectedly, leaving 11 kids. He was raised by a family friend, who was a U.S. senator from Ohio. Sherman's older brother was a federal judge and a younger brother was a U.S. senator. Sherman married his foster sister at age 30 and they had eight kids. Known as "Cump" by his friends and family, he graduated 6th out of 42 from West Point. His roommate was George Thomas. Sherman excelled academically, but received lots of demerits, caring nothing about neatness or form.

After graduation, Sherman served in the army for 13 years, but saw no combat. He held an administrative position in California and was then stationed in Georgia and South Carolina where, as the son

---

[576] Ibid pp. 844, 846; https://www.historynet.com/battle-of-chattanooga, p. 6, accessed May 29, 2021..

[577] Hallock, pp. 127–149; Woodworth (1990), pp. 245–257; https://www.ncpedia.org/biography/bragg-braxton, p. 4, accessed May 24, 2021.

[578] McFeely, pp. 148–150.

of a prominent politician, he moved "within the upper circles of Old South society." Sherman then retired from the army to pursue business interests, managing a bank in San Francisco and later in New York. By the time the Civil War broke out, however, he was the superintendent of what is now LSU.[579]

Sherman was not an abolitionist before the Civil War, but he was adamantly opposed to secession. When he learned of the secession of South Carolina, he burst out crying, pacing the floor and fearing that the whole country might be destroyed. He declared: "This country will be drenched in blood and God only knows how it will end . . . You people speak so lightly of war; you don't know what you're talking about. War is a terrible thing!"[580]

When Lincoln called for 75,000 volunteers for three months to quell the secession, Sherman ridiculed it, saying: "Why, you might as well attempt to put out the flames of a burning house with a squirt-gun." Nevertheless, he rejoined the army, saying "I still think it is to be a long war—very long—much longer than any politician thinks." Throughout the war, he declined to use black troops in his armies.[581]

While serving under Grant at the siege of Vicksburg, Mississippi, Sherman watched as Grant abandoned his supply line and foraged to maintain his troops. At first, Sherman expressed reservations about this unusual strategy, but then went all in on it, strengthening his ties to Grant. One newspaper called Grant a drunkard and his confidential adviser, Sherman, a lunatic.[582]

George Thomas

George Thomas was 47 years old and had graduated from West Point 12th out of a class of 42 cadets more than two decades earlier. He and

---

[579] McDonough, pp. 148–149; Walsh, p. 32; Sherman, pp. 16, 160–162; Hirshson, p. 21; Dougherty, pp. 96–100.

[580] Walters, p. 9; Exchange between W.T. Sherman and Prof. David F. Boyd, December 24, 1860, quoted in Lewis, p. 138.

[581] Bowman and Irwin, p. 25; Sherman to Halleck, September 4, 1864, Civil War Official Records Vol. 38, part 5, pp. 792–793, https://www.archives.gov.

[582] Smith (2001), pp. 235–236; Reid, vol. 1, p. 387.

Sherman were roommates. He had also fought in the Mexican-American War, working closely with Braxton Bragg in an artillery unit. Thomas then taught at West Point, where John Bell Hood was one of his students. And he was close friends with Lee, who was the superintendent at the time. Another one of his students was Jeb Stuart. At Stones River, Rosecrans had considered retreating during a council of war among his officers. Thomas was present, though he had his eyes closed and appeared to be asleep. When the word *retreat* was spoken, Thomas opened his eyes, said "This army does not retreat," and then resumed his nap.[583]

Born in Virginia, Thomas grew up in an upper-class lifestyle on a plantation. He witnessed first-hand the life of slaves, many of whom he taught to read, in violation of Virginia law. When he decided to stay with the Union, his family never spoke to him again.[584]

George Thomas, The Rock of Chickamauga

[583] Einolf, pp. 22–29, 39–57; Cleaves, pp. 24–42; https://en.m.wikipedia.org/wiki/George_Henry_Thomas, pp. 4, 6, 8, accessed June 3, 2021; Foote, vol. 2, p. 94.

[584] https://en.m.wikipedia.org/wiki/George_Henry_Thomas, pp. 5, 6, 12 accessed June 3, 2021. Cleaves, pp. 6–7; O'Connor, p. 60; Furgurson, p. 57;; Einoff, pp. 13, 87–88.

Jefferson Davis

Before the Civil War, Jefferson Davis had served as a United States congressman and senator from Mississippi, as well as secretary of war under Franklin Pierce. Born as the youngest of ten children in Kentucky, he grew up in Louisiana and Mississippi and graduated 23rd out of a class of 33 at West Point. Davis served in the United States army for six years, fighting in the Mexican-American War. He then operated an 800-acre cotton plantation with 113 slaves south of Vicksburg, Mississippi.[585]

As a senator, Davis pushed to annex Texas in order to increase territory for the expansion of slavery. After the Mexican-American War, Davis likewise sought to annex Cuba, declaring it "must be ours to increase the number of slaveholding constituencies." Jefferson Davis believed blacks to be inferior to whites. He also believed that the right to secede was without question. However, he advocated against secession in 1858, later explaining that he did so because he knew the South did not possess the military resources for war. When Mississippi seceded in January of 1861, Davis resigned from the United States Senate, calling it the "saddest day of my life." Eighteen days later, he was chosen as president of the Confederacy, though he would have preferred to be the military commander of the Confederate armies. He was 53 years old.[586]

Davis was in poor health most of his life from Mexican-American War battle wounds, repeated bouts of malaria, and a chronic eye infection that made bright light painful. He also had a nerve disorder that caused severe facial pain.[587]

---

[585] Johnson (1997), p. 452; *U.S. Military Academy, Register of Officers and Graduates of the U.S. Military Academy from March 16 to January 1, 1850.* Compiled by Capt. George W. Cullum. West Point, New York: 1850, p. 148; Cooper (2000), pp. 81–83, 616.

[586] Rives, pp. 634–636; McPherson (1989), p. 104; Dodd, pp. 12, 171–172; Cooper (2000), pp. 3, 574–575, 602–603; Cashin, pp. 102–103; Coulter, pp. 24–25.

[587] Allen (1999), pp. 197–198; Potter, p. 74.

Jefferson Davis

Lincoln refused to deal with Davis, whom he viewed as an insurrectionist with no legal standing in government affairs. Dealing with Davis would have appeared to give legitimacy to the rebellion. Davis soon moved the Confederate government from Montgomery to Richmond, were he resided at the "White House of the Confederacy" 100 miles from Washington. He had few military advisers, preferring instead to make strategic decisions on his own. But he did respect Lee. Davis decided that, with limited resources, the South should fight primarily on the defensive. He maintained this view throughout the war, though he did approve of Lee's offensives at Antietam and Gettysburg, both of which ended in defeat.[588]

Joseph Johnston

There was increasingly bad blood between Joe Johnston and Jefferson Davis during the course of the war. Davis considered firing Johnston, but

[588] Strode (1959), pp. 90–94; Cooper (2000), pp. 401–402; "Jefferson Davis and the Confederacy's 'Offensive–Defensive' Strategy in the U.S. Civil War." Joseph G. Dawson III, *Journal of Military History*. April 2009, 73 (2): 591–607.

did not. Throughout, Johnston resented other officers being ranked ahead of him. As historian Phil Leigh comments: "Johnston complained and equivocated. Rather than finding solutions, he spent his time worrying about problems." Jefferson Davis communicated directly with Johnston's subordinates, so Johnston often did not know what was going on.[589]

Many times, Johnston simply would not act. Even before the war, he had accompanied a friend in South Carolina on a quail hunt, but failed to shoot most of the time, claiming that the birds were too far away or blocked by underbrush or that the sun was in his eyes. His friend concluded that Johnston would not shoot unless the conditions were perfect. "The bird flew too high or too low; the dogs were too far or too near. Things never did suit exactly."[590]

Likewise, during the six-week siege of Vicksburg, Johnston stood nearby but never went into action. At one point, the Confederate secretary of war concluded that Lee should go ahead and invade the north in an effort to gain a victory in the Eastern Theater before Johnston lost Vicksburg in the Western Theater. Though other officers urged Jefferson Davis to save Vicksburg, he instead permitted Lee to invade the North, ultimately resulting in both Lee's defeat at Gettysburg and Johnston's loss of Vicksburg the next day.[591]

John Bell Hood

At Chickamauga, Hood led the assault at the gap in the Union line, leading to the defeat of Rosecrans. After the assault, his injured right

---

589 Eicher and Eicher, p. 69; Symonds (1992), pp. 123–130; "A Failure in Strategic Command: Jefferson Davis, J. E. Johnston and the Western Theater." Joseph E. Wasiak, Jr., U.S. Army War College, Carlisle Barracks, Pennsylvania. 1998; "The Wrong Man." Phil Leigh, *New York Times*, November 21, 2012, p. 2.

590 Foote, vol. 1, p. 417; "The Wrong Man." Phil Leigh, *New York Times*, November 21, 2012, p. 2.

591 "The Wrong Man." Phil Leigh, *New York Times*, November 21, 2012, pp. 3–4; "'We Should Assume the Aggressive': Origins of the Gettysburg Campaign," Stephen W. Sears, *North and South: The Official Magazine of the Civil War Society*, March 2002, pp. 58–66; "Robert E. Lee," https://en.wikipedia.org/wiki/Robert_E._Lee, p. 13, accessed April 28, 2021.

leg was amputated four inches below the hip. From then on, he wore an artificial leg and rode strapped to his horse. Based on his bravery, he was promoted to lieutenant general. But the higher Hood rose and the more men he commanded, the less effective he became.[592]

1864
The Eastern Theater:
Grant and Lee Sidle to Petersburg

George McClellan

While the war was still going, McClellan ran as the Democratic candidate for president against Lincoln in 1864. McClellan's platform included the position that, if elected, he would allow the Confederate states to go their own way peacefully. Lincoln won handily.[593]

Jeb Stuart

Ten months after Gettysburg, in the spring of 1864, Grant attacked Lee in Virginia in a series of battles known as the Overland Campaign, targeting Richmond. Jeb Stuart was there, fighting against Custer again, this time at the Battle of the Wilderness, where he skillfully delayed the advance of Grant's army. Then, at an abandoned stage coach inn known as the Yellow Tavern, Stuart led an attack with 4,500 men against 12,000 Union soldiers, including Custer. He was apparently operating under his standard approach of substituting esprit for numbers.[594]

As Foote explains it, Jeb Stuart considered his gaudy uniform to be necessary for esprit, including the "red-lined cape, bright yellow sash, black ostrich plume, and golden spurs—he wore with such flamboyance,

[592] Woodworth, (1990), p. 271; McMurry (1992), p. 83; Castel, p. 62; Foote, vol. 3, p. 660.

[593] McPherson (1988), p. 805.

[594] Wert (2008), pp. 338–346; Davis (1957), pp. 378–384; Foote, vol. 3, pp. 226–230.

on and off the field of battle."[595] Not surprisingly, Stuart was a conspicuous target on the battlefield.

At the Battle of Yellow Tavern, Stuart led a counterattack, firing his revolver at the retreating Union soldiers. A dismounted, retreating Union private shot Stuart from 30 feet away. Stuart died a few days later in Richmond at the age of 31. One author describes Stuart: "Amid a slaughterhouse, he had embodied chivalry, clinging to the pageantry of a long-gone warrior. He crafted the image carefully, and the image befitted him. He saw himself as the Southern people envisaged him. They needed a knight; he needed to be that knight."[596]

Ulysses S. Grant

Grant was given command of the entire Union army in March of 1864. He also took over the field command of the Eastern Theater. That field command had passed from McClellan to Ambrose Burnside who, like McClellan, was slow to move forward. At one point, Burnside had sat for a week while waiting for pontoon bridges. By the time the bridges arrived, so had 77,000 Confederates, though one out of every six was barefoot. Later, Burnside decided to strike Lee where he least expected it—at Lee's strongest point. It did not go well. Burnside retreated after suffering very heavy losses.[597]

Lincoln and Grant worked well together, with Lincoln allowing Grant to devise his own strategies. Grant set up his headquarters in Culpepper, Virginia, 90 miles northwest of Richmond, and met weekly with Lincoln in Washington. Finally, after going through several commanders, each of whom failed in one way or another to take Richmond, Lincoln had found Grant. Even as the head of the army, Grant wore mud-caked boots and an ordinary private's coat with his rank stitched on it. Grant smoked cigars constantly. He was described by one observer as an "ordinary,

---

[595] Foote, vol. 3, p. 228.

[596] Ibid., pp. 231–234; Smith (2005), p. 242; Salmon, p. 283; Starr, p. 107; Rhea, pp. 209, 390; Thomas (1986), p. 292; Wert (2008), p. 370.

[597] Foote, vol. 1, pp. 766–767, 782.

scrubby-looking man, with a slightly seedy look, as if he was out of office on half-pay."[598]

The Union had tried, unsuccessfully, to invade Richmond three times. Similarly, the Confederates had tried, unsuccessfully, to advance north four times, with each foray ending up farther south than where it had started. The likelihood of foreign intervention on behalf of the South decreased with each setback[599]

Grant sought to defeat Lee by attrition, hoping to pin Lee against Richmond by superior numbers in both troops and resources. However, Lee kept sidling south, heading from Richmond towards Petersburg.

Earlier in the war, both sides had used the parole and exchange system to deal with prisoners. Under it, a prisoner could be released if he promised not to return to the battlefield until he was formally exchanged for an enemy captive of equal rank. At one point, Grant and Lee entertained the idea of exchanging prisoners. However, Lee refused to have captured black Union soldiers be a part of that, insisting instead that they were property that was not eligible for exchange. So exchange failed. As time went by, both sides realized that the parole and exchange system that was in effect elsewhere was in fact prolonging the war, since soldiers were ultimately returning to the battlefield. In fact, parole and exchange was the primary means for the Confederates to maintain troop strength. So the do-overs stopped, with both sides instead using prison camps for the remainder of the war.[600]

The worst prison camp was at Andersonville, 120 miles south of Atlanta. Built in early 1864, it only operated for fourteen months, but imprisoned 45,000 Union soldiers during that time. Of those, 13,000 died from disease, starvation, or exposure. When Sherman took Atlanta

---

598 Foote, vol. 3, p.123; https://www.history.com/news/10-things-you-may-not-know-about-ulysses-s-grant, p. 3, accessed June 14, 2021; Chernow (2017), pp. 343–44, 352; McFeely, p. 156; White, p. 636; Waugh, p. 277.

599 Foote, vol. 1, pp. 795–797.

600 Letter from Robert E. Lee to Ulysses S. Grant, October 3, 1864. *Encyclopedia Virginia*, Virginia Humanities (December 7, 2020), accessed June 27, 2021; "The Myth of the Kindly General Lee." Adam Serwer, *Atlantic*, June 4, 2017, p. 5; https://www.theatlantic.com/politics/archive/2017/06/the-myth-of-the-kindly-general-lee/529038/; Faust, pp. 603–604.

in September of 1864, the prisoners were moved elsewhere before he approached. Henry Wirz, the Confederate commander of Andersonville, was found guilty of murder by a military tribunal and hanged in Washington, D.C., after the war.[601]

In May and June of 1864, Grant and Lee slugged it out in the three-day Battle of the Wilderness, where Stonewall Jackson had been mistakenly killed by his own soldiers one year before. Total casualties were more than 28,000. Grant then tried to go around Lee in order to get between him and Richmond at Spotsylvania Courthouse, but Lee got there first and they battled for thirteen days with heavy casualties.[602]

Grant was determined to maneuver Lee to a decisive battle and then capture Richmond.[603] But, unlike his predecessors, Grant did not retreat after battles. Instead, he repeatedly moved south towards Richmond. This kept Lee on the defensive, having to sidle towards Richmond as Grant moved.

Ulysses S. Grant

---

601 https://www.nps.gov/ande/learn/historyculture/camp_sumter_history.htm; "History of the Andersonville Prison," National Park Service, https://www.nps.gov, accessed July 17, 2021.

602 Chernow (2017), pp. 378–379, 384–395; Bonekemper (2012), p. 463; McFeely, pp. 165, 169.

603 Welsh, p. 96; Eicher, pp. 661, 691–92; Davis (1986), p. 18; Salmon, p. 251; Fuller, pp. 207–208.

At Cold Harbor, Virginia, Grant was convinced that a breakthrough would bring about both the capture of Richmond and an end to the war. Lee had no fortifications at Cold Harbor. But he quickly constructed them overnight and, to Grant's surprise, the Confederates were entrenched the next day. Grant nevertheless launched a frontal assault with 120,000 men, knowing that his larger army could better sustain a war of attrition. Predictably, he suffered heavy losses. The Northern newspapers called him a "butcher." He had 50,000 casualties, which was 41 percent of his army. Of Lee's 69,000 men, there were 32,000 casualties, which was 46 percent of his army. Grant later called Cold Harbor his "greatest regret" of the war. At Cold Harbor, Grant was at the same location near Richmond that McClellan had been two years earlier prior to retreating. More than 360,000 Union and Confederate soldiers had died over those two years.[604]

One month later, Grant moved south again without Lee knowing it. He planned to cross the James River and go past Richmond down to Petersburg in order to seize the railroad junction there. Grant's army built a 2,100-foot-long pontoon bridge and crossed the James. When Lee found out about it, he initially thought that Grant was heading to Richmond, so he did not send many soldiers to Petersburg. With 18,000 inhabitants, Petersburg was the junction for five railroads, and served as the main supply base for Richmond and Lee's army. However, Lee soon sent soldiers to Petersburg and Grant established his headquarters at City Point, 25 miles southeast of Richmond and 10 miles northeast of Petersburg, where Lincoln visited him to assess the situation.[605]

---

[604] Welsh, pp. 96, 101; Eicher, pp. 663–687; Hattaway and Jones, pp. 540–546, 552–567, 577–580; Salmon, pp. 251–258; "The Butcher's Bill: Ulysses S. Grant Is Often Referred To As A 'Butcher,' But Does Robert E. Lee Actually Deserve The Title?" Edward H. Bonekemper, *Civil War Times*, 52 (1): pp. 36–43, OCLC 67618265, https//www.history.net.com/the-butchers-bill.htm; McFeely, pp. 170–171; Furgurson (2007), pp. 120–121, 235; Chernow (2017), pp. 403–404; Foote, vol. 3, p. 380; https://www.facinghistory.org/resource-library/statistics-civil-war, accessed June 27, 2021.

[605] McFeely, pp. 157–175; Smith (2001), pp. 313–339, 343–368; Chernow (2017), p. 414; White, pp. 369–370.

By mid-July of 1864, 70,000 Union troops were at Petersburg, facing 36,000 Confederates. At Richmond, 40,000 Union soldiers faced 21,000 rebels. A series of skirmishes and battles occurred at Petersburg with some horrendous casualties, but neither side gained advantage. Then the Union army decided to dig trenches of its own, starting a ten-month standoff that extended from Richmond down to Petersburg. Grant tried several times to cut off the rail lines to Petersburg, but failed. In late July, he sent some of his forces northward in an effort to entice Lee to remove some of his soldiers from Petersburg. Lee responded by sending soldiers north to protect Richmond.[606]

Then the big explosion at Petersburg occurred. The Union army had dug a tunnel more than 500 feet long under the Confederate line and planted 8,000 pounds of gunpowder in there. The plan was to blow up the Confederate line and then have Union soldiers rush through the tunnel and around the edge of the hole in order to attack the enemy lines from behind. The explosion on July 30, 1864 created a massive hole 170 feet long, 80 feet wide, and 30 feet deep.

Due to a last-minute change in plans, however, the Union soldiers who rushed in after the explosion were not the same ones who had been trained for the invasion. They waited a full ten minutes before rushing in after the blast and, when they finally did so, they went into the crater, rather than going around it. By that time, the Confederates had gathered around the edges of the crater, firing down upon the invaders in what one Confederate general described as a "turkey shoot." The Union commander (Burnside) who was in charge of the invasion sent in more troops, who likewise got slaughtered. Burnside was relieved of his command, with Grant calling it a "stupendous failure." Known as "The Crater," the hole from the explosion is still visible today. For eight months after the Crater, attacks and counterattacks continued between the two entrenched armies.[607]

---

606 Davis (1986), pp. 18, 49–52, 64; Welsh, p. 121; Eicher, p. 690; Salmon, pp. 406, 411–413, 416; Trudeau (1991), pp. 53–55, 63–65; Bonekemper (2004), p. 313; Kennedy (1998), p. 353; Welsh, p.122; Longacre (2001), pp. 289–290; Starr, pp. 191–193; Davis (1986), 69–70; Horn, pp. 102–107.

607 Eicher, pp. 720–723; Davis (1986), pp. 67–69, 72, 88–89; Trudeau (1991), pp. 99–128; Kennedy (Frances), pp. 355–356; Salmon, pp. 418–421; Welsh, p. 122;

1864
The Western Theater: Sherman Pushes Ahead

Braxton Bragg

In February of 1864, Bragg was summoned to Richmond. He had resigned his command after the loss at Chattanooga three months earlier. In Richmond, Bragg was put in charge of military operations, but had no direct command. Instead, he organized military hospitals, prisons, and army supplies.[608]

Joseph Johnston

As Sherman advanced from Chattanooga to Atlanta, Johnston used a strategy similar to the one he had employed on the Peninsula against McClellan. Sherman rarely assaulted frontally; he preferred flanking an opponent. This usually involved a frontal "demonstration attack" to hold the opponent in place, while moving soldiers around the right or left flank. So Johnston prepared strong positions, which Sherman then went around, causing Johnston to fall back in Georgia at Resaca, Adairsville, Dalton, and Cassville. By using this strategy, Johnston slowed the Union advance and inflicted more losses than he sustained. Sherman reported to Lincoln: "We gain ground daily, fighting all the time . . . As fast as we gain one position the enemy has another already." Nevertheless, Sherman's army continued to advance toward Atlanta, covering 110 miles in two months. Meanwhile, Grant had returned to Virginia and was slugging it out with Lee.[609]

In late June of 1864, Johnston set up his army at Kennesaw Mountain, Georgia, 22 miles north of Atlanta. It had rained for nearly two weeks and the wet roads were impassable, preventing Sherman from

---

Bonekemper (2004), p. 315; Chernow (2017), p. 429; McFeely, p. 179; Smith (2001), pp. 369–395; Catton (2015), pp. 308–309.

608 Hallock, pp 163–164, 171–179, 204–208; Eicher and Eicher, p. 141; Woodworth (1990), p. 256.

609 Kennedy (Frances), pp. 326–331, 336; Welcher, pp. 447–448.

flanking him. Johnston's cannon on Kennesaw Mountain threatened Sherman's railroad supply line, so Sherman decided to surprise Johnston with a frontal attack at Kennesaw, first feinting right and then left, before charging the center. Johnston had 50,000 soldiers. Sherman had 98,500.[610]

Sherman's forces were repulsed and sustained heavy losses, with three times as many casualties as Johnston. However, an attack by one of Sherman's officers on the left side broke through, placing a portion of the Union army closer to Atlanta than any of the Confederate forces, so Johnston withdrew toward Atlanta. Sherman soon crossed the Chattahoochee River near the mouth of Sope Creek, two miles from where I grew up 100 years later. It's no wonder we found Civil War bullets in the woods behind our house. There were dark gray ones and some white ones that must have hit something, because they were all bent into a shape that looked like a curled up white worm.[611]

Nine days after Kennesaw Mountain, Johnston was removed from command. He was succeeded by John Bell Hood. Sherman then placed Atlanta under siege for a month, while sending forces south of the city to cut off its last remaining railroad connection. Originally named Terminus, Atlanta had a population of 20,000 civilians and stood at the intersection of four railroad lines. It manufactured guns and ammunition. Atlanta was captured on September 2, 1864.[612]

In 1964, when I was seven years old, I went to the centennial commemoration of the Battle of Kennesaw Mountain. There I saw guys charging with open sabres on horses through a smoke-filled field while cannon fired. The ceremony had an exciting, disturbing aspect to it all around.

---

[610] Livermore, pp. 120–121; Eicher, pp. 696–697; McMurry (2000), p. 109; Bailey (1985), pp. 20–21, 66, 74; Kennedy (Frances), pp. 326–331, 336–338; Luvaas and Nelson, pp. 173–246; Welcher, pp. 447–449; Castel, pp. 311–313.

[611] McMurry (2000), p. 109; Bailey (1985), p. 74; Welcher, p. 451; Sherman frontally assaulted at Chickasaw Bayou, Vicksburg, and Chattanooga. All such efforts were unsuccessful.

[612] Livermore, pp. 120–121; Eicher, pp. 696–697; Bailey (1985), pp. 20–21; Kennedy (Frances), pp. 339–343; McPherson (1988), pp. 774–775; Symonds (1992), pp. 302–319; Castel, pp. 255–347.

John Bell Hood

Hood inherited a "virtually impossible situation" at the outskirts of Atlanta. Up until then, Johnston had been engaging in a "campaign of maneuver" against Sherman and Hood had secretly sent letters to Jefferson Davis complaining of Johnston's lack of aggressiveness. So Davis sent Braxton Bragg (of all people) to Atlanta to assess. Even Bragg concluded that Johnston should be replaced. At the age of 33, John Bell Hood became the youngest soldier on either side to command an army.[613]

Two of Sherman's officers had been at West Point with Hood and they told Sherman of Hood's recklessness. In Atlanta, Hood resorted to his usual aggressive tactics, launching four frontal assaults in an effort to break Sherman's siege. All failed and nearly 20,000 of his soldiers were killed or injured. Hood evacuated Atlanta 47 days after taking command and Jefferson Davis was not happy about it, but he kept Hood in command. In fact, Davis met with Hood in Palmetto, Georgia, 25 miles southwest of Atlanta, one month after Atlanta fell. When Davis arrived, some of the Confederate soldiers hollered, "Johnston! Give us Johnston!"[614]

Jefferson Davis approved a plan by Hood to march north and strike at Sherman's supply line. The following morning, Davis spoke in Macon, Georgia, saying: "Sherman cannot keep up his long line of communications; retreat sooner or later he must. And when that day comes, the fate that befell the army of the French Empire in its retreat from Moscow will be re-enacted. Our cavalry and our people will harass and destroy his army, as did the Cossacks that of Napoleon . . ."[615]

So Hood headed north into Tennessee, assuming that Sherman would give chase to protect his supply line. In fact, Hood even hoped to defeat Sherman in a battle and then move through the Cumberland Gap to help Lee in Petersburg, Virginia. Sherman did not take the bait.

---

[613] Castel, p. 562; Symonds (1992), pp. 321–324; Woodworth (1990), p. 284.

[614] Dyer, pp. 251–252; Woodworth (1990), pp. 286–290; "Sherman Unleashes Total War on Confederacy." Pat Horan, *Real Clear History*. Archived from the original on April 2, 2015; Sword, pp. 46–49; Jacobson, pp. 30–32; Foote, vol. 3, pp. 604–605.

[615] Foote, vol. 3, pp. 607–608.

Instead, he sent troops under George "the Rock" Thomas and John Schofield to deal with Hood. In fact, Sherman was delighted that Hood was getting out of his path to Savannah, saying "If he will go to the Ohio River, I'll give him my rations . . . my business is down south."[616] Sherman expressly ordered that the Union troops heading north remain as one large fighting unit in order to avoid being attacked by Hood as separate, smaller forces. But those troops got separated in Tennessee.

Hood tried to trap Schofield's part of the separated Union army before it could reach Nashville. But Schofield's men slipped past him in the night, quietly sneaking by Hood's army in Spring Hill, Tennessee, 45 miles south of Nashville. The Union soldiers were so close that a few of them unwisely came over to the Confederate campfires to light their pipes and were captured.[617]

The next morning, on November 30, 1864, Hood was furious when he found out about it, blaming almost everyone in sight. He made his way to Franklin, Tennessee, 26 miles south of Nashville, where he found Schofield's army entrenched on the near side of the Harpeth River. From a hill three miles to the south, Hood studied the naked plain that lay between his army and the Union entrenchment. Then he declared, "We will make the fight." His officers were stunned, given the clearly unfavorable conditions. They tried to talk him out of it, to no avail. Hood had 30,000 men and no artillery. The Union army, led by one of Hood's West Point classmates, John Schofield, had 34,000 men and 60 cannon.[618]

---

[616] "Sherman Unleashes Total War on Confederacy." Pat Horan, *Real Clear History*. Archived from the original on April 2, 2015

[617] Foote, vol. 3, p. 661.

[618] Ibid., pp. 661–666.

John Bell Hood

Hood also decided that flanking maneuvers were out of the question and that a headlong assault would set things right. So, one hour before sundown, he launched 18,000 of his men in a frontal assault across two miles of open ground without artillery support. The assault failed and a lot of Confederates got killed. As historian Wiley Sword describes the battle of Franklin, "Never had there been such an overwhelming victory during the Civil War—indeed, never in American military history." One Union officer observed, "I never saw the dead lay near so thick."[619]

Then, after dark, Hood sent in more soldiers. In all, he had 6,252 casualties, including 1,750 dead soldiers. As Foote puts it, "Hood had wrecked his army, top to bottom, and the army knew it; or soon would . . . Hood did not know this yet, however—and would not have been likely to admit it if he had . . ."[620]

Hood ordered another attack to begin at daybreak, but by morning the Union army had disappeared, burning its own makeshift bridge after

[619] Ibid., pp. 661, 667–670; Sword, p. 425.

[620] Ibid., p. 672.

crossing the Harpeth River on its way to Nashville.[621] All in all, Hood was a hard-charging dumbass.

John Bell Hood proceeded to Nashville the next day with 24,000 men in his "last and manful effort to lift up the sinking fortunes of the Confederacy." But he dug in south of town, waiting to be attacked. In effect, he used an approach once referred to by Napoleon as a form of "deferred suicide." Somehow Hood believed that he could defeat the Union army if it attacked him. Then an ice storm hit and the two armies remained at a standoff for two weeks. During this delay, Hood first realized the full scope of danger that he was in. The Union army was well equipped and had 54,000 soldiers ready to strike. Another 17,000 were nearby.[622]

On December 16, 1864, the Union army finally attacked Hood under the command of George Thomas, who had been Hood's instructor at West Point. Thomas had taken so long to launch the attack that Grant was now calling the Rock of Chickamauga "Slow Trot" Thomas. The Union forces smashed into Hood's army, sending it a few miles south in retreat across the thawed, muddy footing. Thomas sent a telegram to Washington declaring that he would attack again in the morning if the enemy chose to stand and fight. One of his officers, who had been Hood's roommate at West Point, told Thomas, "You don't know Hood . . . He'll be right there, ready to fight you in the morning." He was right. The Union army attacked the next day in a bloody battle that eventually sent the Confederates in flight south toward Franklin.[623]

During the two days of fighting in Nashville, the Confederate casualties were 6,000 killed, wounded, missing, or captured. Union casualties were 3,061. As one of Hood's privates later wrote of Hood, "As a soldier, he was brave, good, noble, and gallant, and fought with the ferociousness of the wounded tiger, and with the everlasting grit of the bulldog; but as a general he was a failure in every particular."[624] As Shelby Foote puts it: "For all its harshness, Franklin and Nashville

---

[621] Ibid., pp. 672–673.

[622] Ibid., pp. 674–681.

[623] Ibid., pp. 684, 696–697.

[624] Ibid., pp. 705–706.

had confirmed and reconfirmed this assessment . . . not only because he fought them with so little tactical skill . . . but also because he fought them at all. Within a span of just over two weeks, these two battles had cost him 12,000 casualties . . ." As one Confederate stated, "Ain't we in a hell of a fix: a one-eyed President, a one-legged general, and a one-horse Confederacy!"[625]

The union army pursued Hood more than 200 miles south, all the way to Tupelo, Mississippi. Though Hood had started out from Atlanta with 38,000 soldiers, he now had only 14,500 left. He was removed from command in January of 1865.[626]

John Schofield

John Schofield had given Hood the slip during the night at Spring Hill, Tennessee and then soundly defeated Hood the next day at the Battle of Franklin. Meanwhile, Thomas and the other part of the Union troops had safely reached the Union fortifications at Nashville. Schofield was the 32-year-old son of a New York Baptist preacher and had graduated from West Point ranking 7th out of 52. He had taught philosophy at West Point for five years and physics at Washington University in St. Louis until the war broke out.[627] After the Battle of Franklin, however, Schofield fed false information to Grant about George Thomas in an unsuccessful effort to take over the command in Nashville.[628]

625 Ibid., pp. 706, 709.

626 Sword, p. 425.

627 https://en.m.wikipedia.org/wiki/George_Henry_Thomas, p. 19, accessed June 3, 2021; Eicher and Eicher, pp. 472–473; https://en.m.wikipedia.org/wiki/John_Schofield, p. 4, accessed May 29, 2021.

628 Bobrick, pp. 287–288, 329–331, 336–337.

John Schofield

George Thomas

At Nashville, the Rock waited until he was damned good and ready to attack Hood, driving Grant and others crazy in the meantime. Grant was even on his way from Virginia to Nashville to take over when "Slow Trot" finally attacked in mid-December of 1864, destroying Hood's army.[629]

William Tecumseh Sherman

The fall of Atlanta ensured Lincoln's reelection two months later. Five days after the fall, Sherman and Hood engaged in an unusual exchange of correspondence. Sherman wrote: "General: I have deemed it to the interest of the United States that the citizens now residing in Atlanta should remove, those who prefer it to go south and the rest north . . . Atlanta is no place for families or non-combatants, and I have no desire

[629] https://en.m.wikipedia.org/wiki/George_Henry_Thomas, p. 20, accessed June 3, 2021; Chisholm, pp. 866–867.

to send them North if you will assist in conveying them South . . . I have the honor to be, your obedient servant, W.T. Sherman."[630]

Hood replied two days later: "I shall render all assistance in my power to expedite the transportation of citizens in this direction . . . And now, sir, permit me to say that the unprecedented measure you propose transcends, in studied and ingenious cruelty, all acts ever before brought to my attention in the dark history of war. In the name of God and humanity I protest, believing that you will find that you are expelling from their homes and firesides the wives and children of a brave people. I am, general, very respectfully, your obedient servant, J.B. Hood"[631]

The next day, Sherman wrote back: "General . . . I say that it is kindness to these families of Atlanta to remove them now at once from scenes that women and children should not be exposed to, and the 'brave people' should scorn to commit their wives and children to the rude barbarians who thus, as you say, violate the laws of war . . . In the name of common sense I ask you not to appeal to a just God in such a sacrilegious manner; you who, in the midst of peace and prosperity, have plunged a nation into war, dark and cruel war . . . God will judge us in due time . . . W.T. Sherman"[632]

Hood replied: "General . . . I see nothing in your communication which induces me to modify the language of condemnation with which I characterized your order . . . And because I characterized what you call a kindness as being real cruelty you presume to sit in judgment between me and my God and you decide that my earnest prayer to the Almighty Father to save our women and children from what you call kindness is a 'sacrilegious, hypocritical appeal.' You came into our country with your army avowedly for the purpose of subjugating free white men, women, and children, and not only intend to rule over them, but you make negroes your allies and desire to place over us an inferior race, which we have raised from barbarism to its present position . . . You say, 'let us fight it out like men.' To this my reply is, for myself, and, I believe, for

---

630 https://www.historynet.com/fighting-words-sherman-hood.htm, p. 1–2, accessed June 5, 2021.

631 Ibid., pp. 2–3, accessed June 5, 2021.

632 Ibid., p. 3, accessed June 5, 2021.

all the true men, aye, and women and children, in my country, we will fight you to the death. Better die a thousand deaths than submit to live under you or your Government and your negro allies . . . Respectfully, your obedient servant, J.B. Hood"[633]

Sherman responded: "General . . . I agree with you that this discussion by two soldiers is out of place and profitless . . . I was not bound by the laws of war to give notice of the shelling of Atlanta, a 'fortified town' with magazines, arsenals, foundries, and public stores. You were bound to take notice. See the books . . . I am, with respect, your obedient servant, W.T. Sherman."

Sherman ordered civilians to leave the city and all military and government buildings to be burned. Though not ordered, many private homes and shops also went up in flames.[634]

Sherman's March to the Sea began on November 15, 1864. He had obtained approval to abandon his supply line as had been done in Vicksburg, assuring Grant that he would "make Georgia howl." Grant and Sherman believed that the war would end if the South's capacity for warfare was decisively broken. Sherman's March also put pressure on Lee by having Grant in front of Lee and Sherman behind, though far away.[635]

Engaged in what he called "hard war," Sherman implemented a scorched earth policy on all military, economic, and transportation resources between Atlanta and Savannah. He had no supply line and was deep within enemy territory. Sherman's 62,000 union soldiers began the march southward and were joined by another 5,500 soldiers along the way. They marched in two columns 60 miles apart. The Confederates had 12,000 men.[636] In an order, Sherman laid out the scope of the March:

---

[633] Ibid., pp. 4–6, accessed June 5, 2021.

[634] Ibid., p. 7, accessed June 5, 2021.

[635] Telegram W.T. Sherman to Gen. Ulysses S. Grant, October 9, 1864, reproduced in Simpson and Berlin, p. 731; Senour, p. 293; Hirshson, pp. 246–247, 431 n.23; Eicher, p. 739.

[636] https://en.wikipedia.org/wiki/William_Tecumseh_Sherman, p. 14, accessed June 27, 2021; Sherman's March to the Sea, https://www.thecivil-war.com, accessed May 12, 2021; Savannah Campaign Union Order of Battle (Official Records, Series I, Volume XLIV, pp. 19–25, National Archives, https://www.archives.gov); Effective

> The army will forage liberally on the country during the march . . . (and) will gather, near the route traveled, corn or forage of any kind, meat of any kind, vegetables, corn-meal, or whatever is needed . . . Soldiers must not enter the dwellings of the inhabitants, or commit any trespass . . . To army corps commanders alone is entrusted the power to destroy mills, houses, cotton-gins, &c., and for them this general principle is laid down: In districts and neighborhoods where the army is unmolested no destruction shall be permitted; but should guerrillas or bushwhackers molest our march, or should the inhabitants burn bridges, obstruct roads, or otherwise manifest local hostility, then army commanders should order and enforce a devastation more or less relentless according to the measure of such hostility. As for horses, mules, wagons, &c., belonging to the inhabitants, the cavalry and artillery may appropriate freely and without limit . . . and will endeavor to leave with each family a reasonable portion for their maintenance.[637]

Sherman's route took 300 miles to cover the 250-mile distance between Atlanta and Savannah. His two columns meandered initially, in order to make it unclear whether they were headed to Augusta, Macon, or Savannah. Sherman's army was escorted by a cavalry regiment of union soldiers who were all Southerners loyal to the Union. The march involved nearly 3,000 wagons and 5,000 head of cattle that crossed seven rivers with no bridges unless they built them along the way. Sherman's solders referred to him as "Uncle Billy." Unlike McClellan, he shared the

---

strength of the army in the field under Maj. Gen. William T. Sherman, November and December, 1864 (Official Records, Series I, Volume XLIV, page 16, National Archives, https://www.archives.gov).

[637] William T. Sherman, Military Division of the Mississippi, Special Field Order 120, November 9, 1864. https://civil.war.monitor.com; ehistory.osu.edu.

lifestyle of his soldiers, eating hardtack and sitting on a cracker box in worn-out clothes.[638]

The Union troops "lived off the land," seizing food from local farms. For Sherman, this eliminated the need to protect the supply line running from Nashville to Chattanooga to Atlanta and beyond. Along the way, his army destroyed the railroads and the manufacturing and agricultural infrastructure of Georgia.

Sherman had even studied livestock and crop production data from the 1860 census in order to move his men through areas where they would be able to forage most effectively.[639] The torn-up railroad rails that they heated over fires and wrapped around trees became known as "Sherman's neckties." Confederate resistance was mild, since Hood had taken off with most of his army from Atlanta toward Chattanooga in the unfulfilled hope that Sherman would chase him.

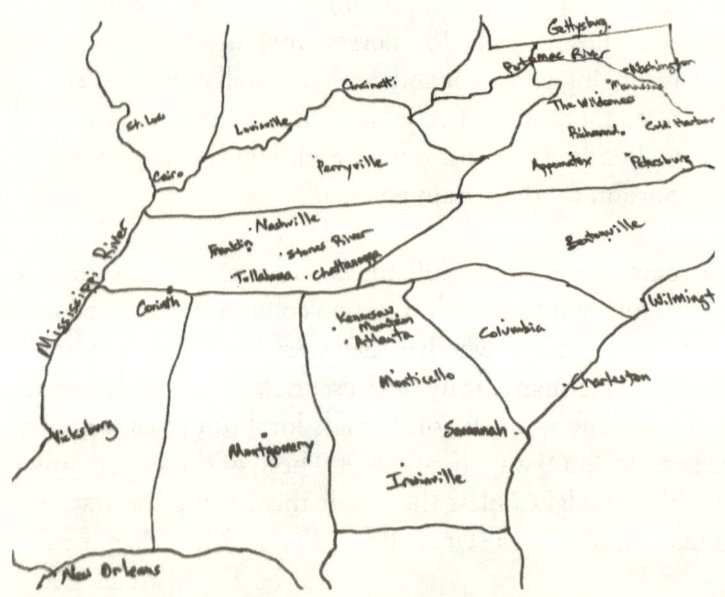

Points of Interest Map for the Eastern and Western Theaters

[638] Nevin, p. 48; "What We Don't Know About Sherman's March," https://www.npr.org January 4, 2009, accessed May 12, 2021; Sherman, Memoirs, p. 589; Foote, vol. 3, p. 492.

[639] Trudeau (2008), p. 52.

William Tecumseh Sherman

As many as 10,000 freed slaves followed Sherman's army. The March to the Sea was devastating, inflicting $1.6 billion in today's dollars by Sherman's estimate. Three hundred miles of train track were destroyed and more than nine million pounds of corn seized. As well, 13,000 cattle, 5,000 horses, and 4,000 mules were taken. As historian David Eicher asserts, Sherman "had defied military principles by operating deep within enemy territory and without lines of supply or communication. He destroyed much of the South's potential and psychology to wage war."[640]

When he reached the outskirts of Savannah in early December of 1864, Sherman expected to connect with the U.S. navy for the attack. Instead, he found 10,000 Confederates entrenched to protect the town. He captured nearby Fort McAllister to open up the connection with the navy so that he could obtain supplies and artillery for a siege. Then he wrote to the opposing Confederate officer, William Hardee:

> I have already received guns that can cast heavy and destructive shot as far as the heart of your city; also, I have for some days held and controlled every avenue by which the people and garrison of Savannah can be

[640] Catton (1965), pp. 415–416; Eicher, p. 768.

> supplied, and I am therefore justified in demanding the surrender of the city of Savannah . . . and shall wait a reasonable time for your answer, before opening with heavy ordnance. Should you entertain the proposition, I am prepared to grant liberal terms to the inhabitants and garrison; but should I be forced to resort to assault, or the slower and surer process of starvation, I shall then feel justified in resorting to the harshest measures, and shall make little effort to restrain my army—burning to avenge the national wrong which they attach to Savannah and other large cities which have been so prominent in dragging our country into civil war.[641]

Hardee did not surrender. Instead, he escaped across the Savannah River. The following day, however, the mayor of Savannah presented Sherman with the key to the city. The March to the Sea had taken 36 days, with Savannah being captured on December 21, 1864. One month later, Sherman issued an order providing for the settlement of free slaves on land taken from white landowners. Known as the "forty acres and a mule" promise, it redistributed approximately 400,000 acres of land in 40-acre parcels stretching from Charleston, South Carolina, to the St. John's River in Florida and 30 miles inland. This order was later revoked by President Andrew Johnson.[642]

Jefferson Davis

Though Davis had considerable military experience, he was less effective than Lincoln, who had none. Historian William Cooper observes: "Lincoln was flexible; Davis was rigid." As the war dragged on, the

[641] William T. Sherman, Message to William J. Hardee, December 17, 1864, recorded in Sherman (*Memoirs)*.

[642] Sherman (*Memoirs)*, p. 693; William T. Sherman, Military Division of the Mississippi, Special Field Order 15, January 16, 1865, https://www.georgiaencyclopaedia.org/articles/history-archaeology/shermans-field-order-no-15, https://www.britannica.com/topic/Field-Order-No-15, accessed May 22, 2022.

Confederates printed more and more money, with inflation increasing from 60 percent in 1861 to 600 percent in 1864. Davis was seemingly unable to grasp the gravity of the problem.[643]

1865
The Eastern Theater: Breakthrough at the Shad Bake

In March of 1865, Abraham Lincoln gave his second inaugural address. Believing that the war was God's punishment for the sins of human slavery, he proclaimed:

> Fondly do we hope—fervently do we pray—that this mighty scourge of war may speedily pass away. Yet, if God wills that it continue, until all the wealth piled by the bond-men's two hundred and fifty years of unrequited toil shall be sunk, and until every drop of blood drawn with the lash, shall be paid by another drawn by the sword, as was said three thousand years ago, so still it must be said 'the judgments of the Lord, are true and righteous altogether.'

In his closing words, hoping for the nation's reconstruction, Lincoln offered:

> With malice toward none; with charity for all; with firmness in the right, as God gives us to see the right, let us strive on to finish the work we are in; to bind up the nation's wounds; to care for him who shall have borne the battle, and for his widow, and his orphan—to do all which may achieve and cherish a just, and a lasting peace, among ourselves, and with all nations.

---

[643] Cooper (2000), pp. 351–352; Escott, pp. 146, 269; Cooper (2010), p. 161.

Nine days after Lincoln gave his second inaugural address, Jefferson Davis issued an order allowing slaves to enlist in the Confederate army, with a promise of freedom afterwards.[644]

Petersburg was not a siege in the classic military sense of surrounding a foe and severing supply lines. Instead, it was nine and a half months of trench warfare from June 15, 1864, until April 2, 1865. Lee had dug 35 miles of trenches from Richmond to south of Petersburg, which was critical to the supply of Richmond and Lee's army.

In late March of 1865, Lee's army of 50,000 was still faced-off against Grant's army of 125,000. An additional 50,000 Union forces were on the way. Meanwhile, after capturing Savannah, Sherman was working his way north through the Carolinas to join Grant in Virginia. Lee's troops were deserting in droves due to starvation and trench warfare conditions. Lee launched a surprise attack, but it was unsuccessful and incurred high casualties. His defeat was imminent.[645]

Grant then launched a dawn attack on April 2, 1865, along the entire Confederate line. He broke through at Petersburg. At the time of Grant's attack, George Pickett and another Confederate commander were behind the lines at Petersburg enjoying a shad bake and their men had no idea where they were. By the time Pickett realized what was going on, the Union army had broken through and half of his men had been shot or captured. Lee and his army withdrew overnight from both Petersburg and Richmond, heading west. Jefferson Davis fled by train. The Union army captured Richmond the next day and, two days later, Abraham Lincoln was sitting in Davis's office chair there. Vice President Andrew Johnson offered a $100,000 reward for the capture of Jefferson Davis.[646]

Lee made it as far as Appomattox Court House, 90 miles away, before his path was blocked by Custer's Union cavalry. He surrendered

---

[644] "General Orders No. 14." *Civil War on the Western Border: The Missouri-Kansas Conflict, 1855–1865.* Kansas City: The Kansas City Public Library, https://web.archive.org/web/20141105001859/http://www.civilwaronthewesternborder.org/timeline/general-orders-no-14, accessed May 23, 2022.

[645] Bonekemper (2012), pp. 319, 323, 353, Kennedy (Frances), p. 373; Salmon, p. 450; Horn, p. 216; Korn, p. 39; Greene, pp. 114–115; Salmon, pp. 467–468.

[646] Foote, vol. 3, p. 870; "Battle of Five Forks." Peter Luebke, *Encyclopedia Virginia.* https://encyclopediavirginia.org, accessed May 25, 2022.

to Grant one week later on April 9, 1865. Custer was present at Lee's surrender to Grant and received, as a gift for his wife, the table on which Lee signed.[647] The Richmond-Petersburg campaign had been costly, with 42,000 Union casualties and 28,000 casualties for the Confederacy. Lincoln was assassinated five days after Lee surrendered.[648]

1865
The Western Theater:
Crossing the Swamp toward Richmond

Sherman rested his troops in Savannah for a month before turning east. In February of 1865, he then marched through the Carolinas in an effort to join forces with Grant, who was still battling Lee in Petersburg at the time. Grant had wanted Sherman to load his army onto steamships bound for Virginia, but Sherman had persuaded him that a march through the Carolinas would be of military value in terms of breaking morale in the South, particularly in South Carolina, which had seceded from the Union first.[649]

By then, Joe Johnston had returned to action. After being relieved of his command in Atlanta, he had gone to Columbia, South Carolina, to retire. But when Sherman headed into the Carolinas, Jefferson Davis had come under public pressure to call Johnston back into duty, and he did so on February 25, 1865. Johnston provided only light resistance to Sherman in South Carolina. Sherman's army marched 12 miles per day through the Salkehatchie swamps on "corduroy" roads built of logs that were laid side by side as thousands of horses, men, wagons, and cannon rolled over them at a right angle. Johnston was convinced that there had been no such army since the days of Caesar. The winter of 1865 was

---

[647] Wert (1996), p. 225.

[648] Salmon, pp. 448, 450, 467–468; Horn, pp. 33–36, 209, 215–216; Greene, pp. 108–112; Trudeau (1991), pp. 333–342; Bonekemper (2012), pp. 319, 323, 365–366; White, pp. 403–404.

[649] Marszalek (1992), p. 311.

one of the coldest on record for South Carolina, so Sherman's soldiers climbed trees to sleep above the frigid swamp water.[650]

Columbia, South Carolina, was burned in mid-February. Sherman then marched across North Carolina to capture Wilmington. Severely outnumbered, Johnston attacked an isolated portion of Sherman's army in Bentonville, North Carolina, where he "gained some tactical successes" before having to retreat.

In late March, Sherman traveled by boat from the North Carolina coast to Grant's headquarters at City Point, Virginia, to meet with Grant and Lincoln. It was the only time that the three men met during the war. Lee surrendered before Sherman's army reached Grant.[651]

Shortly after Lee surrendered, Joseph Johnston met with Sherman for three days in Durham, North Carolina, to negotiate his own surrender. After learning the terms of the proposed surrender, Jefferson Davis, who was still fleeing, ordered Johnston to escape. But Johnston refused, instead making the largest surrender of the war on April 26, 1865. All 89,270 soldiers active in North Carolina, South Carolina, Georgia, and Florida were turned in.[652]

In May of 1865, Braxton Bragg was captured in Monticello, Georgia. Jefferson Davis was captured the following day in Irwinville, Georgia. Davis was found scampering through the woods with a black shawl over his head, which his wife claimed to have thrown over him in an effort to hide his identity. The newspapers had a heyday with this, creating a long-lasting rumor and caricatures of Davis fleeing in a woman's clothes. During his flight, Davis had considered escaping to Cuba to set up base there.[653]

---

[650] Cox, (1900), vol. 2, pp. 531–532; Cox, (1882), p. 168; https://en.wikipedia.org/wiki/William_Tecumseh_Sherman, p. 12, accessed May 16, 2021.; https://www.researchonline.net/catalog/04178.htm, accessed May 19, 2021.

[651] Sherman (1990), pp. 806–817; Pfanz, (1989), pp. 1–2, 24–29, 94–95.

[652] Symonds (1992), pp. 339–342, 356–357; Bradley, pp. 22–25, 45–46; North Carolina Historic Sites: Bennett Place Archived January 29, 2015 at the Wayback Machine; Eicher and Eicher, p. 323; http://www.wadehamptoncamp.org/"Johnston's Surrender" accessed May 25, 2022.

[653] Dodd, pp. 353–357; Cooper (2000), pp. 533, 629; From Varina Banks Howell Davis to Francis Preston Blair, Savannah, Ga., June 6, 1865. In Blair, Gist. Annals

Davis Fleeing in a Woman's Clothing

In his post-war justifications, Jefferson Davis put forth: "The negroes' servile instincts rendered them contented with their lot, and their patient toil blessed the land of their abode with unmeasured riches. Their strong local and personal attachment secured faithful service . . . never was there happier dependence of labor and capital on each other. The tempter came, like the serpent of Eden, and decoyed them with the magic word of 'freedom' . . ."

John Bell Hood surrendered in Natchez, Mississippi, in late May of 1865.

---

of Silver Spring, Records of the Columbia Historical Society, Washington, D.C., Vol. 21 (1918), pp. 155–185; "Capture of Jefferson Davis." *The New Georgia Encyclopedia*. https://www.georgiaencyclopaedia.org/articles/history-archaeology/capture-of-jefferson-davis, accessed May 23, 2022.

After the War

George McClellan

George McClellan is widely considered to have been a poor battlefield general. As historian Stephen Sears says, McClellan "could be both comfortable and successful performing as an executive officer, and also, if somewhat less successfully, as grand strategist; as battlefield commander, however, he was simply in the wrong profession."[654]

Five flaws that McClellan demonstrated (according to some online leadership coach!) were: (1) hesitating to take definitive action; (2) complaining about insufficient resources; (3) refusing to take responsibility; (4) abusing the privileges of leadership; and (5) engaging in acts of insubordination.[655] Though constantly preparing his army, he was never quite ready, refusing to engage the enemy even when he had the clear advantage.

McClellan blamed everyone else for his mistakes. As historian Michael Hyatt puts it, "While his troops were struggling in almost unbearable conditions, McClellan lived in near-royal splendor. He spent almost every evening entertaining guests with elaborate dinners and parties . . . His lifestyle . . . stood in distinct contrast to that of Gen. Ulysses S. Grant . . ." And McClellan was passive-aggressive. "Even when Lincoln gave him a direct order, McClellan found a way to avoid obeying it." Though he was energetic and focused and could train the daylights out of an army, he was, as one fervent critic characterizes him, "an imperious, obstinate, arrogant, pseudo-intellectual patrician who saw almost everyone as his inferior."[656]

George McClellan could not adapt as a situation changed, causing him to be overly cautious and passive. Lincoln referred to this as having a case of "the slows." Of course, McClellan thought that Lincoln was

---

[654] Carlson, Cody K. "This week in history: McClellan Becomes the Army's Commanding General." *Deseret News*, October 29, 2014; Sears (1999), pp. 19–20.

[655] Hyatt, Michael, https://michaelhyatt.com/5-characteristics-of-weak-leaders, May 2, 2021.

[656] Ibid., p. 2; https://bobcivilwarhistory.wordpress.com, pp. 1–2, accessed October 5, 2021.

a fool, calling him "the original Gorilla" to his wife. He was possessed with the constant belief that he was outnumbered, wildly overestimating the opposing force and convincing himself that he could not possibly proceed without more men and supplies. At Richmond he insisted that his 128,000 soldiers were outnumbered by the Confederate force, which only had 54,000 men. After winning a battle, he exaggerated the brilliance of his victory. When Lee appeared and counterattacked, McClellan withdrew, even though he had far superior numbers. He then blamed Lincoln for his defeat.[657]

After the war, McClellan went to Europe with his family for three years. He then served as chief engineer for the docks in New York and as president of a railroad for a few years before taking another three-year family trip to Europe. He later served one term as governor of New Jersey. McClellan died of a heart attack 20 years after the war at the age of 58. In his obituary, the *New York Evening Post* commented: "Probably no soldier who did so little fighting has ever had his qualities as a commander so minutely, and we may add, so fiercely discussed." Yet when Lee was asked who he thought was the ablest general on the Union side, he replied without hesitation: "McClellan, by all odds."[658]

Fort McClellan in Anniston, Alabama, was founded by the United States government in 1917. During World War II it served as one of the country's largest army posts, training roughly 500,000 troops. It closed in 1999. Gigantic statues of McClellan exist in Washington and Philadelphia. It is puzzling to me why the government erected statues and built a military base honoring an arrogant soldier who did so little.

Joseph Johnston

Joseph Johnston lost most of the military campaigns that he commanded.Yet Grant and Sherman both spoke highly of him, with Sherman describing him as a "dangerous and wily opponent." Grant said that he thought Johnston's tactics "were right." After the war the three men became friends, corresponding frequently and meeting for

[657] https://bobcivilwarhistory.wordpress.com, pp. 2–3, accessed October 5, 2021.
[658] Sears (1988), p. 393, 400–401; Lee, p. 416; Foote, vol. 1, p. 757.

dinner whenever Johnston was in Washington. Johnston would allow no criticism of Sherman in his presence.[659]

After the war, Johnston lived in Washington and worked in the railroad and insurance businesses. He served one term in the U.S. House of Representatives. Joe Johnston was a pall bearer at Grant's and Sherman's funerals. Sherman died of pneumonia and at his February 1891 funeral in New York City, the weather was cold and rainy. As a sign of respect, Johnston kept his hat off. When someone concerned for his health asked that he put his hat on, Johnston said: "If I were in his place, and he were standing here in mine, he would not put on his hat." Johnson indeed caught a cold that day and died of pneumonia ten days later at the age of 84. In accordance with his wishes, he had a funeral "of the simplest sort" without any military ceremony.[660]

Why did Johnston retreat so much? Was he tentative by nature? Or did he know that he was overpowered militarily and therefore tried simply to delay the inevitable and minimize casualties? He sometimes attacked. And he was injured several times in battle during the Mexican-American War and the Civil War. So it does not seem that Johnston was afraid to fight. He was smart, much like McClellan, but without the big ego.

Debate continues even today about Johnston's actions and lack thereof. One blogger vehemently states that Joe Johnston was not Fabian and that any characterization of him as such is "both inaccurate and at the same time protective of Johnston's legacy." Unlike Fabius Maximus, who is said to have been very aggressive on *all* facets except a direct confrontation with Hannibal's army, Johnston was defensive and inactive. Throughout the Civil War, Johnston was up against numerically superior armies and went by the book, retreating until forced to defend an important location that could not be abandoned. This is far from Fabian.[661]

---

[659] Symonds (1992), p. 370.

[660] Ibid., pp. 380–381; Flood, pp. 397–398; "A Much-Respected, And Conflicted, General of the Confederacy." Frederick N. Rasmussen, *Baltimore Sun*, July 29, 2011, accessed May 25, 2022.

[661] https://civilwartalk,com/threads/joe-johnston-was-not-a-fabian-general/pp. 1–2, accessed July 23, 2021.

Jeb Stuart

In June of 2018, J.E.B. Stuart Elementary School in Richmond was renamed Barack Obama Elementary School. The student population of the school is 90 percent black. In July of 2020, his statue was removed from Monument Avenue in Richmond.[662]

Stonewall Jackson

Considered by military historians to be one of the most talented tactical commanders in U.S. history, Stonewall Jackson believed that he was fighting in a holy war and that the Creator had sanctioned slavery. He is an important figure in the Lost Cause ideology.[663]

The Jackson stained-glass windows in the Washington National Cathedral depicted him reading the Bible in Confederate camp and entering heaven, among other things. They were removed in 2017. In July of 2020, Virginia eliminated Jackson's birthday as a state holiday. His statue in Richmond was likewise removed.[664]

Ulysses S. Grant

Grant prevailed upon the government to drop its case of treason against Lee. In his memoirs, Grant referred to the Southern cause as "one of the worst for which a people ever fought."[665] He was a skillful military

---

[662] "Richmond's J.E.B. Stuart Elementary School—Honoring a Confederate—Will Be Renamed for Barack Obama." Justin Mattingly, *Richmond Times-Dispatch*, June 19, 2018; https://abcnews.go.com/amp/US/wireStory/richmond-removing-statue-confederate-gen-jeb-stuart-71646648.

[663] See Robertson, p. 191; See Hettle.

[664] "Washington National Cathedral to Remove Stained Glass Windows Honoring Robert E. Lee, Stonewall Jackson." Michelle Boorstein, *Washington Post*, September 6, 2017; "Virginia Senate Votes to Eliminate Lee-Jackson Day, Create New Election Day Holiday." Laura Vozzella, *Washington Post,* January 21, 2020; "Stonewall Jackson Removed from Richmond's Monument Avenue." *AP News*. July 1, 2020; Virginia General Assembly SB 601: Legal holidays, Election Day.

[665] https://www.history.com/news/10-things-you-may-not-know-about-ulysses-s-grant, p. 4, accessed June 14, 2021; Grant, Chapter LXVII; Smith (2001), p. 404

leader with a natural understanding of strategy and tactics. Over time, his reputation has shifted from the role of victor by brute force to that of a skillful, modern military strategist.

After the war, Grant differed with President Andrew Johnson on Reconstruction, wanting to enforce civil rights for recently free slaves while Johnson did not. Banking on Grant's popularity, Johnson included Grant (and Custer) on his "Swing Around the Circle" tour, which was an attempt to gain support for leniency for the South. Grant left the tour early, calling it a "national disgrace." As historian Ethan Rafuse sees it, "After the war, Confederate apologists launched a brutally effective campaign against Grant to obscure the true history of slavery, the Civil War and the white Southern terrorist campaigns against Reconstruction."[666]

As president beginning in 1868, Grant supported female suffrage. He also appointed more than 50 Jews to federal office, apparently in an effort to atone for his overturned order in Mississippi during the war. He is generally considered to have been an effective advocate for civil rights, creating (with Congress) the Justice Department that prosecuted the Ku Klux Klan. Grant's presidency was plagued, however, by internal corruption among his subordinates and colleagues. He was "naive in matters of finance" and was "honest, trusting, and gullible."[667]

For his second term, Grant defeated Horace Greeley, who advocated amnesty for Confederates, literacy tests for voting, and the removal of federal troops from the South. Greeley had previously posted bail for Jefferson Davis. After Grant's second term ended, federal troops were

---

[666] Chernow (2017), pp. 569, 672; Brands, pp. 396–398, 437–446; Simon (2002), pp. 244, 248; Utley, pp. 39–40. "Still A Mystery? General Grant and the Historians, 1981–2006." Ethan S. Rafuse, July 2007, *Journal of Military History*, 71(3): 849–874.

[667] Chernow (2017), pp. 643–644, 749–50; Kahan, p. XII, 61, 76, 119; Calhoun, pp. 130, 384–385; Sarna, pp. ix–xiv; Foner, pp. 119–121; "The Lowest Ebb." C. Vann Woodward, *American Heritage*. (1957) 8 (3): 53–108, 156. ISSN 0002-8738; White, pp. 538–541; Smith (2001), pp. 587, 592; McFeely, pp. 407–415; "Toppling of the Ulysses Grant Statue is No Way to Treat History." Gregory Downs, *San Francisco Chronicle*, June 25, 2020.

indeed removed from the South and Reconstruction was dead. The Jim Crow era then set in for the next 80 years.[668]

After his presidency, Grant spent most of the money he had on a two-and-a-half year world tour, meeting with the Pope and Queen Victoria along the way. He had money troubles from then on, eventually losing the title to his home and worrying constantly about leaving his wife enough money to live on. Then Mark Twain, knowing how dire Grant's financial situation was, offered him a gigantic 70 percent royalty to write his memoirs. Grant did so, working on it at a friend's cottage on Mount McGregor in upstate New York and finishing only a few days before his death from throat cancer at the age of 63. His memoirs were a success, providing more than $12 million in today's dollars for his wife.[669]

More than 1.5 million people attended Grant's funeral in New York City and his cortege was seven miles long. Joseph Johnston served as a pall bearer, as did Sherman. Grant's final resting place took 12 years to complete. Grant's Tomb is the largest mausoleum in North America. Oddly, his presidential library is located at Mississippi State University.[670]

Braxton Bragg

After the war, Bragg served as superintendent of the New Orleans waterworks, as a life insurance agent, and as a railroad inspector. At one point, he even considered joining the Egyptian army. Bragg's shortcomings included poor battlefield strategy, heavy reliance on the frontal assault, and a lack of follow-up at Perryville, Stones River, and

---

[668] Wang, pp. 103–104; Simon, p. 250; Chernow (2017), pp. 735, 740, 858; Smith (2001), p. 604; Strode (1955), p. 305.

[669] Chernow (2017), p. 872; White, pp. 632–633, 646; Brands, pp. 620–21, 629–630; Marzalek et. al. (2017), p. xx; McFeely, pp. 501–505.

[670] Brands, pp. 633–635; Smith (2001), p. 19; See http://www.usgrantlibrary.org/; "New Ulysses Grant Presidential Library at Home in the South." *Associated Press,* November 16, 2017; https://www.pbs.org/wgbh/americanexperience/features/grant-funeral/p. 2, accessed May 4, 2021; https://www.pbs.org/wgbh/americanexperience/features/grant-funeral/, pp. 2–3, accessed May 4, 2021.

Chickamauga. He had a sour disposition and a tendency to blame others. However, some say he was a good organizer.[671]

Bragg was quarrelsome and "thorny." He is widely considered to be one of the worst generals of the Civil War, with his losses playing a primary role in the defeat of the Confederacy.[672] Braxton Bragg died of a massive heart attack on the streets of Galveston, Texas, at the age of 59. Fort Bragg was established in 1918 in Fayetteville, North Carolina, and is one of the largest military posts in the world, covering 250 square miles and having 545,000 military personnel. As with McClellan, I am puzzled why the government named a prominent military base after a cantankerous Confederate traitor who lost most of the battles that he fought.

John Bell Hood

Hood and Bragg have been called the "bumblers" who lost the Western Theater. After the war, Hood moved to Louisiana, working in the cotton business and the insurance business. He lived 14 more years, had 11 kids, and died of yellow fever in New Orleans. On January 1, 2021, the U.S government passed a law requiring that Fort Hood in Texas be renamed, along with Fort Bragg. Hood's leg is believed to be buried under a monument in Tunnel Hill, Georgia, near Chickamauga.[673]

William Rosecrans

The military career of William Rosecrans was wrecked by his devastating defeat at Chickamauga. After his removal from command in Chattanooga, he played no further large part in the war. Later, he and others started the

---

[671] Hallock, pp. 260–264; McPherson (1988), p. 857; Woodworth (1990), pp. 29–30.

[672] Cashin, pp. 102–103; McPherson (1988), p. 857; https://en.wikipedia.org/wiki/Braxton_Bragg, pp. 2, 13, accessed April 28, 2021.

[673] McPherson, (1988), p. 857; https://www.kcentv.com/article/news/military-matters/fort-hood-facing-potential-name-change-with-congressional-override-of-military-bill/500-41c6f941-882e-4e77-bbad-5d2268d84283, May 4, 2021; https://www.roadsideamerica.com, "Leg of the Gallant Hood," accessed May 21, 2021.

Southern Pacific Railroad. Rosecrans also served as a U.S. congressman representing California. He died at the age of 78 in Redondo Beach.[674]

Jefferson Davis

Jefferson Davis tried to defend the whole South with the same amount of effort, spreading resources too thin and rendering it vulnerable to attacks. He even allowed Lee to invade the North while things were going to hell at Vicksburg, resulting in the simultaneous Gettysburg and Vicksburg defeats.[675]

After the war, Davis was imprisoned for two years on the Virginia coast. Though indicted for treason, no trial occurred for him—nor for any other Confederate—for several reasons, including likelihood of conviction, interference with the reconciliation between the North and South, and potential validation by a court of the constitutionality of secession (though secession was in fact held unconstitutional by the Supreme Court five years later).[676]

Davis was released on bail, which was posted by Horace Greeley, Cornelius Vanderbilt, and others. Andrew Johnson later pardoned him and all others who participated in the insurrection. Jefferson Davis blamed the Union for "whatever of bloodshed, of devastation, or shock to republican government has resulted from the war."[677]

---

[674] https://en.m.wikipedia.org/wiki/William_Rosecrans, pp. 4–5, 49, 53, accessed May 29, 2021.

[675] Woodworth (1999), pp. 1–22.

[676] Dodd, pp. 366–368; Blackford, p. 62; "United States vs. Jefferson Davis, 1865–1869." Roy Franklin Nichols, *American Historical Review* (1926), 31 (2): p. 266, doi: 10.2307/1838262, JSTOR 1838262; Blight, p. 57; See "United States v. Jefferson Davis: Constitutional Issues in the Trial for Treason." Eberhard P. Deutsch, *American Bar Association Journal*, February 1966, vol. 52 (2), pp. 139–145. ISSN 0747-0088. JSTOR 25723506. OCLC 72582745; See also "United States v. Jefferson Davis: Constitutional Issues in the Trial for Treason." Eberhard P. Deutsch, *American Bar Association Journal*, March 1966, vol. 52 (3), pp. 263–268. ISSN 0747-0088. JSTOR 25723552. OCLC 725827455; Davis (1865), p. 96; Kennedy (James and Walter), p. 104.

[677] Strode (1955), p. 305; Blackford, p. 62; Blight, p. 57; "United States vs. Jefferson Davis, 1865–1869." Roy Franklin Nichols, *American Historical Review* (1926), 31

Davis then lived in the Peabody Hotel in Memphis, where he ran a life insurance company for four years. He gave occasional speeches, saying in 1871 that the South had been "cheated not conquered" and asserting that it never would have surrendered if it had known that Reconstruction lay in store. He declined positions offered by the University of the South at Sewanee, Tennessee, and by Randolph-Macon College in Virginia, but served as the commencement speaker at Sewanee six years after the war.[678]

In an 1885 article in the *North American Review*, Teddy Roosevelt likened Davis to Benedict Arnold. Jefferson Davis had been both a United States senator and secretary of war before turning his back on the Union. He died of acute bronchitis in New Orleans at the age of 81. His United States citizenship was restored posthumously by Jimmy Carter in 1978.[679]

Considered a poor leader by many, Davis was preoccupied with detail and reluctant to delegate, showing favoritism to old friends and unable to get along with those who disagreed with him. He was loathed by much of the Confederate army. The statue of Jefferson Davis was removed from the rotunda at the capitol in Kentucky in June of 2020. But his birthday is celebrated in Florida, Kentucky, Louisiana, Tennessee, Alabama, Mississippi, and Texas.[680] Two years after Davis died, his wife,

---

(2): p. 266, doi: 10.2307/1838262, JSTOR 1838262; Blight (2001), p. 57; Foster, p. 232; See "United States v. Jefferson Davis: Constitutional Issues in the Trial for Treason." Eberhard P. Deutsch, *American Bar Association Journal*, February 1966, vol. 52 (2), pp. 139–145. ISSN 0747-0088. JSTOR 25723506. OCLC 72582745; See also "United States v. Jefferson Davis: Constitutional Issues in the Trial for Treason." Eberhard P. Deutsch, *American Bar Association Journal*, March 1966, vol. 52 (3), pp. 263–268. ISSN 0747-0088. JSTOR 25723552. OCLC 725827455.

678 Cooper (2000), pp. 586–588, 594; Collins, p. 21.

679 Cooper (2000), pp. 623–624; "Jimmy Carter: Restoration of Citizenship Rights to Jefferson F. Davis Statement on Signing S. J. Res. 16 into Law." American Presidency Project. https://www.presidency.ucsb.edu, October 17, 1978, accessed June 11, 2022.

680 Cooper (2000), pp. 3–4; "Jefferson Davis: An Appraisal." Bell I. Wiley, *Civil War Times Illustrated.* (1967) 6 (1): 4–17; Escott, pp. 197, 256–274; Cooper (2010), p. 161; Woodworth (1990), p. 309; "Why Jefferson Davis Was Loathed in the Confederacy He Led." Avi Selk, *Washington Post*, December 8, 2018; "The 2010 Florida Statutes (including Special Session A)". The Florida Legislature; "2.110 Public holidays." Kentucky Legislative Research Commission; "Days of public rest,

Varina, moved to New York City, where she became friends with Grant's widow and declared that the right side had won the Civil War.[681]

George Armstrong Custer

Custer stole a prize racehorse in Virginia two weeks after the war ended and rode it in the victory parade in Washington. The horse bolted during the parade when someone tossed a wreath from the curb, making quite a scene. As Foote puts it, "A reporter, watching the general's hat fly off and 'his locks, unskeined, stream a foot behind him,' was put in mind—more prophetically than he knew—of 'the charge of a Sioux chieftain.'" Ulysses S. Grant ordered Custer to return the stolen horse. Instead, Custer hid it, winning a race on it the next year shortly before the horse suddenly up and died.[682] Custer was the Union's dumbass version of Confederate John Bell Hood.

After the Civil War, Custer marched from Louisiana to Texas with Union troops to occupy the South during Reconstruction. His soldiers despised him, considering him a "vain dandy." Several of them even planned to ambush him after they were released from service, but Custer found out about it the night before and avoided it. Custer then considered a career in railroading and mining. He also considered running for Congress and accompanied Andrew Johnston on the "Swing Around the Circle" tour that promoted leniency for the South.[683]

Custer later became a lieutenant colonel in the regular army and went to Kansas, where he was suspended for one year for going AWOL. Then he went west to fight in the Indian Wars. At the Battle of Washita

---

legal holidays, and half-holidays." The Louisiana State Legislature; "Memorial Day History." United States Department of Veterans Affairs; "Official State of Alabama Calendar." Alabama State Government; "Mississippi Code of 1972 – SEC. 3-3-7. Legal holiday." LawNetCom, Inc; "State holidays." Texas State Library.

681 Cashin, p. 2.

682 Foote, vol. 3, p. 1015; "That Time When Custer Stole a Horse." T. J. Stiles, *Smithsonian Magazine*. November 2015.

683 Wert (1996), pp. 232–238;"It Is Best to Go Strong-Armed: Army Occupation of Texas, 1865–66." William L. Richter, *Arizona and The West,* Summer 1985, Vol. 27, No. 2, pp. 121–122, 135; Utley, pp. 39–40.

River, he had his men shoot most of the 875 ponies that they captured. His troops called him "Iron Butt," in reference to his strict discipline and his stamina in the saddle. They also called him "Ringlets" for his curling, long blond hair, which he is said to have "frequently perfumed with cinnamon scented hair oil."[684]

George Armstrong Custer

In the Dakota Territory, Custer's expedition into the Black Hills discovered gold in 1874. When President Grant's attempt to buy the Black Hills from the Sioux failed in 1875, Grant ordered that the Sioux be sent to reservations as "hostiles," with Custer in charge. Custer set out with his cavalry in May of 1876 as part of a larger army to round up the Indians. He declined the support of an additional 500–800 men offered by another officer, and he left behind a battery of Gatling guns, though he knew he would be facing superior numbers.

Meanwhile, Sitting Bull had assembled the largest gathering ever of the Plains Indians to determine what to do. The Arapaho, Lakota, and

[684] "Why Jefferson Davis Was Loathed in the Confederacy He Led." Avi Selk, *Washington Post*, December 8, 2018; Woodworth (1999), pp. 1–22.; Schultz, pp. 111–126; Welch, p. 60.

Northern Cheyenne Indians met near the Little Bighorn River. When Custer's scouts detected Sitting Bull's large gathering of Indians in late June, Custer decided to attack immediately since his presence in the area was known. He divided his cavalry of 580 men into three battalions, contrary to basic military strategy. Sitting Bull had between 1,800 and 3,500 Indians. During the battle, Custer's other two battalions never came to his relief.[685]

None of the Indians knew that they were fighting Custer, who was killed by Buffalo Calf Road Woman when she struck a blow that knocked him off his horse. Two Cheyenne women recognized his body on the battlefield and they shooed away a Sioux warrior from desecrating it, telling the warrior: "Stop, he is a relative of ours." Custer had had two children with an Indian woman that they knew. The two women shoved their sewing sticks into his ears so that he would "hear better in the afterlife," because he had broken his promise not to fight against Indians. Custer was later mutilated by others, who forced an arrow up his penis. Grant regarded Custer's sacrifice of troops at the Little Bighorn as being "wholly unnecessary."[686]

George Armstrong Custer died at the Little Bighorn 11 years after the Civil War at the age of 36. He was buried in a shallow grave. When soldiers returned a year later, they found that animals had scavenged the grave and scattered his bones. So, a double handful of bones was gathered and reinterred at West Point with full military honors.[687]

---

685 Tagg, p. 184; Marshall, p. 15; Kappler, pp. 1008–1011; Treaty with the Crows, 1868; Michno, pp. 10–20; Smalley, p. 6; Miles, Nelson Appletion (1896). *Personal recollections and observations of General Nelson A. Miles embracing a brief view of the Civil War, or, From New England to the Golden Gate: And the story of his Indian campaigns, with comments on the exploration, development and progress of our great western empire*. Chicago: Werner. Chapter XXII, pp. 289–290, http://digital.library.wisc.edu/1711.d/History.Miles, accessed May 17, 2022.

686 Michno, p. 293; "Northern Cheyenne Break Vow of Silence." Martin J. Kidston, Helenair.com. June 28, 2005; Powers, Thomas. "How Little Bighorn Was Won." *Smithsonian Magazine*, November 2010; Hardoff, p. 21; Graham, pp. 115–117.

687 "Custer National Cemetery-Big Horn County-Montana." https://www.mrail.net, accessed 2020–02–18.

William Tecumseh Sherman

Sherman's tactics during the March to the Sea broke the back of the Confederacy and helped lead to its eventual surrender. A hero in the North, Sherman was despised in the South, more for his affront to Southern dignity than for his damage to railroads and farms. He is praised for his military strategy and criticized for his scorched-earth policy.[688]

The president of the Georgia Historical Society, however, distinguishes Sherman's "hard war" from the "total war" seen in World War II: "But 'hard war' was not total war. While the march destroyed property and infrastructure and visited suffering and fear on the civilian population, it lacked the wholesale destruction of human life that characterized World War II. Sherman's primary targets—foodstuffs and industrial, government and military property—were carefully chosen to create the desired effect, and never included mass killing of civilians . . . He was fighting to bring rebels back into the Union, not to annihilate them."[689]

Sherman possessed a mastery of maneuver warfare, as demonstrated by his series of turning movements against Johnston on his way to Atlanta. His "hard war" approach was in fact endorsed in advance by Grant and even Lincoln, who were willing to allow drastic measures to save the United States. Sherman remained in the U.S. army for nearly 20 years after the war. When someone proposed him as a presidential candidate in 1884, he forcefully declined: "I will not accept if nominated and will not serve if elected." Sherman died of pneumonia in 1891 at the age of 71 in New York City. He is buried in St. Louis.[690]

---

[688] Woodworth (2005), p. 631 says that Sherman's "genius" for "strategy and logistics . . . made him one of the foremost architects of Union victory."

[689] "Rethinking Sherman's March." W. Todd Groce, *New York Times*, November 17, 2014.

[690] Hirshon, p. 393, quoting B.H. Liddell Hart, "Notes on Two Discussions with Patton, 1944" February 20, 1948, GSP Papers, box 6, USMA Library; https://en.wikipedia.org/wiki/William_Tecumseh_Sherman, p. 14, accessed May 16, 2021; "Rethinking Sherman's March." W. Todd Groce, *New York Times*, November 17, 2014.

George Thomas

George Thomas, the Rock of Chickamauga, was a deliberate general who stayed cool and firm under fire. He was mentally quick, but slow in action. Thomas is considered by many historians to be one of the top three Union generals in the war, along with Grant and Sherman.

After the war, Thomas served in Kentucky and Tennessee during Reconstruction, using troops to protect against violence from the Ku Klux Klan. He wrote: "The greatest efforts made by the defeated insurgents since the close of the war have been to promulgate the idea that the cause of liberty, justice, humanity, equality, and all the calendar of the virtues of freedom, suffered violence and wrong when the effort for Southern independence failed. This is, of course, intended as a species of political cant, whereby the crime of treason might be covered with a counterfeit varnish of patriotism . . . a species of self-forgiveness amazing in its effrontery . . ."[691]

Thomas then commanded the Pacific Region, with his army headquarters in San Francisco, where he died of a stroke at the age of 53. He is buried in Troy, New York. None of his family from Virginia attended his funeral.[692]

John Schofield

After the war, John Schofield lived another 30 years. He served as secretary of war under Andrew Johnson and as superintendent of West Point for five years. Schofield died at the age of 74 in St. Augustine, Florida.

---

691 https://en.m.wikipedia.org/wiki/George_Henry_Thomas, pp. 22, 24–25, accessed June 3, 2021; "Forgotten Heroism." Christopher J. Einolf. *North & South*, December 2008, Volume 11, number 2, page 90; "The Department Reports." George Henry Thomas, *Sacramento Daily Union*, December 4, 1868.

692 "National Register of Historic Places Registration Nomination, Oakwood Cemetery (Javascript)." A. Rebecca Harrison, New York State Office of Parks, Recreation and Historic Preservation, August 3, 1984, p. 11; https://en.m.wikipedia.org/wiki/George_Henry_Thomas, p. 24, accessed June 3, 2021.

Robert E. Lee

Shortly after the war ended, Lee said, "So far from engaging in a war to perpetuate slavery, I am rejoiced that slavery is abolished." To me, this declaration seems to be inconsistent with his words and actions both before and after the war. After the war, Lee did not lead the South toward reconciliation, instead engaging in "forced acquiescence so grudging and pernicious in its effects as to be hardly realized," as Grant put it.

Lee gathered information regarding the comparative strength of the armies during battles, believing that it would "be difficult to get the world to understand the odds against which we fought." As he saw it, "the public mind is not prepared to receive the truth." But the truth is that he got a lot of people killed on both sides by joining the Confederacy and conducting an effective, drawn-out war.[693]

Over time, Lee has become what historian Emory Thomas calls a "suffering Christ-like icon for ex-Confederates." He serves as "the embodiment of the Southern cause," says another. Lee told a colleague that the greatest mistake of his life was taking a military education. Personally, I think he made a much bigger mistake by siding with the Confederates.[694]

In 1868, Lee signed a public letter endorsing Grant's opponent in the presidential campaign. The letter stated: "The idea that the Southern people are hostile to the negroes and would oppress them, if it were in their power to do so, is entirely unfounded." Yet the letter went on to call for "the restoration of white political rule," stating that the people of the South are "inflexibly opposed to any system of laws that would place the political power of the country in the hands of the negro race."[695]

Lee served as president of what is now Washington and Lee University from 1865 until his death five years later from pneumonia at the age of 63. At Lee's funeral, Grant wept openly. Lee is buried on the

---

693 Nolan, p. 24; "The Myth of the Kindly General Lee." Adam Serwer, *Atlantic*, June 4, 2017, p. 5, https://www.theatlantic.com/politics/archive/2017/06/the-myth-of-the-kindly-general-lee/529038/; Gallagher, p. 12.

694 Thomas (1995), pp. 391–392; "The Making and the Breaking of the Legend of Robert E. Lee." Eric Foner, *New York Times*, August 28, 2017.

695 Freeman (1934), pp. 375–376.

campus of Washington and Lee University. Surprisingly, a portrait of Lee in full Confederate uniform hangs in the library at West Point, where it was installed in 1952. As two recent West Point graduates remark in their support of removal of the massive painting, "Robert E. Lee was not just a racist and a slave owner. He chose to betray his country in the defense of his right to subjugate the black race, which now comprises a significant portion of the Army and officer corps."[696]

Robert E. Lee's beliefs on race and slavery were paradoxical. While declaring that he had sympathy for blacks, he considered them inferior. He characterized slavery as evil, yet said it provided some benefit to slaves. In his view, slaves should be free at some future, unspecified date as part of God's plan. Lee wanted to do right, but not right now. Historian Elizabeth Brown Pryor observes: "No visionary, Lee nearly always tried to conform to accepted opinions. His assessment of black inferiority, of the necessity of racial stratification, the primacy of slave law, and even a divine sanction for it all, was in keeping with the prevailing views of other moderate slaveholders and a good many prominent Northerners."[697]

Historian Eric Foner notes that, though Lee was "not a pro-slavery ideologue," he likewise never spoke out against it even though some white Southerners were doing so, and "Lee's code of gentlemanly conduct did not seem to apply to blacks." After the war, Lee told a congressional committee that, as for blacks, he hoped Virginia could "get rid of them." During Reconstruction, he was urged to condemn the Ku Klux Klan, but remained silent. In fact, the students at the university where he served as president formed their own chapter of the KKK during his tenure.[698]

---

[696] Thomas (1995), pp. 374–402; "Robert E. Lee's Last Stand: His Dying Words and the Stroke That Killed Him." Andrew Southerland, *Neurology*, 82 (10 Supplement), p. 294. ISSN 0028-3878; Smith (2001), pp. 409–412; "What Should West Point Do About Its Robert E. Lee Problem?" Jimmy Burn and Gabe Royal, Modern War Institute at West Point, June 22, 2020; https://www.mwi.usma.edu, accessed June 21, 2021.

[697] Fellman (2000), pp. 73–74; Cox (2017), p. 157; "Robert E. Lee, Slavery, and the Problem of Providence." R. David Cox, EerdWord (publisher blog), May 18, 2017, accessed June 11, 2022; Pryor, p. 151.

[698] "What Robert E. Lee Wrote to The *Times* about Slavery in 1858." Jacey Fortin, *New York Times*, August 18, 2017. ISSN 0362-4331; "The Making and the Breaking of the Legend of Robert E. Lee." Eric Foner, *New York Times*, August 28, 2017. ISSN

Unlike Jefferson Davis, Lee was never arrested nor punished. He also applied to Grant and to Andrew Johnson for reinstatement of his citizenship, but he was not pardoned and his citizenship was not restored. In 1972, the Stone Mountain Confederate Memorial was completed, depicting Robert E. Lee, Jefferson Davis, and Stonewall Jackson riding their horses to glory in the world's largest high relief sculpture. Stone Mountain Park had officially opened seven years earlier on the 100th anniversary of Lincoln's assassination. To this day, Lee serves as an icon of Lost Cause mythology. As Serwer puts it, "Lee's elevation is a key part of a 150-year-old propaganda campaign designed to erase slavery as the cause of the war and whitewash the Confederate cause as a noble one."[699]

Lee's 60-foot statue in New Orleans was removed in 2017. His statue in Charlottesville was set to be removed in 2017, but sparked the violent Unite the Right rally in August of that year. It finally came down on July 10, 2021. The stained-glass window of Lee that was placed in the Washington National Cathedral in 1953 has been removed. So has Lee's statue in the United States Capitol, to be replaced with a statue of civil rights activist Barbara Johns. Fort Lee in New Jersey retains its name, however, since it is named after Revolutionary War General Charles Lee rather than Robert E. Lee. Lee's statue has also disappeared from the Hall of Fame for Great Americans in Bronx, New York. The State of Virginia,

---

0362-4331; "Book review: 'Clouds of Glory: the Life and Legend of Robert E. Lee' by Michael Korda." Eric Foner, *Washington Post*, May 30, 2014. ISSN 0190-8286; "The Myth of the Kindly General Lee." Adam Serwer, *Atlantic*, June 4, 2017, page 5; https://www.theatlantic.com/politics/archive/2017/06/the-myth-of-the-kindly-general-lee/529038/; Pryor, p. 5.

[699] Fremantle, Arthur (1864). *Three Months in the Southern States, April-June, 1863*. Republished 2008, Applewood Books. ISBN 978–1429016667; Freeman (1934), pp. 376, 526; Fellman (2000), pp. 258–263, 275–277; Seidule, p. 55; "The Myth of the Kindly General Lee." Adam Serwer, *Atlantic*, June 4, 2017, p. 2, https://www.theatlantic.com/politics/archive/2017/06/the-myth-of-the-kindly-general-lee/529038/; "Stone Mountain, A Monumental Dilemma." Debra McKinney, Southern Poverty Law Center Intelligence Report No. 164, Spring 2018, pp. 18–22, https://en.m.wikipedia.org/wiki/Stone_Mountain, accessed June 26, 2021; See generally Reeves.

however, offers an optional license plate showing a picture of General Robert E. Lee with the phrase *The Virginia Gentleman.*[700]

Robert E. Lee's birthday is commemorated in Texas. Alabama and Mississippi celebrate it on the same day as Martin Luther King, Jr. Day. Georgia stopped celebrating it in 2016 and Virginia dropped it in 2020. As author Adam Serwer opines, "The most fitting monument to Lee is the national military cemetery the federal government placed on the grounds of his former home in Arlington." In 1975, Gerald Ford for some reason signed a Senate bill introduced by Harry Bird of Virginia posthumously restoring Lee's citizenship.[701]

George Pickett

George Pickett surrendered with Lee at Appomattox. When asked by reporters why his charge at Gettysburg failed, Pickett replied: "I've always thought the Yankees had something to do with it." He has received criticism from historians about his staying far to the rear of his attacking troops at Gettysburg. Others defend him, with one saying he "went as far as any Major General, commanding a division, ought to have gone, and farther." The image of a commander sending his barefoot

---

700 "Citizenship For R. E. Lee." *Gettysburg Times,* August 7, 1975; "'The Lees Are Complex': Descendants Grapple With a Rebel General's Legacy." Simon Romero, *New York Times*, August 22, 2017; Konstam, p. 48.

701 Fellman (2005), p. 19; "The Myth of the Kindly General Lee." Adam Server, *Atlantic*, June 4, 2017, page 8; https://www.theatlantic.com/politics/archive/2017/06/the-myth-of-the-kindly-general-lee/529038; "Robert E. Lee's Last Stand: His Dying Words and the Stroke That Killed Him." Andrew Southerland, *Neurology,* April 8, 2014, 82 (10 Supplement), P1.294. ISSN 0028-3878; "Today in History: May 13: Arlington National Cemetery." lcweb2.loc.gov. Library of Congress; "Arlington House." *Encyclopedia Virginia.* https://encyclopediavirginia.org/entries/arlington-house accessed May 26, 2022; "The Day White Virginia Stopped Admiring Gen. Robert E. Lee and Started Worshiping Him." Steve Hendrix, *Washington Post,* October 8, 2017; "Robert E. Lee Statue Removed from U.S. Capitol." *NBC News.* https://www.nbcnews.com/news/us-news/robert-e-lee-statue-removed-u-s-capitol-n1251925, accessed May 26, 2022; "Stone Mountain History." Stone Mountain Memorial Association, http://www.stonemountainpark.org/text/Stone%20Mountain%20History.pdf, accessed May 26, 2022.

men to their deaths is indeed an ugly one. Yet it also does little good if the commanding officer is killed by the first bullet.[702]

Decades after Pickett's death from a liver abscess at age 50, his wife became a well-known writer and speaker about him. But her writings have been characterized as "unreliable" and "fictionalized," with Pickett being "partially obscured by 'Lost Cause' mythology." He is said to be "a tragic hero of sorts—a flamboyant officer who wanted to lead his troops into a glorious battle, but always missed the opportunity until the disastrous charge at Gettysburg."[703]

Parting Thoughts: The Gloves Come Off

I considered writing this chapter without any reference whatsoever to slavery. But the motives and actions of these soldiers very clearly involved that issue, requiring mention of it for context and understanding. The Civil War was about slavery, and the more I read about it, the angrier I get at those who denied it then and now. It was brother versus brother, North versus South, White versus Black, tradition versus morality, right versus wrong. The Civil War seems as alive today as it was 160 years ago, with many still writing about it vigorously. The South would be well served by acknowledging its wrong, rather than clinging to the Lost Cause myth and denying the fundamental issue in the Civil War.

The Lost Cause myth recharacterizes the Confederacy as being based on family and heritage, rather than as an effort to sustain slavery. When Mississippi declared secession, the lawmakers there declared: "Our position is thoroughly identified with the institution of slavery—the greatest material interest of the world." Alexander Stephens, the Confederate vice president, acknowledged slavery as "the immediate cause of the late rupture and present revolution," adding that the Confederacy

---

702 Hess, p. 177; Gordon (1998), p. 115; Robbins (2006), p. 292; Boritt, p. 19.

703 "LaSalle Corbell Pickett (1843–1931)." Lesley J. Gordon, *Virginia Encyclopedia*. October 27, 2015; Eicher and Eicher, p. 429; Brown, p. 730; "Book Review: General George E. Pickett in Life and Legend." UNC Press. Archived from the original on February 24, 2013; "The Fame of Pickett's Charge." https://www.scienceviews.com, accessed May 14, 2022.

was founded on "the great truth that the negro is not equal to the white man."

The Lost Cause is also romanticized in the movies *The Birth of a Nation*, *Gone With the Wind*, *Song of the South*, and *Gods and Generals*. These have been said to "recast the antebellum South as a moonlight and magnolia paradise of happy slaves, affectionate slave owners and villainous Yankees." As historian David Blight observes: "From this combination of Lost Cause voices, a reunited America arose pure, guiltless, and assured that the deep conflicts in its past had been imposed upon it by otherworldly forces. The side that lost was especially assured that its cause was true and good." Of *Gods and Generals*, Roger Ebert said it is "a film that Trent Lott might enjoy" and that if World War II had been handled this way, "there'd be hell to pay."[704]

As a kid, it always struck me as odd that even after the Civil War had been over for 100 years, the Southern states observed "Confederate Memorial Day" separately from Memorial Day. In 1965, I saw cars with vanity license plates on the front that depicted a fat, old Confederate soldier holding the stars-and-bars flag and saying: "Forget, Hell!" After church, we often ate at Johnny Reb's cafeteria near Kennesaw Mountain. The food was delicious and the place was swarming with Civil War paraphernalia and Stars and Bars flags. On my grandmother's farm in South Georgia, I often heard the somber story of my great-great-grandfather, who is said to have walked home from the Civil War. As a teenager in 1972, when I saw the 90-foot carving at Stone Mountain of Stonewall Jackson, Robert E. Lee, and Jefferson Davis on horseback with their hats over their hearts, I did not know what to think. It all seemed proud, sad, and muddled.

Only much later did I learn that the Klan, which had been largely eliminated by federal forces during Reconstruction, was reestablished at Stone Mountain in 1915 by a former Methodist preacher who scaled the mountain with a few others and set a cross on fire at the summit. When

---

[704] "How Trump's Victory Turns Into Another 'Lost Cause.'" John Blake, *CNN*. December 28, 2016, accessed July 8, 2020; Blight (2001), pp. 283–284; "Gods and Generals: Movie Review."Roger Ebert, https://www.rogerebert.com, February 21, 2003, accessed June 11, 2022; Gallagher, pp. 24–25.

the carving on Stone Mountain was in the planning phase, the head of the local chapter of the Daughters of the Confederacy had unsuccessfully urged the sculptor to include klansmen in the image: "Why not represent a small group of them in their nightly uniform approaching in the distance?"[705]

Historian Caroline Janney states that the tenets of the Lost Cause include the following:

- Having joined the Union, states can likewise withdraw.
- The defense of states' rights was the primary cause of the Civil War.
- Secession was in response to the cultural and economic aggression of the North against the superior and chivalric Southern way of life, which included slavery.
- Secession, not slavery, caused the Civil War.
- The motive of the North was economic.
- Slavery was a benign institution under which slaves were happy and much better off.
- Southern soldiers were chivalrous, aristocratic, and manly, and were good horsemen.
- Sherman destroyed property out of meanness.
- Slaves were loyal to the Confederate cause and unprepared for the responsibilities of freedom.
- The South lost only because the North had more soldiers and resources.
- The most heroic and saintly of all was Robert E. Lee.
- White dominance is God's will.[706]

Though I am a born-and-bred Southerner, it is my opinion that the South was doing wrong and it damned well knew it. Slavery had become so entrenched in its agricultural society that it was not willing

[705] "How the Birthplace of the Modern Ku Klux Klan Became the Site of America's Largest Confederate Monument." Jess Engebretson, https://www.kqed.com, July 24, 2015, accessed June 21, 2021.

[706] See Janney; Foster, pp. 4–8.

to set the moral record straight. Instead, Southerners diverted the issue by calling the conflict the War of Northern Aggression and insisting that the issue was not slavery but states rights and the preservation of a way of life. To me, worst of all was Robert E. Lee who, after being the head of West Point, resigned from the United States army in order to side with the South rather than do what was morally right. And all the while he claimed to be conflicted about it. Lee was a traitorous, self-righteous son of a bitch who, by siding with the South, prolonged the war with his military prowess, thereby getting lots of men killed on both sides.

The Lost Cause myth is said to be an "American pseudo-historical, negationist ideology." It is, in essence, revisionist history. It furthers the belief that slavery was moral, because the enslaved people were happy, even grateful. Many religious white Southerners are said to interpret the defeat of the Confederacy as God's punishment for their sins, turning to religion for solace. I am not sure how this is supposed to work if they are also unwilling to admit to any sin in the first place.[707] The constitutional legitimacy of secession is, of course, critical to the Lost Cause myth; otherwise the Confederates were traitors.

Surprisingly, many historians agree, however, that the Lost Cause somehow served to facilitate reunification of the country. As Janney observes: "Providing a sense of relief to white Southerners who feared being dishonored by defeat, the Lost Cause was largely accepted in the years following the war by white Americans who found it to be a useful tool in reconciling North and South." Historian Bruce Catton says: "The things done during the Civil War have not been forgotten, of course, but we now see them through a veil . . . It is a part of American legend, a

[707] "The Confederacy Was Built on Slavery. How Can So Many Southern Whites Think Otherwise?" Paul Duggan, *Washington Post*, November 28, 2018, accessed March 2, 2020; "The Black and the Gray: An Interview with Tony Horwitz." *Southern Cultures*, 1998: 4: 5–15. doi:10.1353/scu.1998.0065; "Confederate Symbols Are Making Way for Better Things." *Los Angeles Times*. Associated Press, February 27, 2021. p. A-2, accessed May 23, 2021; See generally Domby; "The Not-So Lost Cause of Moses Ezekiel." Lara Moehlman, *Moment* magazine, September 21, 2018; Wilson, p. 11; "The Religion of the Lost Cause: Ritual and Organization of the Southern Civil Religion, 1865–1920." Charles Reagan Wilson, *Journal of Southern History*, May 1980: 46 (2): 219–238. doi:10.2307/2208359. JSTOR 2208359.

part of American history, a part, if you will, of American romance." The Confederate Museum in Richmond, in addition to depicting slavery as benevolent, also puts forth the premise that Jim Crow laws were a proper solution to heightening racial tensions during Reconstruction.[708]

The Lost Cause myth was also used to condemn Reconstruction, which was portrayed as a Union strategy to exploit the South economically and politically. In essence, the Lost Cause involves bitter resentment. Yet as writer Mike LaSalle observes: "They say that history is written by the victors, but the Civil War has been the rare exception. Perhaps the need for the country to stay together made it necessary for the North to sit silently and accept the South's conception of the conflict."[709]

The Lost Cause portrays the South as being more adherent to Christian values than the greedy North, and slavery as being more benevolent than cruel. An enormous effort has been expended to preserve the South's honor. Religion of course confounds things further, with the burning of crosses by the Klan beginning after the publication of *The Clansman*, a Lost Cause book featuring an illustration of a burning cross. Slavery was predominately practiced in the South, the Bible Belt. By relegating blacks to the status of an "inferior race," it was perhaps easier for Southerners to reconcile their Bible teachings of "love one another" and "love thy neighbor" with their enslavement of blacks—beings whom they considered to be neither one of them nor a neighbor.[710]

Interestingly, and painfully, the Stop the Steal movement is said to be a reemergence of the Lost Cause idea, a manifestation of white backlash. It involves a false narrative (the Big Lie about the 2020 election

---

708 Gallagher, p. 28; "The Lost Cause." Caroline E. Janney, *Encyclopedia Virginia* (Virginia Foundation for the Humanities), 2009. https://www.encyclopediavirginia.org; accessed May 3, 2022; "Relics of Reconciliation: The Confederate Museum and Civil War Memory in the New South." Reiko Hillyer, *Public Historian*, November 2011, Vol. 33 Issue 4, pp. 35–62; see generally Catton, *Reflections on the Civil War*.

709 See Wilson; "Romanticizing Confederate Cause Has No Place Onscreen." Mick LaSalle, *San Francisco Chronicle*, July 24, 2015.

710 "Facts – The Civil War (U.S. National Park Service)." Nps.gov. Accessed June 11, 2022; "Civil War Sesquicentennial: The Lost Cause," Gaines Foster, Civil War Book Review (Fall 2013) online; See generally Dixon; https://en.m.wikipedia.org/wiki/Lost_Cause_of_the_Confederacy, p. 4, accessed June 21, 2021.

results), a revisionist history claiming that the January 6 insurrection was a peaceful tour of the Capitol, threats of secession, and a good old Southern helping of religious zeal to fuel it all.[711]

[711] https://edition.cnn.com/2016/12/28/us/lost-cause-trump/index.html; https://www.rollcall.com/2020/12/03/donald-trump-confederates-and-the-gop-brethren-in-the-new-lost-cause/; https://millercenter.org/election-2020-and-its-aftermath#lost-cause; https://www.trtworld.com/perspectives/why-donald-trump-s-lost-cause-can-never-stop-winning-41361

Bibliography

Adams, Randolph Greenfield (1928). "Arnold, Benedict." In Allen Johnson (ed.). *Dictionary of American Biography*. Scribner.

Alden, John R. (1996). *George Washington, a Biography*. Louisiana State University Press. ISBN 978–0–8071–2126–9.

Allen, Felicity (1999). *Jefferson Davis: Unconquerable Heart*. Columbia, Missouri: The University of Missouri Press. ISBN 9780826212191.

Allen, Thomas B. (2010). *Tories: Fighting for the King in America's First Civil War*. HarperCollins. ISBN 978–0–06–124180–2.

Anarumo, Theresa and Seaburg, Maureen (2017). *Hidden History of Staten Island*. New York, New York: The History Press. ISBN 9781467138680.

Bailey, Ronald H., and the Editors of Time-Life Books (1983). *Forward to Richmond: McClellan's Peninsular Campaign*. Alexandria, Virginia: Time-Life Books. ISBN 0–8094–4720–7.

Bailey, Ronald H., and the Editors of Time-Life Books (1985). *Battles for Atlanta: Sherman Moves East*. Alexandria, Virginia: Time-Life Books. ISBN 0–8094–4773–8.

Bauer, Karl Jack (1992). *The Mexican War: 1846–1848*. University of Nebraska Press. ISBN 978–0–8032–6107–5.

Beagle, Jonathan M (2000). "George Brinton McClellan." *Encyclopedia of the American Civil War: A Political, Social, and Military History*, edited by David S. Heidler and Jeanne T. Heidler. New York: W.W. Norton & Company. ISBN 0–393–04758–X.

Bearss, Edwin C. (2006).. *Fields of Honor: Pivotal Battles of the Civil War*. Washington, D.C.: National Geographic Society. ISGN 0–7922–7568–3.

Beatie, Russel H. (2004). *Army of the Potomac: McClellan Takes Command, September 1861 – February 1862.* New York: Da Capo Press. ISBN 0–306–81252–5.

Bell, William Gardner (2005). *Commanding Generals and Chiefs of Staff, 1775–2005: Portraits & Biographical Sketches of the United States Army's Senior Officer.* Washington, D.C.: Center of Military History. ISBN 978–0–1608–7330–0.

Bicheno H. (2003). *Rebels and Redcoats: The American Revolutionary War.* Harper Collins. ISBN 0007156251. ISBN 13: 9780007156252.

Billias, George Athan (1964). *George Washington's Generals.* New York: William Morrow.

Billias, George Athan (1969). *George Washington's Opponents.* New York: William Morrow. OCLC 11709.

Black, Jeremy (1992). "Naval Power, Strategy and Foreign Policy, 1775–1791." In Michael Duffy (ed.). *Parameters of British Naval Power, 1650–1850.* Exeter, United Kingdom: University of Exeter Press. ISBN 978–0–85989–385–5.

Blackford, Charles M. (1901). *The Trials and Trial of Jefferson Davis.* Vol. XXIX, Southern Historical Society, edited by R. A. Brock. Richmond, Virginia: William Ellis Jones.

Blassingame, John W. (1977). *Slave Testimony: Two Centuries of Letters, Speeches, Interviews, and Autobiographies.* Louisiana State University Press. ISBN 978–0807102732.

Blight, David W. (2001). *Race and Reunion: The Civil War in American Memory.* Belknap Press. ISBN 978–0–674–00332–3.

Bobrick, Benson (2009). *Master of War: The Life of General George H. Thomas.* New York, New York: Simon & Schuster. ISBN 978–0–7432–9025–8.

Bonekemper, Edward H. (2004). *A Victor, Not a Butcher: Ulysses S. Grant's Overlooked Military Genius.* Washington, DC: Regnery. ISBN 0–89526–062–X.

Bonekemper, Edward H. (2010). *Ulysses S. Grant: A Victor, Not a Butcher: The Military Genius of the Man Who Won the Civil War.* Regnery Publishing. ISBN 978–1–5969–8641–1.

Bonekemper, Edward H. (2012). *Grant and Lee.* Washington, DC: Regnery History; ISBN 978–1–62157–010–3.

Borick, Carl P. (2003). *A Gallant Defense: The Siege of Charleston, 1780.* University of South Carolina Press. ISBN 1–57003–487–7. OCLC 5051139.

Boritt, Gabor S. (1992). *Why the Confederacy Lost.* Gettysburg Civil War Institute Books. New York: Oxford University Press. ISBN 0–19–507405–X.

Bowman, Samuel M. and Irwin, Richard B. (1865). *Sherman and His Campaigns.* Republished 2000, Vivisphere Publishing. ISBN 10: 1587760169. ISBN 13: 978–158770167.

Boylston, James R.; Wiener, Allen J. (2009). *David Crockett in Congress: The Rise and Fall of the Poor Man's Friend.* Houston, Texas: Bright Sky Press. ISBN 978–1–933979–51–9.

Bradley, Mark L. (1995). *Last Stand in the Carolinas: The Battle of Bentonville.* Campbell, California: Savas Publishing Co., ISBN 978–1–882810–02–4.

Brands, H. W. (2012). *The Man Who Saved the Union: Ulysses S. Grant in War and Peace.* New York, New York: Doubleday. ISBN 978–0–385–53241–9.

Brandt, Clare (1994). *The Man in the Mirror: A Life of Benedict Arnold.* New York: Random House. ISBN 0–679–40106–7.

Brooks, Noah (1900). *Henry Knox, a Soldier of the Revolution: Major-General in the Continental Army, Washington's Chief of Artillery, First Secretary of War Under the Constitution, Founder of the Society of the Cincinnati; 1750–1806.* New York: G.P. Putnam's Sons. OCLC 77547631.

Brooks, Victor (1999). *The Boston Campaign.* Conshohocken, Pennsylvania; Combined Publishing. ISBN 1–58097–007–9. OCLC 42581510.

Brown, Fred R. (1909). *History of the Ninth U.S. Infantry, 1799–1909.* Chicago, Illinois: R.R. Donnelley & Sons Co.

Buchanan, John (1997). *The Road to Guilford Courthouse: The American Revolution in the Carolinas.* John Wiley & Sons. ISBN 978–0–4711–6402–9.

Burrough, Bryan; Tomlinson, Chris; Stanford, Jason (2021). *Forget the Alamo: The Rise and Fall of an American Myth.* New York, New York: Penguin Press. ISBN 9781984880093.

Burrows, Edwin G. (2008). *Forgotten Patriots: The Untold Story of American Prisoners During the Revolutionary War*. Basic Books. New York. ISBN 978–0–7867–2704–9.

Burton, Brian K. (2007). *The Peninsula & Seven Days: A Battlefield Guide*. Lincoln, Nebraska: University of Nebraska Press. ISBN 978–0–8032–6246–1.

Cadwalader, Richard McCall (1901). *Observance of the One Hundred and Twenty-third Anniversary of the Evacuation of Philadelphia by the British Army: Fort Washington and the Encampment of White Marsh, November 2, 1777*. Press of the New Era Printing Company.

Calhoun, Charles W. (2017). *The Presidency of Ulysses S. Grant*. Lawrence, Kansas: University Press of Kansas. ISBN 978–0–7006–2484–3.

Callahan, North (1958). *Henry Knox: General Washington's General*. New York: Rinehart.

Calloway, Colin G. (2007). *The Scratch of a Pen: 1763 and the Transformation of North America*. Oxford University Press. ISBN 978–0195331271.

Calore, Paul (2014). *The Texas Revolution and the U.S.-Mexican War: A Concise History*. Jefferson, North Carolina: McFarland. ISBN 978–0–7864–7940–5.

Camnitzer, Luis (2009). Weiss, Rachel (ed.). *On Art, Artists, Latin America, and Other Utopias*. University of Texas Press. ISBN 9780292783492.

Cantrell, Gregg (2001). *Stephen F. Austin: Empresario of Texas*. New Haven, Connecticut: Yale University Press. ISBN 10: 0300090935; ISBN 13: 978–0300090932.

Carhart, Tom (2003). *Lost Triumph: Lee's Real Plan at Gettysburg and Why It Failed*. New York, New York: G. P. Putnam & Sons.

Cartmell, Donald (2001). "The Legend of Stonewall". *The Civil War Book of Lists*. Franklin Lakes, New Jersey: The Career Press Inc. ISBN 1–56414–504–2.

Cashin, Joan E. (2006). *First Lady of the Confederacy: Varina Davis's Civil War*. Belknap Press of Harvard University Press. ISBN 978–0674030374.

Castel, Albert E. (1992). *Decision in the West: The Atlanta Campaign of 1864*. Lawrence, Kansas: University Press of Kansas. ISBN 978–0–7006–0748–8.

Catton, Bruce (1960). *The Civil War*. New York, New York: American Heritage. ISBN 0–618–00187–5.

Catton, Bruce (1965). *The Centennial History of the Civil War. Vol. 3, Never Call Retreat*. Garden City, New York: Doubleday. ISBN 0–671–46990–8.

Catton, Bruce (1982). *Reflections on the Civil War*. Penguin Publishing. ISBN 0425057372; ISBN 13: 9780425057377..

Catton, Bruce (2015). *Grant Takes Command*. Boston, Massachusetts: Little, Brown. ISBN 978–0–316–13210–7.

Chandler, Jonathan (2017). "To Become Again Our Brethren': Desertion and Community During the American Revolutionary War, 1775–83." Historical Research. Oxford University Press. 90, March 2017: 363–380. doi:10.1111/1468–2281.12183, retrieved March 20, 2020.

Chariton, Wallace O. (1992). *Exploring the Alamo Legends*. Wordware Publishing. ISBN 1–55622–255–6.

Chernow, Ron (2010). *Washington: A Life*. Penguin Press. ISBN 978–1–59420–266–7.

Chernow, Ron (2017). *Grant*. New York, New York: Penguin Press. ISBN 978–1–59420–487–6.

Chesnut, Mary (1905). *Diary of Mary Chesnut*. Fairfax, Virginia: D. Appleton and Company. OCLC 287696932.

Chisholm, Hugh, ed. (1911). "Thomas, George Henry." *Encyclopædia Britannica*. 26 (11th ed.). Cambridge University Press.

Christensen, Carol and Thomas. *The U.S.-Mexican War Companion to The U.S.-Mexican War, 1846–1848*. Public Television Series. San Francisco: Bay Soma Publishing, 1998. ISBN 0912333448.

Clark, Champ, and the Editors of Time-Life Books (1985). *Gettysburg: The Confederate High Tide*. Alexandria, Virginia: Time-Life Books. ISBN 0–8094–4758–4.

Cleaves, Freeman (1948). *Rock of Chickamauga: The Life of General George H. Thomas*. Norman, Oklahoma: University of Oklahoma Press. ISBN 0–8061–1978–0.

Clode, Charles M. (1869). *The Military Forces of the Crown: Their Administration and Government.* 1. London, J. Murray.

Cobia, Manley F., Jr. (2003). *Journey into the Land of Trials: The Story of Davy Crockett's Expedition to the Alamo.* Franklin, Tennessee: HIllsboro Press. ISBN 978–1–57736–268–5.

Coddington, Edwin B (1968). *The Gettysburg Campaign: A Study in Command.* New York, New York: Scribner's. ISBN 0–684–84569–5.

Collins, Donald E. (2005). *The Death and Resurrection of Jefferson Davis.* Lanham, Maryland: Rowman & LIttlefield Publishers. ISBN 9780742543041.

Cooke, Jacob E. (2002). "George Washington." In Graff, Henry (ed.) *The Presidents: A Reference History.* (3rd ed.). Scribner. ISBN 978–0–684–31226–2.

Cooper, William J. (2000). *Jefferson Davis, American.* Knopf Doubleday Publishing Group. ISBN 978–0–3077–7264–0.

Cooper, William J. (2010), "A Reassessment of Jefferson Davis as War Leader," in Hewitt, Lawrence Lee; Bergeron, Jr., Arthur W. (eds.), *Confederate Generals in the Western Theater, Volume 1: Classic Essays on America's Civil War.* Knoxville: University of Tennessee Press, p. 161, ISBN 9781572337008.

Coski, John M (2005). *The Confederate Battle Flag: America's Most Embattled Emblem.* Cambridge, Massachusetts: Belknap Press of Harvard University Press. ISBN 0–674–01983–0.

Coulter, Ellis Merton (1950). *The Confederate States of America, 1861–1865, Volume 7.* Baton Rouge, Louisiana: Louisiana State University Press. ISBN 9780807100073.

Cox, Jacob D. (1882). *The March to the Sea—Franklin and Nashville.* Reprinted 2004, Digital Scanning Inc. ISBN 10: 1582185360. ISBN 13: 978–1582185361.

Cox, Jacob D. (1900). *Military Reminiscences of the Civil War.* New York, New York: Charles Scribner's Sons. Reprinted 2008, Herron Press. ISBN 10: 1408687593. ISBN 13: 978–1408687598.

Cox, R. David (2017). *The Religious Life of Robert E. Lee.* Wm. B. Eerdmans Publishing. ISBN 978–0–8028–7482–5.

Cozzens, Peter (1990). *No Better Place to Die: The Battle of Stones River.* Urbana, Illinois: University of Illinois Press. ISBN 0–252–01652–1.

Cozzens, Peter (1992). *This Terrible Sound: The Battle of Chickamauga.* Urbana, Illinois: University of Illinois Press. ISBN 0–252–02236–X.

Cozzens, Peter (1997). *The Darkest Days of the War: The Battles of Iuka and Corinth.* Chapel Hill, North Carolina: University of North Carolina Press. ISBN 0–8078–2320–1.

Crockett, David (1834). *A Narrative of the Life of David Crockett of the State of Tennessee Written By Himself.* Contained within The Autobiography of David Crockett. New York: Charles Scribner's Son 1923; Bison Books Reprint Edition 1987, ISBN-10: 0803263253; ISBN-13: 978–0803263253.

Cullum, George W. (1850). *Biographical Register of the Officers and Graduates of the U.S. Military Academy.* Boston, Massachusetts: Houghton Mifflin And Company.

Cullum, George W. (1891). *Biographical Register of the Officers and Graduates of the U.S. Military Academy. Vol. 2.* Boston, Massachusetts: Houghton Mifflin And Company. ISBN 9780608428628.

Davies, K.G., ed. (1972–1981). *Documents of the American Revolution, 1779–1783.* Shannon, Ireland: Irish University Press. ISBN 9780716520856. OCLC 836225.

Davis, Burke (1957). *Jeb Stuart: The Last Cavalier.* New York: Random House. ISBN 0–517–18597–0.

Davis, William C. (1999). *The Commanders of the Civil War.* London: Salamander Books Ltd. ISBN 978–1–84065–105–8.

Davis, William C. (2004). *Lone Star Rising: The Revolutionary Birth of the Texas Republic.* New York, New York: Free Press. ISBN 978–0–68486–510–2.

Davis, William C., and the Editors of Time-Life Books (1986). *Death in the Trenches: Grant at Petersburg.* Alexandria, VA: Time-Life Books. ISBN 0–8094–4776–2.

de Bachelle Seebold, Herman Boehm (1941). *Old Louisiana Plantation Homes and Family Trees.* New Orleans: Pelican Press.

Dixon Jr., Thomas (1905). *The Clansman: An Historical Romance of the Ku Klux Klan.* ASIN B08DMK98VB.

Dodd, William E. (1907). *Jefferson Davis.* Philadelphia: George W. Jacobs and Company. Reprinted 1997, Bison Books. ISBN 10: 080326609X. ISBN 13: 978–0803266094.

Domby, Adam H. (2020). *The False Cause: Fraud, Fabrication, and White Supremacy In Confederate Memory*. Univ. of Virginia Press. ISBN 978–0–8139–4376–3. OCLC 1151896244.

Donald, David Herbert (1995). *Lincoln*. New York, New York: Simon & Schuster. ISBN 0–684–80846–3.

Dougherty, Kevin (2007). *Civil War Leadership and Mexican War Experience*. Jackson, Mississippi: University of Mississippi Press, 2007. ISBN 1–57806–968–8.

Dull, Jonathan R (2015) [1975]. *The French Navy and American Independence: A Study of Arms and Diplomacy, 1774–1787*. Princeton, New Jersey: Princeton University Press. ISBN 978–0–691–06920–3. OCLC 1500030.

Dyer, John P. (1995). *The Gallant Hood*. New York: Smithmark. ISBN 978–0–8317–3285–1.

Eclov, Jon Paul (2013). "Informal Alliance: Royal Navy And U.S. Navy Co-Operation Against Republican France During The Quasi-War And Wars Of The French Revolution." (PhD) University of North Dakota.

Eicher, David J. (2001). *The Longest Night: A Military History of the Civil War*. New York, New York: Simon & Schuster. ISBN 0–684–84944–5.

Eicher, John H. and Eicher, David J. (2001). *Civil War High Commands*. Stanford, California: Stanford University Press. ISBN 0–8047–3641–3.

Einolf, Christopher J. (2007). *George Thomas: Virginian for the Union*. Norman, Oklahoma: University of Oklahoma Press. ISBN 978–0–8061–3867–1.

Ellis, Joseph J. (2004). *His Excellency: George Washington*. Alfred A. Knopf. ISBN 978–1–4000–4031–5.

Escott, Paul (1978). *After Secession: Jefferson Davis and the Failure of Confederate Nationalism*. Baton Rouge, Louisiana: Louisiana State University Press. ISBN 9780807118078.

Esposito, Vincent J. (1959). *West Point Atlas of American Wars*. New York, New York: Frederick A. Praeger. OCLC 5890637; https://www.worldcat.org/oclc/5890637.

Farina, William (2007). *Ulysses S. Grant, 1861–1864: His Rise from Obscurity to Military Greatness.* Jefferson, North Carolina: McFarland & Co. ISBN 978–0–7864–2977–6.

Faust, Patricia L. ed. (1991). *Historical Illustrated Encyclopedia of the Civil War*. Perennial. ISBN 10: 0062731165; ISBN 13: 9780062731166.

Fellman, Michael (2000). *The Making of Robert E. Lee*. Random House. ISBN 978–0–679–45650–6.

Fellman, Michael (2005). "Robert E. Lee: Myth and Man" in *Virginia's Civil War*. University of Virginia Press (Peter Wallenstein; Bertram Wyatt-Brown, eds). ISBN 978–0–8139–2315–4. Paperback (2009), ISBN 10: 0813928281. ISBN 13: 978–0813928289.

Ferling, John (2002). *Setting the World Ablaze: Washington, Adams, Jefferson, and the American Revolution*. Oxford University Press. ISBN 978–0–19–513409–4.

Ferling, John (2003). *A Leap in the Dark: The Struggle to Create the American Republic*. Oxford University Press. ISBN 978–0–1997–2870–1.

Ferling, John (2009). *Almost a Miracle: The American Victory in the War of Independence*. New York: Oxford University Press. ISBN 978–0–19–538292–1.

Ferling, John (2009). *The Ascent of George Washington: The Hidden Political Genius of an American Icon*. Bloomsbury Press. ISBN 978–1–6081–9182–6.

Fischer, David Hackett (2004). *Washington's Crossing*. Oxford University Press. ISBN 978–0–1951–7034–4.

Fleming, Thomas (2006). *Washington's Secret War*. Harper Collins. ISBN 978–1–4391–0533–7.

Flood, Charles Bracelen (2005). *Grant and Sherman: The Friendship That Won the Civil War*. New York, New York: Harper Perennial. ISBN 0–06–114871–7.

Foner, Eric (2019). *The Second Founding: How The Civil War And Reconstruction Remade The Constitution*. New York, New York: W.W. Norton & Company, Inc. ISBN 978–0–393–35852–0.

Foote, Shelby (1958). *The Civil War: A Narrative. Vol. 1, Fort Sumter to Perryville*. New York, New York: Random House. ISBN 0–394–49517–9.

Foote, Shelby (1958). *The Civil War: A Narrative. Vol. 2, Fredericksburg to Meridian.* New York, New York: Random House. ISBN 0–394–74621–X.

Foote, Shelby (1958). *The Civil War: A Narrative. Vol. 3, Red River to Appomattox.* New York, New York: Random House. ISBN 0–394–74622–8.

Ford, John Salmon (1963). *Rip Ford's Texas.* Austin, Texas: University of Texas Press. Reissued 1987, University of Chicago Press. ISBN 10: 0292770340. ISBN 13: 978–0292770348.

Ford, Paul Leicester, (1896). *The True George Washington.* Philadelphia: J.B. Lippincott Company.

Foster, Gaines M. (1988). *Ghosts of the Confederacy: Defeat, the Lost Cause and the Emergence of the New South, 1865–1913.* Oxford University Press (1987). ISBN 978–0–19–505420–0.

Fowler, Will (2007). *Santa Anna of Mexico.* Lincoln, Nebraska: University of Nebraska Press. ISBN 13: 978–0–8032–1120–9.

Freedman, Russell (2008). Washington at Valley Forge. Holiday House. ISBN 978–0–8234–2069–8.

Freeman, Douglas S. (1934). *R. E. Lee, A Biography.* Charles Scribner's Sons. ASIN: B00NFPZR9G.

Freeman, Douglas S. (1946). *Lee's Lieutenants: A Study in Command,* 3 Vol. New York: Scribner. ISBN 978–0–684–85979–8.

Frost, Lawrence A. (1976). *General Custer's Libbie.* Seattle, Washington: Superior Publishing Co. ISBN 10: 0875648061. ISBN 13: 978–0875648064.

Frothingham, Richard (1903). *History of the Siege of Boston, and of the Battles of Lexington, Concord, and Bunker Hill: Also an Account of the Bunker Hill Monument.* Little, Brown, & Company.

Fuller, Maj. Gen. J. F. C. (1957). *Grant and Lee: A Study in Personality and Generalship.* Bloomington, Indiana: Indiana University Press. ISBN 0–253–13400–5.

Furgurson, Ernest B. (2007). *Not War But Murder.* Knopf Doubleday Publishing Group. ISBN 978–0–3074–2704–5.

Gallagher, Gary W. and Alan T. Nolan ed. (2000). *The Myth of the Lost Cause and Civil War History.* Indiana University Press. ISBN 0–253–33822–0.

Garland, Hamlin (1898). *Ulysses S. Grant: His Life and Character*. New York, New York: Doubleday & McClure. ISBN 9780795019111.

Glatthaar, Joseph T. (2008). *General Lee's Army: From Victory to Collapse*. New York, New York: Free Press. ISBN 978–0–684–82787–2.

Goodwin, Doris Kearns (2005). *Team of Rivals*. New York, New York: Simon & Schuster. ISBN 978–0–684–82490–1.

Gordon, John W.; Keegan, John (2007). *South Carolina and the American Revolution: A Battlefield History*. University of South Carolina Press. ISBN 9781570034800.

Gordon, Lesley J. (1998). *General George E. Pickett in Life and Legend*. Chapel Hill, North Carolina: University of North Carolina Press. ISBN 978–0–8078–2450–4.

Graham, William A. (1953). *The Custer Myth: A Source Book of Custeriana*. The Stackpole Co. ISBN 0811703479.

Grainger, John D. (2005). *The Battle of Yorktown, 1781: A Reassessment*. Boydell Press. ISBN 978–1–8438–3137–2.

Grant, Ulysses S. (1885–1886). *Personal Memoirs of U. S. Grant*. 2 vols. Charles L. Webster & Company. ISBN 0–914427–67–9.

Greene, A. Wilson (2008). *The Final Battles of the Petersburg Campaign: Breaking the Backbone of the Rebellion*. Knoxville, Tennessee: University of Tennessee Press,. ISBN 978–1–57233–610–0.

Greene, Jack P.; Pole, J.R. (2008). *A Companion to the American Revolution*. Blackwell Publishers. ISBN 978–0–4707–5644–7.

Groneman, William (2005). *David Crockett: Hero of the Common Man*. New York: Forge Books, ISBN 978–0–7653–1067–5.

Groom, Winston (2012). *Shiloh 1862*. National Geographic Society. ISBN 978–1–4262–0879–9.

Gruber, Ira (1972). *The Howe Brothers and the American Revolution*. New York: Atheneum Press. ISBN 978–0–8078–1229–7. OCLC 1464455.

Guardino, Peter (2017). *The Dead March: A History of the Mexican-American War*. Cambridge: Harvard University Press. ISBN 9780674244740.

Hadden, James M. and Rogers, Horatio (1884). *A Journal Kept in Canada and Upon Burgoyne's Campaign in 1776 and 1777 by Lieut. James M. Hadden*. J. Munsell's Sons. OCLC 2130358.

Hallock, Judith Lee (1991). *Braxton Bragg and Confederate Defeat.* Vol. 2. Tuscaloosa, Alabama: University of Alabama Press. ISBN 0–8173–0543–2.

Hamilton, Sir Frederick William (1874). *The Origin and History of the First Or Grenadier Guards.* John Murray, London.

Hardin, Stephen (1994). *Texian Iliad-A Military History of the Texas Revolution.* Austin, Texas: University of Texas Press. ISBN 0–292–73086–1.

Hardin, Stephen (2004). *The Alamo 1836: Santa Anna's Texas Campaign.* Westport, Connecticut: Osprey Publishing. ISBN 978–1–84176–090–2.

Hardoff, Richard (1989). *The Custer Battle Casualties: Burials, Exhumations, and Reinterments.* El Segundo, California: Upton and Sons. ISBN 0912783141.

Hattaway, Herman, and Archer Jones (1983). *How the North Won: A Military History of the Civil War.* Urbana, Illinois: University of Illinois Press. ISBN 0–252–00918–5.

Henderson, Timothy J. (2008). *A Glorious Defeat: Mexico and Its War with the United States.* New York, New York: Hill and Wang. ISBN 978–0–8090–4967–7.

Hess, Earl J. (2001). *Pickett's Charge – The Last Attack at Gettysburg.* Chapel Hill, North Carolina: University of North Carolina Press. ISBN 978–0–8078–2648–5.

Hesseltine, William B. (1957) [1935]. *Ulysses S. Grant: Politician.* New York, New York: F. Ungar Pub. Co. ISBN 1–931313–85–7.

Hettle, Wallace (2011). *Inventing Stonewall Jackson: A Civil War Hero in History and Memory.* Louisiana State University Press. ISBN 10: 0807137812. ISBN 13: 978–0807137819.

Higginbotham, Don (1983). *The War of American Independence: Military Attitudes, Policies, and Practice, 1763–1789.* Northeastern University Press. ISBN 0930350448.

Hine, Robert V; Faragher, John Mack (2000). *The American West: A New Interpretive History.* New Haven, Connecticut: Yale University Press. ISBN 978–0300078350.

Hirshson, Stanley P. (1997). *The White Tecumseh: A Biography of General William T. Sherman.* John Wiley & Sons. ISBN 0–471–28329–0.

Hood, John Bell (1880). *Advance and Retreat: Personal Experiences in the United States and Confederate States Armies.* Lincoln, Nebraska: University of Nebraska Press (2011). ISBN 978–0–8032–7285–9.

Horgan, Lucille E. (2002). *Forged in War: The Continental Congress and the Origin of Military Supply and Acquisition Policy.* Greenwood Publishing Group. ISBN 978–0–313–32161–0.

Horn, John (1999). *The Petersburg Campaign: June 1864 – April 1865.* Conshohocken, Pennsylvania: Combined Publishing. ISBN 978–1–58097–024–2.

Howe, Archibald (1908). *Colonel John Brown, of Pittsfield, Massachusetts, the Brave Accuser of Benedict Arnold.* Boston: W. B. Clarke.

Hoyt, Edwin P. (1999). *The Alamo: An Illustrated HIstory.* Dallas, Texas: Taylor Publishing Company, ISBN 087833–204–9.

Hurt, R. Douglas (1994). *American Agriculture: A Brief History.* Iowa State Press. ISBN 0813823765.

Jacobson, Eric A., and Richard A. Rupp (2007). *For Cause And For Country: A Study of the Affair at Spring Hill and the Battle of Franklin.* Franklin, Tennessee: O'More Publishing. ISBN 0–9717444–4–0.

Janney, Caroline E. (2009). "The Lost Cause." *Encyclopedia Virginia.* Virginia Foundation for the Humanities. https://www.encyclopediavirginia.org.

Jermann, Donald R. (2012). *Civil War Battlefield Orders Gone Awry: The Written Word and Its Consequences in 13 Engagements.* McFarland. ISBN 10: 0786469498. ISBN 13: 978–0786469499.

Johnson, Paul (1997). *A History of the American People.* New York, New York: HarperCollins. ISBN 0–06–016836–6.

Johnson, Robert Underwood (1885). *Battles and Leaders of the Civil War (4 vol).* New York, New York: The Century Company. Reprinted 1956, Castle Books. ASIN B000AP54H0. Reprinted 1979. ISBN 9780890095690.

Johnston, Henry Phelps (1881). *The Yorktown Campaign and the Surrender of Cornwallis, 1781.* New York: Harper & Bros. OCLC 426009.

Kahan, Paul (2018). *The Presidency of Ulysses S. Grant: Preserving the Civil War's Legacy.* Yardley, Pennsylvania: Westholme Publishing, LLC. ISBN 978–1–59416–273–2.

Kappler, Charles J. (1904). *Indian Affairs. Laws and Treaties. Vol. II.* Washington. Treaty with the Crows, 1868.

Kennedy, Frances H. (1998). *The Civil War Battlefield Guide*, 2nd ed. Boston: Houghton Mifflin Co. ISBN 0–395–74012–6.

Kennedy, James R; Kennedy, Walter Donald (1998). *Was Jefferson Davis Right?* Gretna, Louisiana: Pelican Publishing Co. ISBN 156554370X.

Ketchum Richard M. (2014). *Victory at Yorktown: The Campaign That Won the Revolution*. Henry Holt and Company. ISBN 978–1–4668–7953–9.

Ketchum, Richard M. (1997). *Saratoga: Turning Point of America's Revolutionary War*. New York: Henry Holt. ISBN 978–0–8050–6123–9. OCLC 41397623.

Ketchum, Richard M. (1999). *Decisive Day: The Battle of Bunker Hill.* New York: Owl Books. ISBN 0–385–41897–3.

Ketchum, Richard M. (1999). *The Winter Soldiers: The Battles for Trenton and Princeton*. Henry Holt. ISBN 978–0–8050–6098–0.

Kilgore, Dan and Crisp, James E. (2010). *How Did Davy Die? And Why Do We Care So Much?* College Station, Texas: Texas A&M University Press. Commemorative Ed.,originally published 1978.

Kilmeade, Brian (2019). *Sam Houston and the Alamo Avengers: The Texas Victory That Changed American History*. Sentinel. ISBN 978–0525540533.

Konstam, Angus; Bryan, Tony (2004). *Confederate Blockade Runner 1861–65*. Wisconsin: Osprey Publishing. ISBN 9781841766362.

Korn, Jerry, and the Editors of Time-Life Books (1985). *The Fight for Chattanooga: Chickamauga to Missionary Ridge*. Alexandria, Virginia: Time-Life Books. ISBN 0–8094–4816–5.

Krauze, Enrique (1997). *Mexico: Biography of Power*. New York: Harper Collins. ISBN 0–06–016325–9.

Lack, Paul D. (1992). *Texas Revolutionary Experience: A Political and Social History, 1835–1836*. College Station, Texas: Texas A&M University Press. ISBN-10: 0890967210; ISBN-13: 978–0890967218.

Lamers, William M. (1965). *The Edge of Glory: A Biography of General William S. Rosecrans*. U.S.A. Baton Rouge, Louisiana: Louisiana State University Press. ISBN 0–8071–2396–X.

Lee, Robert E. Jr. (1904). *Recollections and Letters of General Robert E. Lee*. St. Petersburg, Florida: Red and Black Publishers, 2008. ISBN 978–1–934941–13–3. First published in 1904 by Doubleday, Page & Co.

Lengel, Edward G. (2005). *General George Washington: A Military Life*. Random House. ISBN 978–1–4000–6081–8.

Levy, Janey (2003). *The Alamo: A Primary Source History of the Legendary Texas Mission*. Rosen Publishing Group, Inc. ISBN 0–8239–3681–3.

Lewis, Lloyd (1993). *Sherman: Fighting Prophet*. University of Nebraska Press, ISBN 0–8032–7945–0. First published by Harcourt, Brace & Co., 1932.

Lind, Michael (1997). *The Alamo: An Epic*. Houghton Miffllin. ISBN 0–395–82758–2.

Lindley, Thomas Ricks (2003). *Alamo Traces: New Evidence and New Conclusions*. Plano, Texas: Republic of Texas Press. ISBN 1–55622–983–6.

Livermore, Thomas L. (1986). *Numbers and Losses in the Civil War in America, 1861–65*. Dayton, Ohio: Morningside House, 1986. ISBN 0–527–57600–X. First published by Houghton Mifflin, 1901.

Loewen, James W. (1999). *Lies Across America: What American Historic Sites Get Wrong*. New York, New York: Touchstone, Simon & Schuster, Inc. ISBN 9780743296298.

Longacre, Edward G. (1986). *The Cavalry at Gettysburg: A Tactical Study of Mounted Operations during the Civil War's Pivotal Campaign, 9 June–14 July 1863*. Lincoln, Nebraska: University of Nebraska Press. ISBN 978–0–8032–7941–4.

Longacre, Edward G. (2001). *Lincoln's Cavalrymen: A History of the Mounted Forces of the Army of the Potomac, 1861–1865*. Mechanicsburg, Pennsylvania: Stackpole Books. ISBN 10: 0806142294. ISBN 13: 978–0806142296.

Longacre, Edward G. (2002). *Lee's Cavalrymen: A History of the Mounted Forces of the Army of Northern Virginia*. Mechanicsburg, Pennsylvania: Stackpole Books. ISBN 978–0–8117–0898–2.

Longacre, Edward G. (2006). *General Ulysses S. Grant: The Soldier and the Man*. Cambridge, Massachusetts: First Da Capo Press. ISBN 978–0–306–81636–9.

Longstreet (1896). *From Manassas to Appomattox: Memoirs of the Civil War in America*. Philadelphia, Pennsylvania: J. B. Lippincott.

Lossing, Benson John (1852). *The Pictorial Field-Book of the Revolution*. Harper & Brothers.

Loveman, Brian (2010). *No Higher Law: American Foreign Policy and the Western Hemisphere Since 1776*. Chapel Hill: University of North Carolina Press. ISBN 9780807895986.

Luvaas, Jay, and Harold W. Nelson, eds. (2008). *Guide to the Atlanta Campaign: Rocky Face Ridge to Kennesaw Mountain*. Lawrence, Kansas: University Press of Kansas. ISBN 978–0–7006–1570–4.

Mackesy, Piers (1992). *The War for America: 1775-1783*. Lincoln Nebraska: Bison Books. ISBN 10: 0803281927; ISBN 13: 9780803281929.

Marshall, Joseph M. III. (2007). *The Day the World Ended at Little Bighorn: A Lakota History*. New York, New York: Viking Press. ISBN 9780670038534.

Marszalek, John F. (1992). *Sherman: A Soldier's Passion for Order*. Free Press. ISBN 0–02–920135–7; reissued with new preface, Southern Illinois University Press, 2007.

Martin, David G. (1993). *The Philadelphia Campaign: June 1777 – July 1778*. Conshohocken, Pennsylvania: Combined Books. ISBN 0–938289–19–5. 2003. Da Capo reprint, ISBN 0–306–81258–4.

Martin, David G. (1996). *Gettysburg July 1*. Conshocken, Pennsylvania: Combined Publishing. ISBN 0–938289–81–0.

Martin, James Kirby (1997). *Benedict Arnold: Revolutionary Hero (An American Warrior Reconsidered)*. New York University Press. ISBN 0–8147–5560–7.

Mays, Terry M. (2019). *Historical Dictionary of the American Revolution*. Rowman & Littlefield. ISBN 978–1–5381–1972–3.

McCullough, David (2005). *1776*. Simon & Schuster. ISBN 978–0–7432–2671–4.

McDonough, James Lee (2016). *William Tecumseh Sherman: In the Service of My Country, A Life*. W. W. Norton & Company. ISBN 978–0–393–24157–0.

McFeely, William S. (1981). *Grant: A Biography*. Norton. ISBN 0–393–01372–3.

McGuire, Hunter. "Death of Stonewall Jackson." *Southern Historical Society Papers* 14 (1886).

McMurry, Richard M. (1992). *John Bell Hood and the War for Southern Independence*. Lincoln, Nebraska: University of Nebraska Press. ISBN 0–8032–8191–9.

McMurry, Richard M. (2000). *Atlanta 1864: Last Chance for the Confederacy*. Lincoln, Nebraska: University of Nebraska Press. ISBN 0–8032–8278–8.

McNeese, Tim (2003). *The Alamo*. Chelsea House. ISBN 10:079107529X. ISBN 13: 978–0791075296.

McPherson, James M. (1988). "Battle Cry of Freedom: The Civil War Era." *Oxford History of the United States*. Oxford University Press. ISBN 0195038630.

McPherson, James M. (2002). *Crossroads of Freedom: Antietam, The Battle That Changed the Course of the Civil War*. New York: Oxford University Press. ISBN 0–19–513521–0.

McPherson, James M. (2008). *Tried By War: Abraham Lincoln as Commander in Chief*. Penguin Press. ISBN 978–1–4406–5245–5.

McWhiney, Grady (1969). *Braxton Bragg and Confederate Defeat*. Vol. 1. New York, New York: Columbia University Press. ISBN 0–8173–0545–9. Reprinted Tuscaloosa, Alabama: University of Alabama Press (1991). ISBN 978–0–8173–5914–0.

Merry Robert W. (2010). *A Country of Vast Designs: James K. Polk, the Mexican War and the Conquest of the American Continent*. Simon & Schuster America Collection. ISBN 074329744X.

Michno, Gregory F. (1997). *Lakota Noon: The Indian Narrative of Custer's Defeat*. Mountain Press Publishing Company. ISBN 0–87842–349–4.

Middleton, Richard (2013). "The Clinton-Cornwallis Controversy and Responsibility for the British Surrender at Yorktown." *History*. 98 (331).

Middleton, Richard (2014). "Naval Resources and the British Defeat at Yorktown, 1781." *The Mariner's Mirror*. 100 (1): 29–43. doi:10.1080/00253359.2014.866373. S2CID 154569534.

Miller, Donald L. (2019). *Vicksburg: Grant's Campaign That Broke the Confederacy*. Simon and Schuster. ISBN 978–1–4516–4137–0.

Miller, John C. (1959). *Origins of the American Revolution*. Stanford University Press. ISBN 9780804705936.

Mintz, Max M. (1990). *The Generals of Saratoga: John Burgoyne and Horatio Gates*. New Haven, Connecticut: Yale University Press. ISBN 978–0–300–04778–3. OCLC 644565187.

Moore, Stephen L. (2004) *Eighteen Minutes: The Battle of San Jacinto and the Texas Independence Campaign*. Plano, Texas: Republic of Texas Press. ISBN 1–58907–009–7.

Nevin, David, and the Editors of Time-Life Books (1986). *Sherman's March: Atlanta to the Sea*. Alexandria, Virginia: Time-Life Books. ISBN 0–8094–4812–2.

Nickerson, Hoffman (1967)]. *The Turning Point of the Revolution*. Port Washington, New York: Kennikat. OCLC 549809.

Nolan, Alan T. (1991). *Lee Considered: General Robert E. Lee and Civil War History*. University of North Carolina Press. ISBN 978–0–8078–4587–5.

O'Connor, Richard (1948). *Thomas, Rock of Chickamauga*. New York, New York: Prentice-Hall. OCLC 1345107.

Paine, Thomas (1982). Kramnick, Isaac (ed.). *Common Sense*. Penguin Classics. ISBN 978–0–1403–9016–2.

Pancake, John (1985). *This Destructive War*. University of Alabama Press. ISBN 0–8173–0191–7.

Pfanz, Donald C. (1989). *Abraham Lincoln at City Point: The Petersburg Campaign, March 20 – April 9, 1865*. Lynchburg, Virginia: H. E. Howard, Inc. ASIN B0785J5C7X.

Pfanz, Harry W. (2001). *Gettysburg–The First Day*. Chapel Hill, North Carolin: University of North Carolina Press. ISBN 0–8078–2624–3.

Philbrick, Nathaniel (2010). *The Last Stand: Custer, Sitting Bull, and the Battle of the Little Bighorn*. Penguin. ISBN 10: 0143119605. ISBN 13: 978–0143119609.

Philbrick, Nathaniel (2016). *Valiant Ambition: George Washington, Benedict Arnold, and the Fate of the American Revolution.* Penguin Books. ISBN 978–0–14–311019–4.

Piecuch, Jim (2006). *The Battle of Camden: A Documentary History.* Charleston, South Carolina: The History Press. ISBN 978–1–59629–144–7. OCLC 70219827.

Poore, Benjamin and Tiffany, O.H. (1885). *Life of Ulysses S. Grant.* Edgewood Publishing Company. Reprinted 1999, Reprint Services Corp. ISBN 10: 0781287642. ISBN 13: 978–0781287647.

Potter, Robert (1994). *Jefferson Davis: Confederate President.* Heinemann/Raintree. ISBN 10: 0811423301. ISBN 13: 978–0811423304.

Poyo, Gerald Eugene (1996). *Tejano Journey, 1770–1850.* Austin, Texas: University of Texas Press. ISBN 978–0–29276–570–2.

Pryor, Elizabeth Brown (2007). *Reading the Man: A Portrait of Robert E. Lee Through His Private Letters.* Viking Press. ISBN 978–0–6700–3829–9.

Puls, Mark (2008). *Henry Knox: Visionary General of the American Revolution.* New York, New York: Palgrave Macmillan. ISBN 978–0–230–62388–0.

Rafuse, Ethan S. (2005). *McClellan's War: The Failure of Moderation in the Struggle for the Union.* Bloomington, Indiana: Indiana University Press. ISBN 0–253–34532–4.

Randall, Willard Sterne (1990). *Benedict Arnold: Patriot and Traitor.* William Morrow and Inc. ISBN 1–55710–034–9.

Randall, Willard Sterne (1997). *George Washington: A Life.* Henry Holt & Co. ISBN 978–0–8050–2779–2.

Randall, William Sterne and Nahra, Nancy (1999). *Forgotten Americans: Footnote Figures Who Changed American History.* De Capo Press. ISBN 978–0–738–20150–4.

Reeves, John (2018). *The Lost Indictment of Robert E. Lee: The Forgotten Case against an American Icon.* Roman & Littlefield Publishers. ISBN 10: 1538110393, ISBN 13: 978–1538110393.

Reid, Whitelaw (1893). *Ohio in the War: Her Statesmen, Generals, and Soldiers.* Columbus, Ohio: Eclectic Publishing Company. Republished 2010, Nabu Press. ISBN 10: 1177893010. ISBN 13: 978–1177893015.

Rhea, Gordon C. (1997). *The Battles for Spotsylvania Court House and the Road to Yellow Tavern, May 7–12, 1864*. Baton Rouge, Louisiana: Louisiana State University Press. ISBN 978–0–8071–2136–8.

Richardson, Heather Cox (2020). *How the South Won the Civil War*. New York, New York: Oxford University Press. ISBN 9780190900908.

Risch, Erna (1981). *Supplying Washington's Army*. Univeristy of Michigan Library. ASIN B006ZOIPMU. Center of Military History, United States Army. ISBN-10: 1508436789.

Robbins, James S. (2006). *Last in Their Class: Custer, Pickett and the Goats of West Point*. New York, New York: Encounter Books. ISBN 1–59403–141–X.

Robertson, James I., Jr. (1997). *Stonewall Jackson: The Man, The Soldier, The Legend*. New York, New York: Macmillan Publishing. ISBN 0–02–864685–1.

Rose, Alexander (2006). *Washington's Spies: The Story of America's First Spy Ring*. Random House Publishing Group. ISBN 978–0–553–80421–8.

Rowland, Thomas J. (1998). "George Brinton McClellan." *Leaders of the American Civil War: A Biographical and Historiographical Dictionary*. Edited by Charles F. Ritter and Jon L. Wakelyn. Westport, Conecticut: Greenwood Press. ISBN 0–313–29560–3.

Salmon, John S. (2001). *The Official Virginia Civil War Battlefield Guide*. Mechanicsburg, Pennsylvania: Stackpole Books. ISBN 0–8117–2868–4.

Sarna, Jonathan D. (2012). *When General Grant Expelled the Jews*. New York: Schocken Books. ISBN 978–0–8052–4279–9.

Savas, Theodore P.; Dameron, J. David (2006). *A Guide to the Battles of the American Revolution*. Savas Beatie LLC. ISBN 978–1–6112–1011–8.

Schultz, Duane (2010). *Custer: Lessons in Leadership*. New York, New York: St. Martin's Press. ISBN 978–0–230–11424–1.

Scott, Hamish M (1988). "Sir Joseph Yorke, Dutch Politics and the Origins of the Fourth Anglo-Dutch War." *The Historical Journal*. 31 (3): 571–589. doi:10.1017/
S0018246X00023499. JSTOR 2639757.

Sears, Stephen W. (1988). *George B. McClellan: The Young Napoleon*. New York, New York: Da Capo Press. ISBN 0–306–80913–3.

Sears, Stephen W. (1992). *To the Gates of Richmond: The Peninsula Campaign*. New York, New York: Ticknor and Fields. ISBN 978–0–89919–790–6.

Sears, Stephen W. (1999). *Controversies & Commanders: Dispatches from the Army of the Potomac*. Boston, Massachusetts: Houghton Mifflin Co. ISBN 0–395–86760–6.

Sears, Stephen W. (2003). *Gettysburg*. Boston, Massachusetts: Houghton Mifflin. ISBN 0–395–86761–4.

Seidule, Ty (2021). *Robert E. Lee and Me: A Southerner's Reckoning with the Myth of the Lost Cause*. St. Martin's Publishing Group. ISBN 9781250239266.

Seineke, Kathrine Wagner (1981). *George Rogers Clark: Adventure in the Illinois and Selected Documents of the American Revolution at the Frontier Posts*. Polyanthos. ISBN 99920–1–653–1.

Senour, Faunt Le Roy (1865). *Major General William T. Sherman And His Campaign*. Republished BiblioBazaar, 2012. ISBN 1275786936. Hansebooks, 2019. ISBN 978–3337810566.

Sheinkin, Steve (2010). *The Floating Vulture: The Notorious Benedict Arnold*. Square Fish. ISBN 978–1–250–02460–2.

Sherman, William T. (1990). *Memoirs of General W.T. Sherman*. 2nd ed. New York: Library of America. ISBN 0–940450–65–8. First published in 1890 as Personal Memoirs of Gen. W.T. Sherman, Vol. I and II. New York : Charles L. Webster & Co.

Shevitz, Amy Hill (2005). "General Orders No. 11 (1862)." Richard S. Levy (ed.) *Antisemitism: A Historical Encyclopedia of Prejudice and Persecution*. 1. Santa Barbara, California: ABC CLIO.

Shy, John. "Arnold, Benedict (1741–1801)" *Oxford Dictionary of National Biography*. Oxford University Press. ISBN 10: 019956244X. ISBN 13: 9780199562442.

Simon, John Y. (ed.) (1967). *The Papers of Ulysses S. Grant, Volume 1: 1837–1861*. Mississippi State University Libraries (electronic): Southern Illinois University Press. National Archives, https://www.archives.gov; Library of Congress, https://www.loc.gov/collections/ulysses-s-grant-papers/about this collection.

Simon, John Y. (ed.) (2002). "Ulysses S. Grant." Graff, Henry (ed.). *The Presidents: A Reference History* (7th ed.). ISBN 0–684–80551–0.

Simpson, Brooks D. (2014). *Ulysses S. Grant: Triumph Over Adversity, 1822–1865*. Boston, Massachusetts: Houghton Mifflin. ISBN 978–0–395–65994–6.

Simpson, Brooks D. and Berlin, Jean V. (1999). *Sherman's Civil War: Selected Correspondence of William T. Sherman*. Chapel Hill, North Carolina: Univ. of North Carolina Press. ISBN 978–1469615141.

Smalley, Vern (2005). *Little Bighorn Mysteries: Issues Concerning the Approach To and Conduct of the Battle of the Little Bighorn*. Little Buffalo Press. ISBN 13: 9780970854919.

Smith, Derek (2005). *The Gallant Dead: Union & Confederate Generals Killed in the Civil War*. Mechanicsburg, Pennsylvania: Stackpole Books. ISBN 0–8117–0132–8.

Smith, Jean Edward (2001). *Grant*. New York, New York: Simon & Schuster. ISBN 0–684–84927–5.

Smith, Justin Harvey (1907). *Our Struggle for the Fourteenth Colony: Canada and the American Revolution*. New York and London: G.P. Putnam's Sons.

Smith, Justin Harvey (1919). *The War with Mexico*. Reprinted 2018, Sagwan Press. ISBN-10: 1376811863. ISBN-13: 978–1376811865.

Sneiderman, Barney (2006). *Warriors Seven: Seven American Commanders, Seven Wars, and the Irony of Battle*. New York: Savas Beatie. ISBN 978–1932714289.

Stanley, A. P. (1882). *Historical Memorials of Westminster Abbey*. London: John Murray.

Starr, Steven (2007). *The Union Cavalry in the Civil War: The War in the East from Gettysburg to Appomattox, 1863–1865*. Volume 2. Baton Rouge, Louisiana: Louisiana State University Press. ISBN 978–0–8071–3292–0.

Stedman, Charles (1794). *The History of the Origin, Progress, and Termination of the American War*. 1. Republished 2010, BiblioBazaar. ISBN: 1140871978; ISBN 13: 9781140871972.

Stevens, Donald Fithian (1991). *Origins of Instability in Early Republican Mexico*. Durham, North Carolina: Duke University Press. ISBN 0822311364.

Strode, Hudson (1955). *Jefferson Davis, Volume I: American Patriot.* New York, New York: Harcourt, Brace & Company. ISBN 10: 0151463018. ISBN 13: 978–0151463015.

Strode, Hudson (1959). *Jefferson Davis, Volume II: Confederate President.* New York, New York: Harcourt, Brace & Company. ISBN 10: 0151463018. ISBN 13: 978–0151463015.

Stuart, Nancy (2013). *Defiant Brides: The Untold Story of Two Revolutionary-Era Women And the Radical Men They Married.* Beacon Press. ISBN 978–0–8070–0117–2.

Sword, Wiley (1993). *The Confederacy's Last Hurrah: Spring Hill, Franklin, and Nashville.* Lawrence, Kansas: University Press of Kansas. ISBN 0–7006–0650–5. First published under the title Embrace an Angry Wind in 1992 by HarperCollins.

Symonds, Craig L. (1992). *Joseph E. Johnston: A Civil War Biography.* New York, New York: W. W. Norton. ISBN 978–0–393–31130–3.

Symonds, Craig L. (2001). *American Heritage History of the Battle of Gettysburg.* New York, New York: HarperCollins. ISBN 0–06–019474–X.

Tagg, Larry (1998). *The Generals Of Gettysburg: Appraisal Of The Leaders Of America's Greatest Battle.* Savas Publishing Company, ISBN 1–882810–30–9.

Taylor, Alan (2016). *American Revolutions: A Continental History, 1750–1804.* W. W. Norton & Company. ISBN 978–0–3932–5387–0.

The Oxford Companion To American Military History. Oxford University Press (1999). ISBN 0–19–507198–0.

Thomas, Emory M. (1986). *Bold Dragoon: The Life of J.E.B. Stuart.* Norman, Oklahoma: University of Oklahoma Press. ISBN 978–0–8061–3193–1.

Thomas, Emory M. (1995). *Robert E. Lee.* W. W. Norton & Co. ISBN 978–0–393–31631–5.

Tinkle, Lon (1958). *The Alamo* (original title: 13 Days to Glory). McGraw-Hill. ISBN 10: 0451149432. ISBN 13: 9780451149435.

Todish, Timothy J.; Todish, Terry; Spring, Ted (1998). *Alamo Sourcebook, 1836: A Comprehensive Guide to the Battle of the Alamo and the Texas Revolution.* Austin, Texas: Eakin Press. ISBN 978–1–57168–152–2.

Trevelyan, George Otto (1898). *The American Revolution, Part 1.* New York: Longmans, Green, and Co. OCLC 20011020.

Trudeau, Noah Andre (1991). *The Last Citadel: Petersburg, Virginia, June 1864 – April 1865.* Baton Rouge, Louisiana: Louisiana State University Press. ISBN 0–8071–1861–3.

Trudeau, Noah Andre (2002). *Gettysburg: A Testing of Courage.* New York, New York: HarperCollins. ISBN 0–06–019363–8.

Trudeau, Noah Andre (2008). *Southern Storm: Sherman's March to the Sea.* New York, New York: HarperCollins. ISBN 978–0–06–059867–9.

Tuchman, Barbara W. (1988). *The First Salute: A View of the American Revolution.* New York: Ballantine Books.

Tucker, Spencer et. al. (2012). *The Encyclopedia of the Mexican-American War* (3 vol). Santa Barbara, California: ABC-CLIO. ISBN 10: 1851098534; ISBN 13: 9781851098538.

Ulbrich, David (2000). "Lost Cause." *Encyclopedia of the American Civil War: A Political, Social, and Military History.* Heidler, David S., and Heidler, Jeanne T., eds., W. W. Norton & Company. ISBN 0–393–04758–X.

Unger, H.G. (2003). *Lafayette.* New York, New York: Wiley. ISBN-10: 0471468851.

Unger, H.G. (2019). *Thomas Paine and the Clarion Call for American Independence.* Da Capo Press. ISBN-10: 0306921936.

Utley, Robert M. (2001). *Cavalier in Buckskin: George Armstrong Custer and the Western Military Frontier.* Revised edition. Norman, Oklahoma: University of Oklahoma Press. ISBN 0–8061–3387–2.

Van Doren, Carl (1941). *Secret History of the American Revolution: An Account of the Conspiracies of Benedict Arnold and Numerous Others Drawn From the Secret Service Paper.* New York, New York: Viking Press. ISBN 10: 0678031762. ISBN 13: 9780678031766.

Walsh, George (2005). *Whip the Rebellion.* Forge Books. ISBN 0–7653–0526–7.

Walters, John B. (1973). *Merchant of Terror: General Sherman and Total War.* Bobbs-Merrill. ISBN 978–0672517822.

Wang, Xi (1997). *The Trial of Democracy: Black Suffrage and Northern Republicans, 1860–1910.* Athens, Georgia: The University of Georgia Press. ISBN 978–0–8203–4206–1.

Ward, Christopher (1952). *The War of the Revolution* (2 volumes). New York, New York: Macmillan. Reprinted 2011, New York, New York: Skyhorse Publishing. ISBN 9781616080808.

Ward, Geoffrey C. (1996). *The West: An Illustrated History.* Little, Brown and Company. ISBN 0–316–92236–6.

Ware, Susan (2000). *Forgotten Heroes: Inspiring American Portraits From Our Leading Historians.* Portland, Oregon: Simon and Schuster. ISBN 978–0–684–86872–1. OCLC 45179918.

Warren, Richard. "Antonio Lopez de Santa Anna." *Encyclopedia of Latin American History and Culture,* Volume 5. ISBN 10: 0684192535. ISBN 13: 978–0684192536.

Washington, George (1932). Fitzpatrick, John C. (ed.). *The Writings of George Washington: From the Original Manuscript Sources 1745–1799.* Washington: United States Government Printing Office.

Waugh, Joan (2009). *U.S. Grant: An American Hero, American Myth.* The University of North Carolina Press. ISBN 978–0–8078–3317–9.

Weintraub, Stanley (2005). *Iron Tears, Rebellion in America 1775–1783.* London: Free Press. ISBN 978–0–7432–2687–5.

Welch, James, with Paul Stekler. (1994). *Killing Custer: The Battle of Little Bighorn and the Fate of the Plains Indians.* New York, New York: W.W. Norton & Company. ISBN 039303657X.

Welcher, Frank J. (1993). *The Union Army, 1861–1865 Organization and Operations.* Vol. 2, The Western Theater. Bloomington, Indiana: Indiana University Press. ISBN 0–253–36454–X.

Welsh, Douglas (1981). *The Civil War: A Complete Military History.* Greenwich, Connecticut: Brompton Books Corporation. ISBN 1–890221–01–5.

Wert, Jeffry D. (1996). *Custer: The Controversial Life of George Armstrong Custer.* New York, New York: Simon & Schuster. ISBN 10: 0684832755. ISBN 13: 978–0684832753.

Wert, Jeffry D. (2008). *Cavalryman of the Lost Cause: A Biography of J.E.B. Stuart.* New York, New York: Simon & Schuster. ISBN 978–0–7432–7819–5.

White, Ronald Cedric (2017). *American Ulysses: A Life of Ulysses S. Grant.* New York: Random House. ISBN 978081298125.

Wickwire, Franklin and Mary (1970). *Cornwallis: The American Adventure*. Boston: Houghton Mifflin. OCLC 62690.

Wickwire, Franklin and Mary (1980). *Cornwallis: The Imperial Years*. Chapel Hill: University of North Carolina Press. ISBN 0–8078–1387–7.

Wiencek, Henry (2003). *An Imperfect God: George Washington, His Slaves, and the Creation of America*. Farrar, Straus and Giroux. ISBN 978–0–374–17526–9.

Willcox, William (1964). *Portrait of a General: Sir Henry Clinton in the War of Independence*. New York, New York: Alfred A Knopf. OCLC 245684727.

Williams, Charlean Moss (1951). *The Old Town Speaks: Reflections of Washington, Hempstead County Arkansas, Gateway to Texas, 1835, Confederate Capital, 1863*. Houston: Anson Jones Press. ASIN B000HX5GXQ.

Wilson, Charles Reagan (1983). *Baptized in Blood: The Religion of the Lost Cause, 1865–1920*. University of Georgia Press. ISBN 978–0–8203–0681–0.

Winters, John D. (1963). *The Civil War in Louisiana*. Baton Rouge, Louisiana: Louisiana State University Press. ISBN 0–8071–0834–0.

Wittenberg, Eric J., and J. David Petruzzi (2006). *Plenty of Blame to Go Around: Jeb Stuart's Controversial Ride to Gettysburg*. New York: Savas Beatie. ISBN 978–1–932714–20–3.

Wittenberg, Eric J., J. David Petruzzi, and Michael F. Nugent (2008). *One Continuous Fight: The Retreat from Gettysburg and the Pursuit of Lee's Army of Northern Virginia, July 4–14, 1863*. New York, New York: Savas Beatie. ISBN 978–1–932714–43–2.

Woodworth, Steven E. (1990). *Jefferson Davis and His Generals: The Failure of Confederate Command in the West*. Lawrence, Kansas: University Press of Kansas. ISBN 0–7006–0461–8.

Woodworth, Steven E. (1998). *Six Armies in Tennessee: The Chickamauga and Chattanooga Campaigns*. Lincoln, Nebraska: University of Nebraska Press. ISBN 0–8032–9813–7.

Woodworth, Steven E. (1999). "Dismembering the Confederacy: Jefferson Davis and the Trans-Mississippi West" in *No Band of*

Brothers: Problems in the Rebel High Command. Columbia, Missouri: University of Missouri Press. ISBN 0826262120.

Woodworth, Steven E. (2003). *Beneath a Northern Sky: A Short History of the Gettysburg Campaign.* Wilmington, Delaware: SR Books. ISBN 0–8420–2933–8.

Woodworth, Steven E. (2005). *Nothing but Victory: The Army of the Tennessee, 1861–1865.* New York, New York: Alfred A. Knopf. ISBN 10: 0375726608. ISBN 13: 978–0375726606.

www.ingramcontent.com/pod-product-compliance
Lightning Source LLC
Chambersburg PA
CBHW021611120626
46545CB00001B/181
9781959895411